IntraBuilder FrontRunner

Terence Goggin

Esther Schindler

Don Taylor

Matt Telles

CORIOLIS GROUP BOOKS

PUBLISHER	**KEITH WEISKAMP**
PROJECT EDITOR	**DENISE CONSTANTINE**
COVER ARTIST	**SQUARE ONE DESIGN**
COVER DESIGN	**ANTHONY STOCK**
INTERIOR DESIGN	**NICOLE BIRNEY**
LAYOUT PRODUCTION	**JIMMIE YOUNG**
PROOFREADER	**JEFF KELLUM**
INDEXER	**CAROLINE PARKS**

The Coriolis Group, Inc.
14455 North Hayden Road, Suite 220
Scottsdale, Arizona 85260
Phone: (602) 483-0192
Fax: (602) 483-0193
Web address: http://www.coriolis.com

ISBN 1-57610-102-9 : $29.99

Printed in the United States of America

10 9 8 7 6 5 4 3 2 1

I happily dedicate this book to my mother, my wife, Jenny and Rachel, the important women in my life.
Matt Telles

To Bill, who gives all the meaning to my life.
Esther Schindler

For Ron Swartz, who taught me how to think about solving problems; and for Vernon Bouton, who was at a critical time a living example of quiet courage that can overcome any adversity.
Don Taylor

To Dad, for all your help.
Terence Goggin

Contents

Chapter 5   JavaScript From Square One   79

Chapter 8 Using IntraBuilder's Database Power Tools 161

Chapter 11 IntraBuilder Reporting 249

Chapter 12 IntraBuilder Components And Their Properties 287

Acknowledgments

I would like to thank everyone who made this book possible, even Denise. The rest of you know who you are.
—*Matt Telles*

My thanks once again to the dedicated staff at The Coriolis Group—especially Marjory Spraycar for her fine editing, and Denise Constantine, who managed to keep me on track even in the midst of Kitchen Remodel Madness.
—*Don Taylor*

Thanks to Mark for reading and editing my stuff before I submitted it. Thanks also to Brenda and Tim, my friends.
—*Terence Goggin*

The first guy in the door has to turn on the lights.

That's true whether you're the first member of a team to adopt a new technology, or whether you're doing it all by yourself. Being "first" means that you have no one to ask for help—and that you must find the light switch on your own.

There are undeniable benefits to being a technology frontrunner: Those first in the door can set the standards, test new approaches, and be first to market with major products. There could be millions of dollars lying on the table, waiting for the first hand that learns how to grab them.

We at Coriolis Group Books created the FrontRunner Series so that you'd have help on Day One: the day you bring that new technology product home and crank it up. This will be true even if Day One for you is Day One for the product, too. We've built working relationships with the technology leaders in our industry so that our teams of analysts and writers can be working as soon as new technology is out of the labs. When it comes to a new technology product, you're not all alone anymore. The Front Runner is here to help.

Our goal is to provide you with the best possible information on new technology products the day they're released to the public. Not "soft stuff" or hot air, either—just real, useful, practical information that you can put to work right away. We hope that this book gives you whatever additional power you need to make that final sprint over the line—and on to outstanding success in your study or business.

Jeff Duntemann

Orientation: The Enterprise Internet

Esther Schindler

Your journey begins here with Internet basics and then moves on to the new world of IntraBuilder, a tool for building intranet Web sites from your own databases.

*E*arly one morning, I stumbled into the kitchen wanting a cup of coffee—preferably intravenously—but getting one was as complex as building a computer system. The coffee pot was dirty, but I couldn't wash it until I moved the dirty dishes from the sink. I couldn't move the dirty dishes until I unloaded the clean dishes from the dishwasher. Twenty minutes later, I was finally drinking that cup of coffee.

All too often, building a computer system becomes as complex as that cup of coffee. You need to understand X before you can use it to build an effective widget. But when you start using X, you discover that understanding the tool requires a more-than-elementary knowledge of Y. Before you know it, you have to become an expert in two or three subject areas. You're never quite sure what you know or whether you have learned enough to get started, and worst of all, you haven't even *started* yet.

No matter what job you're trying to accomplish with a computer or what the topic—to create an inventory management system, organize conference schedules, or track the migratory habits of Northeastern waterfowl—the underlying purpose is the same: You want the computer to get the job done faster, cheaper, and more efficiently than doing it by hand. At least you want the job done in a manner that makes you smile. Most of all, the system shouldn't create more pain than it cures. That, it seems, is often the unhappy fate of using Internet technology to solve business problems.

The Internet—*anything* connected with the Internet—seems to have an overabundance of associated buzzwords. As you surely know by now, the Internet—both the structure that makes it possible (the gazillions of files and their physical manifestations on servers around the world) and the content hidden therein—is a hot item. Even my 76-year-old mother has enough interest in the topic to read books about the Internet, which is more enthusiasm than she ever expressed for my one-time fascination with FORTRAN.

The Appeal Of The Internet

What makes the Internet—and by extension intranets—worth so much attention? It gives people access to an awesome amount of information. Whether you're interested in recent changes in real-estate law, research in paleontology, or object-oriented programming techniques, you can be certain that the information is out there, someplace, compiled on a Web site in Russia or a FTP site in Cheyenne. All too often, of course, the information is raw and requires the best skills of human beings to turn it into useful knowledge.

If information on the Internet is so rough, why do businesses care so much about it? It's more than the undeniable cachet that being on the Internet is cool: Many businesses have found it financially productive to have an Internet presence. At the very least, a Web page provides an electronic billboard advertising goods and services, some of which earn serious cash online. Naturally, it occurs to some companies that if they can put their catalog ordering online to serve customers, they should be able to provide internal information to themselves as well. Online marketing taught companies the benefits inherent in the Internet organizational structure.

The Internet provides *a level playing field* for the people who use it. The content (i.e., the information shared—no matter the subject) lives on the server; whether that content consists of baseball scores, inventory information, or flight schedules doesn't matter. The user accessing the system could be using nearly anything; as long as the user has a Web browser capable of accessing the site, that information is available. The type of operating system or hardware platform doesn't matter.

Nobody started out touting the Web as a client/server system, but that's what it is. The hard work is all done at the server, using instructions written in one of a handful of languages (CGI, Java, or Perl) or in another mostly-human-readable standard language, Hypertext Markup Language (HTML). Among HTML's benefits is the ability to jump to another location referenced in the text—the hypertext referenced in its name.

The cross platform argument was made even stronger by Sun's Java, an object-oriented interpreted language that can run on the client end of any platform (assuming the browser supports Java, and most do). Java (and its little brother, JavaScript—meant to be a scripting language—or what you might think of as a batch language) has earned a lot of attention for several reasons. Java applets (components) are interpreted at the workstation, and the language is constructed to be highly portable. As a result, the native OS of the client is less important, freeing developers from the nightmare of maintaining separate code bases for Windows, OS/2, and Macintosh applications. Some would even say that Java applications could render operating systems irrelevant (and thus, in some ways, a way to resist Microsoft's dominance over everything upon which it sets its gaze). Java is object oriented, and anyone who has used other object-oriented tools will find it reasonably familiar. While it's easy for programmers to accept, it may not be the magic bullet that management hopes for. (Corporate management always seems to expect new technological solutions to make every project finish on time, under budget, and with new features easily added at the last moment.) Be prepared—Java is a language. It's a good language and a powerful one, but it's unlikely to be individually responsible for peace on earth, the end of world hunger, and certainly not free pizza delivery.

The server uses standard Internet communications protocols (primarily TCP/IP) to send the HTML to the end user, formally called the "client computer." The individual Web browser interprets the HTML and JavaScript at the client end. (JavaScript is a subset of Java suited to small applications, called applets, intended to be downloaded and run on the client computer.) Best of all, it doesn't take a great deal of computing power to interpret HTML or JavaScript instructions. Even a lowly 386 computer running Windows 3.1 can access the most complex of Web sites, not to mention the network computers (standalone machines designed to run Internet access software and not much more) that the computer industry has been talking about recently. Also, remote users (such as a distributed sales staff) can dial in from anywhere and operate as if they were attached to the company network.

Sounds great, right? So that's why so many companies have been putting themselves on the Internet. But it isn't all a rosy picture.

So What's Wrong With This Picture?

Despite the appeal of the Internet and the apparent ease of creating Web pages based on a company's own information, there are significant roadblocks along the way. Today's Internet simply isn't an overall business solution.

One major concern is security. You can build a firewall between your company's server and the outside world to keep the bad guys out, but that doesn't do a lot for information traveling in the other direction or for your employees who are directing their attention outside the company. If everyone in the company is given access to the Internet, how much of their time is spent perusing Web sites that have little to do with the day-to-day details of their jobs? As you probably know (or at least suspect), plenty of your coworkers are using their new-found access to the Internet as an opportunity to check out Web sites that you would really rather they didn't. Aside from the obvious "naked lady" sites, you don't want company employees being distracted by home-brew beer sites or folk music calendars any more than you would like it if they were sitting around the office talking about those topics for hours on end.

Even when security issues can be solved—and most of the control issues can be addressed—another major problem is the time it takes to create a useful site for a company's use. Most of the development tools available were designed by and for people who already know about the intricacies of TCP/IP, CGI programming, and other specialized technologies. Until recently, few of the tools expected any other level of expertise. While many of the tools are powerful, they are not all especially robust and certainly not designed for the average business user. Plus, their complexity throws programmers into the "need to know X before I can do the job and need to know Y before I can understand X" cycle.

The development time is especially irksome when you contemplate the problems of the dynamic nature of the data you're wrestling with. While an ordinary Web site might be updated daily or even hourly, most business purposes require more current information: If you need to know how many chocolate truffles are in stock, you need to know how many are in stock *now*, not yesterday, not three hours ago. Perhaps an intranet can handle the situation.

Intranet Basics

Understanding the basic concept of an intranet is delightfully easy: An intranet is a network that uses Internet technologies to share organized sets of information on a private TCP/IP network. Intranets may have the ability to access the Internet, but traffic is inbound only.

We'll try to minimize the use of technical terms here at the beginning, but let's examine a few (with the help of the diagram in Figure 1.1) so you can understand what an intranet is all about. Over the course of the book you'll learn more about each of these concepts, so let's keep it light for now.

An intranet's components include:

◆ Server hardware

◆ Server software

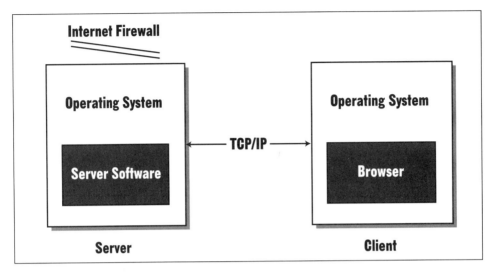

Figure 1.1   The structure of an intranet.

◆ TCP/IP

◆ Browser(s)

◆ Firewall(s)

Server hardware is simply the computer on which the rest of this stuff runs. While you might be familiar with networks from the perspective of file and print servers (on which you run your day-to-day applications), intranets usually have one or more computers dedicated to the job of running the intranet software, as well as any other associated software the intranet needs, such as database engines or other tools.

Server software includes both the operating system that runs on the dedicated intranet hardware (Windows NT, Windows 95, OS/2, Macintosh, or some flavor of UNIX), and the software that makes the Internet run on a particular box. That might include O'Reilly & Associates WebSite, Microsoft Internet Information, Netscape FastTrack, Netscape Enterprise, or any one of the other numerous applications of this kind. Other software makes the server actually do something—which, right now, might be hand-constructed Web pages using HTML, hand-crafted JavaScript, CGI scripts, or other custom applications based on existing database technology. Just remember that hardware plus software equals server.

TCP/IP is nothing more than a communication method across networks. It has been around for eons (at least from a computer historian's perspective) and is supported on every platform you can name. When data has to be transferred over distant, unreliable lines (such as telephone lines), TCP/IP shines. It is the path between server and user.

Browsers are the graphical applications that run on the client's (user's) workstation and give access to information stored on the server. Browsers are easy to learn, although arguably limited. Netscape Navigator is the number-one browser both in sales and mind share, although Microsoft is working hard to chip away at that success.

Firewalls protect one network from another network. Basically, a firewall is two mechanisms that work together: one permits traffic and another blocks traffic. Think of a firewall as a screen door that lets some things in (such as fresh air) and keeps other things from getting out (such as the cats).

Intranets offer businesses several conveniences. As long as the end user has a browser, she can have access to the company's applications or data; this yields the distinct benefit of platform independence. Nobody has to care whether accounting is using OS/2, the boss is using Windows 95, or if marketing is dedicated to Macintoshes. Access from the road is also possible, so employees can see up-to-the-moment information. And I do mean up-to-the-moment: Data on the server can be dynamically tied to company databases, so it is always up to date.

On the other hand, intranets inherit all the limitations of the Internet as well as its benefits. Either you become an expert in a few arcane technologies, or you use products that are not adequately suited for the task at hand. Or, in the worst-case scenario, you're stuck with both simultaneously.

Fortunately for intranet developers, Borland's IntraBuilder came along.

The IntraBuilder Idea

IntraBuilder is a set of tools that helps you easily create intranet Web sites based on your own databases. It is a set of tools for creating and managing databases (with rich data support), and tied to your Web server through service-specific utilities. It's built from the ground up to help mere mortals create intranets without the usual host of superfluous tools or a requirement for technical expertise in Internet intricacies.

IntraBuilder comes in two parts. One runs on the server, integrating itself with one of a handful of Windows 95- or Windows NT-based Web servers, such as O'Reilly & Associates WebSite or Microsoft Internet Information. The other part of IntraBuilder—and where you'll spend most of your time—is in IntraBuilder's *Integrated Development Environment* (IDE). The IDE is used to create database-heavy applications, which IntraBuilder turns into Web pages containing Java programs accessible from your intranet Web site.

The part of IntraBuilder that runs on the server keeps a low profile once it's installed, but let's take a look at it before we set it aside. The server software, too, has two pieces: the IntraBroker, which becomes best buddies with your Web server; and IntraServer, which manages the communication between Borland's database engine and the IntraBroker. (You'll use a different IntraBroker depending on which Web server you choose. You'll learn more about that in the server setup chapter, but Figure 1.2 gives you a picture of how IntraBuilder fits into the intranet setup described earlier.)

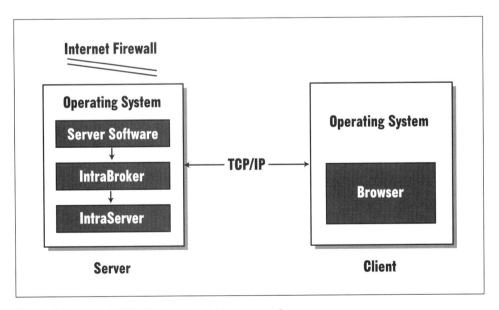

Figure 1.2   IntraBuilder's place in the intranet universe.

As you probably expect from Borland's long involvement with PC-based database administration and its focus on object oriented programming, IntraBuilder is no slouch when it comes to support for serious application development. Databases can use dBase and Paradox tables directly, or they can reach other databases through Borland SQL links and most ODBC data sources.

Here's how the process works:

◆ Create a home page or use one that's already constructed.

◆ Create database tables—if they don't already exist.

◆ Create database queries to filter subsets of the data and tie tables together for useful purposes.

◆ Create forms to enter data and/or examine it, using IntraBuilder's visual development tools.

◆ Create reports that access those databases.

◆ Tell your Web server where to look for these applications, and tell users to begin banging on them.

◆ End-users interactively query and edit live database information using their favorite Web browsers.

Each step can be broken down further and gets much more complex, but that's the basics of what you do with IntraBuilder.

Borland includes plenty of features to make the learning curve a gentle one. IntraBuilder includes Experts to guide you through the creation of common business forms, tables, and reports, which are more than adequate to get you started—especially if, like me, you are graphically challenged. IntraBuilder also provides the structure of common business tables and applications (such as a phone book and a knowledge base) to get you started quickly or help you start customizing from a sensible point.

Once you're ready to go down the IntraBuilder road, you will fast become comfortable with the tools in the IDE. They include the Inspector, the Method Editor, the Component Palette, and the Field Palette—all of which you'll learn about in detail in later chapters. The IDE gives you a visual design surface upon which you drag-and-drop the objects or tools you need; you set their properties with the editors and palettes, or extend their functionality by using IntraBuilder's extended JavaScript. For instance, you can drag and drop a table column (if you're used to programming from a non-database perspective, you'd think of this as a variable) onto the screen, which will later appear as your Web page. You establish the behavior of the object, from user interface (color and font) to more complex behaviors (what to do when the user clicks on the object).

While you might never write a single line of code, you can always view and edit the generated JavaScript in one of IntraBuilder's three text editors (Script Editor, Script Pad, or Method Editor).

IntraBuilder works with standard database formats (or at least the formats that Borland would like you to think of as all the standards you'll ever need). You can design new databases, but since you're using existing standards you also have access to data from other legacy stand alone applications. This helps minimize the necessity of rewriting all of your applications before you can start using your company's intranet; presumably, many or most of your existing data is stored in one of the supported formats. Those applications can continue to work while you create new ones—based on the same data, in the same files—using IntraBuilder. You don't have to transfer data into another proprietary format as you would with, say, Lotus Notes.

What Do You Need?

There's an old story about an alien life form that lands in the middle of New York's Central Park. The police are understandably curious about him and his alien society, and they ask him if he can read and write. "Can write, no read," the alien replies. The police ask the alien to write his name, whereupon the creature scribbles something in an unintelligible scrawl. "What does that say?" the police ask. The alien responds, "Can write. No read."

The power of using a tool geared for beginners is that those beginners may be able to write applications they cannot read. If IntraBuilder is designed for ordinary folks, how much do you *really* need to know? If you're familiar with computer programming (though not necessarily with Internet tools), will IntraBuilder still be useful? Sure.

If you're an accomplished software developer already, you'll be happy to learn that IntraBuilder won't act as a barrier between beginner programming and more expert work. Once you create IntraBuilder applications, you can extend them with Java applets or ActiveX controls. IntraBuilder also supports reuse of components built in Delphi, C++, and Visual Basic through OLE automation and DLL access.

If you're comfortable with databases, IntraBuilder can help you get comfortable (and productive) with Internet development tools. If you're familiar with Internet tools, IntraBuilder can help you get up to speed with database creation and maintenance. But you'll find few assumptions: IntraBuilder is designed for an ordinary business person to be able to grasp. And truly, it does a good job. I was an Internet software neophyte when I started this project, and if I can do it, so can you.

IntraBuilder *will* expect you to know your own business and the applications that you'll want to build and use. It will help considerably if you have ever used a program to create and manage databases, but you won't struggle too hard if you haven't done so. (There's a chapter in this book to give you the database basics, in case you need help on that topic.) And, while using IntraBuilder will probably turn you into a more knowledgeable user of Web tools than you initially expected, you'll never need to become a Web goddess. You'll be able to stop short of being a minor deity.

Ready To Go?

IntraBuilder lets you get started and learn along the way. As you progress past the basics, though, you'll find yourself learning—and you need to learn—the basics of Java programming. IntraBuilder extends the JavaScript language to include elements required for application development, and if you don't gradually learn JavaScript, you'll feel like an alien who has written something that you cannot decipher or understand.

Don't be disheartened by this. The good thing about IntraBuilder is that it lets you accomplish something while you gradually learn JavaScript. You won't be like I was in my kitchen making coffee—having to put in lots of time before you can start brewing.

If you depend upon the Experts, you won't need to know very much about JavaScript. But to accomplish anything nontrivial (or at least out of the ordinary), you will definitely need to learn the language. Our aim in this book is to help you along the way.

Cranking It Up

Esther Schindler

JavaScript is the "native" language of IntraBuilder. It adds considerable power to your toolkit, and in this chapter you'll get a flavor for language basics and how JavaScript's features work together.

I recently went to Stockholm, Sweden, to teach a computer class, though I don't speak a word of Swedish. I had no idea where to go or what to do to get situated; I knew that plenty of information was available, but helpless to find it, I was at the mercy of taxi drivers. Menus, subways, and store names were in a language I didn't understand. Everyone around me seemed to know what was going on, but I was lost and adrift.

That's the way I feel when I start using any new software tool; I need a guide. In this chapter, we'll take a short guided tour to get you oriented to IntraBuilder and get you comfortable enough with its features to create a small but non-trivial project. You'll feel like you can actually accomplish something useful before lunch time.

At this point, I assume that you have installed IntraBuilder in a typical configuration, either by following Borland's instructions or by reading through Chapter 4, "Development System Configuration", later in the *IntraBuilder FrontRunner*, to provide guidance while you set up your Web server.

The Chocolate Conglomeration

Since my initial example was about travel, we'll stick with that theme. You and I are in charge of the computer resources for the Chocolate Conglomeration, an international company bent on dominating the world of chocolate commerce. (Presumably, it's good, dark chocolate; I'd hate to think we're going through all this for any other kind.) The company has dozens of sales people and executives who travel around the world, busily making the world safe for cocoa products. They visit the company's several offices in major cities, they stay in hotels, they probably consume a lot of chocolate.

However, none of the employees tends to remember the rules about travel policies, a fact that causes strife between the sales people who travel and accounting personnel who have to make sense of the travelers' expense forms. Having a travel policy online, instead of on a dusty shelf or holding up a table leg, would probably help matters considerably.

But face it—travel policies are barely more interesting to read than insurance policies, even when they impact the size of the check you see at the end of each month. While it's nice to know how much the Chocolate Conglomerate will pay for a hotel room, the information is dull reading. And moving the data from paper to Web site doesn't necessarily change that. The delivery technology has changed, but the benefits of the medium haven't been exploited. Online services (internal or external to a company) aren't successful just because they make information accessible; their value lies in making data relevant to the people accessing it. The more relevant the information, the more—and the more often—it will be accessed. Instead of thinking in terms of creating a travel policy database, in our example we'll turn it into a company travel guide.

In our hands-on example, we'll note the company's travel policies (or at least pretend to supply the sort of information a company might provide). We'll also give the user information about the places to which he is likely to travel. The Chocolate Conglomeration's intranet will tell the user how to find the company office in each city and will recommend nearby hotels. To further enhance the quality of the information (and to keep users coming back to the site), we'll let people add their own comments. Other company travelers can tell each other about an all-night copy shop, or learn to avoid the Chinese restaurant on Thunderbird Road. Figure 2.1 gives an overview of the site we'll put together in the next several pages.

Starting Out Easy

In the first part of our travel guide project, we'll use a few of the built-in tools to create a simple database and form. Then we'll modify what we created to make it more suitable for our needs. This might be similar to running Borland's initial quick-start tutorial, but it will also give you hands-on experience with using the supplied tools to get work done quickly. Besides, we need a simple location table to identify hotel addresses anyway; there's no point in making the job harder than it has to be.

In this first section, I intentionally provide a lot of hand-holding; if you're new to software development (and hoping that Borland's promises of IntraBuilder being easy are accurate), then the verbal and visual reassurances will help you become comfortable with IntraBuilder. If you're experienced with these kind of tools, don't worry; we'll get progressively more technical as the chapter (and the book) progresses.

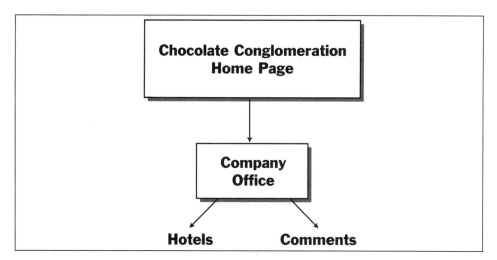

Figure 2.1 The structure of our travel guide project.

You might want to use your favorite OS utility (even if it's just the command line) to create a subdirectory for this project. It would probably make sense to put it under the borland\intrabuilder\apps directory; I put mine in a subdirectory called Travel.

Organizing Your Files Effectively

IntraBuilder doesn't make it especially easy to keep your files organized, so it's a good idea to create directories for each project. While you can throw stuff into directories willy-nilly, you'll probably get yourself hopelessly confused by doing so. Between tables, forms, reports, graphics, and everything else, IntraBuilder generates a lot of files. Because file names and paths can be (and usually are) embedded in the code IntraBuilder generates, finding and fixing these references later on can be a real pain.

IntraBuilder can also seem to lose files because they wind up in a different directory than you'd intended. For example, if you import a graphics file from, say, your personal graphics or download directories, when you save the form a few minutes later IntraBuilder will expect you to save the form in the graphics or download directory, too. Get in the habit of checking to make sure the Look-in directory is the one you had in mind, and double-check where you save files.

In fact, while you're looking at the directory structure, take a few minutes to learn where IntraBuilder keeps all its pieces. It will help you later on, when you have to copy files into the correct directory to make them live.

The IntraBuilder table-creation expert includes a sample table similar to the information we need to maintain about area hotels. The customer information table keeps some information we don't need (such as a contact date), it lacks a few other items (such the hotel's daily rate), but it has the basic address information we want.

Click on the Tables tab, and just for good measure, make sure that the Look In field points to your Travel subdirectory. Double click on the icon on the far left, called Untitled, to start creating a new form. IntraBuilder will display a dialog asking if you want Expert or Designer, as you see in

Figure 2.2. Personally, those terms sound too similar to me (if I'm an expert, do I need a designer?), but at least IntraBuilder is consistent with its terminology. Experts are the tools that walk you through the creation process. Other products call such tools wizards; users describe, as macros on steroids. Use the Designer when you want to start with a blank form, empty table, etc.

This time, we'll use the supplied Expert. Click on Expert and scroll down through the list of sample tables in the dialog, until you find the one called Customer Information. Click on that table definition to highlight it and the column definitions will be displayed. We could pick and choose among the columns (and if we weren't trying so hard to stay simple, we probably would), but for now choose all of the suggested columns by clicking on the button that looks like >>, as you see in Figure 2.3. Click on Next to bring you to the next dialog.

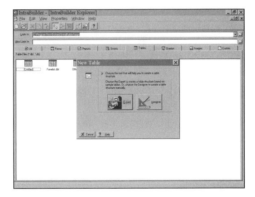

Figure 2.2   The first step in creating a table.

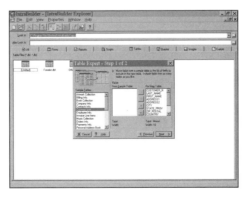

Figure 2.3   Choosing the table to use as a starting point.

There's not much more to it. Choose the database format you prefer (dBase or Paradox—it won't make a difference for our purposes), then click on Run Table. You'll be prompted to save the file. Call it Hotel, and make sure you put the file in the correct directory. IntraBuilder will automatically run the table. That is, it will open a view of the table you just created. The window will look something like what you see in Figure 2.4: an empty table with absolutely no aesthetics, but your own creation, nonetheless.

As dull as the results may appear, you can do real work with the Hotel table at this point. Right-click on the background of the table, and IntraBuilder will display a menu showing what you can do. The options are unexciting without data in the table to work with, and we still have a couple of changes to make before the structure is usable. So after you admire them for a moment, ignore the menu choices. Close the table; we'll come back to it in a few minutes.

If you look at the Tables page in the IntraBuilder Explorer, you'll now see your Hotel table bravely listed. Right-click on the Hotel icon; among the menu options is the ability to edit the table. Choose that one, and IntraBuilder will display the structure of the actual table.

If you have worked with database tables before, this one will look absolutely unremarkable. If you haven't, you can probably discern that the table definition describes the nature and size of the information kept therein as

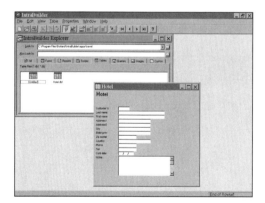

Figure 2.4   IntraBuilder displays the table once you've created it, to ensure that you got everything right.

well as what each column (what you might think of as a field or variable or place to hold stuff, depending on your background) is called. (If you're completely new to databases, you might want to peek ahead at Chapter 7, "Database 101".)

As we noted earlier, this table isn't exactly what we need without some modifications, and even if you have to putter around to figure out your way around, it won't be long before you figure out how to change the fields. Just remember: The Tab key is your friend.

Whatever CUSTOMER_N was intended for, we don't need it. We will, however, need a column to keep track of the general location of this hotel (since, after all, hotels near the New York City offices of the Chocolate Conglomerate might include those in New Jersey), so type over the CUSTOMER_N field and change the name to LOCATION. Make it a numeric field, 3 digits wide. Similarly, change other columns as follows:

1. Turn FIRSTNAME into HOTELNAME

2. Add a RATE, which should be a floating point number (6 digits, 2 decimal points)

3. Add a DIRECTIONS column, which should be a memo

You can right-click on the table definition window to find out what you can do here, too. With anything in the LASTNAME field highlighted, right-click on the item and choose Delete Current Field. Do the same to the contact date. At this point the Hotel table will look something like Figure 2.5.

Field	Name	Type	Width	Decimal	Index
	hotel.DBF - Table Designer				_ □ ×
Updated:	09/30/96	Bytes Used: 190	Type: DBASE		
Rows:	1	Bytes Left: 32,577			
1	LOCATION	Numeric	3	0	Ascend
2	HOTELNAME	Character	30	0	None
3	ADDRESS1	Character	20	0	None
4	ADDRESS2	Character	20	0	None
5	CITY	Character	20	0	None
6	STATE_PROV	Character	20	0	None
7	ZIP_POSTAL	Character	10	0	None
8	COUNTRY	Character	20	0	None
9	PHONE	Character	10	0	None
10	FAX	Character	10	0	None
11	NOTES	Memo	10	0	None
12	RATE	Float	6	2	None
13	DIRECTIONS	Memo	10	0	None

Figure 2.5   The structure of the Hotel table.

Close the table and reply in the affirmative when you're prompted to save the table. (If you had added data earlier, IntraBuilder would also tell you that it needed to rebuild the table to incorporate the changes you just made.)

Finally, the Hotel table is set to hold the data we have to maintain, so let's add some information. Double-click on the Hotel icon, then right-click on the window and choose Add. Type in some information (make it up—who'll know?), then right-click again to choose the option to save the record. You could keep adding information this way, but unless you have been yearning for a way to keep track of hotels, your enthusiasm probably won't last long.

Let's give the Hotel table a more aesthetic appeal, and not coincidentally create what will eventually turn into a Web page on our travel guide intranet site.

Click on the Forms tab in the IntraBuilder Explorer. This time you'll notice that there are two Untitled documents. Assuming that your screen offers enough resolution to peer at the icons to discern the difference, the simpler of the two icons lets you go right into the visual designer. Double-click on the more complex-looking Untitled icon (it's probably the one on the left), and IntraBuilder will prompt you to choose between an Expert and the Designer. We're keeping things simple, so choose the form creation Expert.

In the first dialog, you choose the table from which you'll be constructing the form: the Hotel table. Click on Next, and choose the columns to be included in the table, as in Figure 2.6. To keep it simple choose all of them—we can always yank them out later if we like.

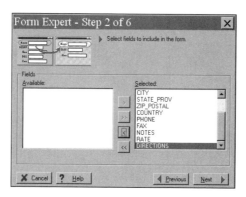

Figure 2.6   Choosing columns to include in the form.

In the third step, choose the form layout (though if your sense of individuality urges you to experiment, feel free to pick the column layout instead).

The fourth step prompts you to choose a scheme, which provides a standard background, font, colors, and so forth, as you can see in Figure 2.7. While schemes are not precisely a style sheet for creating standard Web pages—they won't change on the fly if you make modifications later—you'll discover that they're very useful for giving your site an attractive, uniform appearance. IntraBuilder lets you choose from any of several pretty schemes, or you can fiddle with the settings on your own to create one you prefer. In any case, fool around until you find one you like and choose Next to move to the next dialog.

IntraBuilder lets you control what users can do to the data (in more formal terms, the row operations permitted) that will be displayed on this form. As Figure 2.8 shows, you can limit or grant navigation, updating, and search capabilities. Choose All so that all of them are selected. (If you were doing this for production work, you would probably limit what the user can do, but it's nice for you to be able to see how all the buttons appear.)

◆ The first set of operations are navigational, displaying the first, last, next, and previous records.

◆ The update choices let you control what changes the user can make to the data source: add, delete, edit, save, and abandon. (Abandon is like an Undo—it tells IntraBuilder to ignore any changes that were made to the data.)

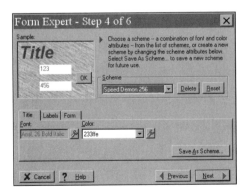

Figure 2.7   Picking a color scheme for the form.

◆ Third, IntraBuilder has options to control whether the user can search or limit the data. When you permit users to Query by Form, they can look for records that match a specific value in a specific field. For instance, users could look up any hotel with a rate of $140. The Filter by Form option lets the user limit the records displayed, to scroll through all the hotels with a room rate of $140.

The form can display either text buttons or small graphic icons; personally, I find the icons unintelligible and a gratuitous use of graphics-for-graphics sake, but you can make your own decision.

Finally, choose Run Form and save the file (this time as hotel.jfm). IntraBuilder will display your newly created form, just like you see in Figure 2.9.

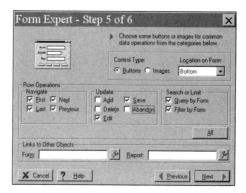

Figure 2.8   Choosing data operations.

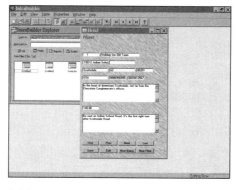

Figure 2.9   The new hotel form.

Using this form, you can add, update, search through the database—anything you would do with an ordinary database manager. Just to prove we can do it (and so we have some data to experiment with, later in this chapter), add the records in Listing 2.1.

LISTING 2.1   DATABASE ENTRIES FOR THE HOTEL TABLE.

```
Location: 2
KunLun Hotel
(make up an address)
Phone: 10-65003388
Fax: 10-65003228
Notes: Near the Liangma River. 5 star hotel.
Directions: 15 minutes to airport. Take a cab.
Rate: $150.00

Location: 2
Wanghu Hotel
2 Huangcheng West Road
Hangzhou, China 310006
571-7071024
fax 571-7071350
Notes: 2 minutes to West Lake. 10 minutes from airport.
Rate: $85.00
```

Add a few more records on your own, to give yourself enough data to play with. Then close the form.

This form looks okay; it's just a bit sparse. By default, the Expert uses the table column names, and not all of them are intuitive. Let's take a first look at the visual development environment by editing the Hotel form. Highlight the Hotel icon in the IntraBuilder Explorer and edit it by pressing Shift+F2. As shown in Figure 2.10, IntraBuilder will display the Form Designer with both the Hotel form and a complex window (called an Inspector) off to the right.

This time, we'll keep the changes simple. Click on the title Hotel; IntraBuilder will put boxes around the text and highlight the rulers on the outside of the form. In the Inspector, click on the field called Text (as in Figure 2.11) and change it to Hotel Information. Press Enter, or an up- or down-arrow. If you click on the Form window, IntraBuilder loses the change you just made.

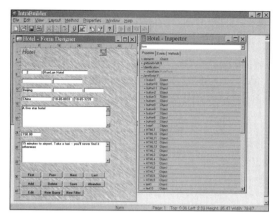

Figure 2.10   Working with the Form Designer.

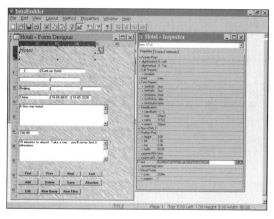

Figure 2.11   Changing a form.

That will result in a tiny heading indeed; we need to do something to perk it up. Click on the icon to the right of the Hotel Information you just typed. Depending on your monitor resolution and your degree of cynicism, it either looks like a wrench (i.e., a tool) or a dog bone. Whenever you choose that tool icon, IntraBuilder will display the relevant tool to customize the piece you're working with. In this case, that means the Text Property Builder, since we're working with text (see Figure 2.12).

In the dialog that's displayed, click on Custom Tags and choose Header 1; press the Add button beneath the drop-down menu. Doing so will insert the proper HTML codes to make the Hotel Information appear in a larger,

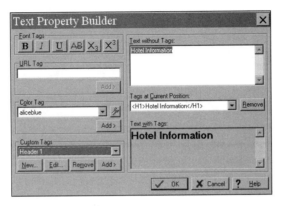

Figure 2.12   Changing Text properties on a form.

bolder font. (You can also poke around to see what other kinds of trouble you can get into with fonts and colors, here, but I'll leave that to your own sense of adventure.)

So far we haven't done much more than use IntraBuilder as a fancy HTML editor. But we can get much fancier. Exit the Form Designer and save the file.

Any time you make changes to the JavaScript inside a form, you need to recompile the form. Right-click on the Hotel icon and choose Compile. IntraBuilder will recompile the JavaScript and tell you about any errors it encounters. (Not that we expect any.)

You might be surprised at how much we've accomplished in the last few minutes. Take a look at the script we generated. Right-click on the Hotel icon and choose Edit as Script. You'll see JavaScript that looks much like Listing 2.2.

LISTING 2.2   THE GENERATED JAVASCRIPT FOR THE HOTEL FORM.

```
// Generated on 10/01/96
//
var f = new HotelForm();
f.open();
class HotelForm extends Form {
    with (this) {
        color = "";
```

```
        height = 35.4706;
        left = 2.3333;
        top = 0.0588;
        width = 79.6667;
        title = "Hotel";
        background = "filename blumtl21.jpg";
    }


    with (this.hotel1 = new Query()){
        left = 52;
        top = 0;
        sql = 'SELECT * FROM "C:\\Program
          Files\\Borland\\IntraBuilder\\APPS\\Travel\\hotel.dbf"';
        active = true;
    }


    with (this.hotel1.rowset) {

    }


    with (this.HTML1 = new HTML(this)){
        height = 1;
        left = 1;
        top = 4;
        width = 14;
        color = "d2d2d2";
        fontName = "Arial";
        fontItalic = true;
        text = "Location";
```

Now it's time to turn this database and its associated form into a real Web page.

You have to copy all your files into the directory that you defined as the ibapps directory when you set up IntraBuilder. In most cases, that will be \program files\borland\intrabuilder\apps on the Web server, but yours might be different. Deploying the files can be slightly awkward (or at least a little less elegant than I'd prefer) because IntraBuilder doesn't provide specific tools to do so. You can't click on something that says, "Make this live." Instead, bop over to the command line to copy all the hotel.* files from the Travel directory to the Apps directory. If you chose a bitmap background rather than a color, don't forget to copy the background jpg file, too.

Connect your workstation to your Web server, if it isn't already running, and make sure that you have started the Borland Web Server and IntraBuilder Server. Then launch your favorite browser from the client workstation. Point the browser at your Web site (you'll probably have a domain name instead of my IP address). It will look something like:

```
http://127.0.0.4/svr/intrasrv.isv?apps/hotel.jfm
```

You should see the application in your browser, as you do in Figure 2.13, and be able to add, edit, and navigate your way around the database.

Look what we've accomplished. It might be the adult equivalent of the hand-scrawled drawings your kids bring home from school and insist deserve a place of honor on the refrigerator, but it's all yours.

But What If It Doesn't Work Right?

At this point, you ought to see the hotel database—but perhaps you don't. Don't be too surprised, especially if you're new to both Web servers and to IntraBuilder. I ran into plenty of these problems myself, and I found that the most likely situations were:

◆ I didn't have the Web server set up correctly. In particular, make sure the Web server points at the right IntraBuilder directories.

◆ I hadn't copied all of the files into the correct directories.

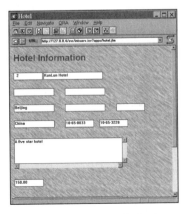

Figure 2.13   Accessing the hotel database through the browser.

◆ The jfm files I had generated with IntraBuilder had references to files in directories, and those files were no longer in those directories because I'd moved them elsewhere. Occasionally, especially when you're getting started, you may have to edit the jfm files to fix directory paths and file names.

◆ I had a typo. (It's humiliating but true.)

◆ The Web server wasn't actually started; I just thought it was.

◆ If had to run the Borland BDE Configuration Utility to convince the database engine I really did want everything to start.

In general, I found that most of the problems I encountered were the result of my communication with the Web server and not with IntraBuilder.

Now that we have a little hands-on experience with IntraBuilder, it's time to construct our Travel Guide Web site, one piece at a time.

Creating A Few More Tables

Because this database project requires a few interrelated databases and forms, it makes sense to finish creating the pieces before we glue them together. We already have the Hotel table complete, so let's move on to the user Feedback table.

The Feedback table is a simple one because it's not much more than a comment form on places the Chocolate Conglomeration employees have visited. IntraBuilder doesn't supply any Expert that comes close, so we'll start with a blank slate. Click on the Tables tab in the IntraBuilder Explorer and click on the Untitled icon to create a new table. This time, choose Designer and fill in the database fields as shown in Table 2.1.

Table 2.1   Structure of the Feedback table.

Name	Type	Width	Decimal	Index
Location	Numeric	3	0	Ascending
EntryDate	Date			None
Comments	Memo			None
UserName	Character	30		None
EmailID	Character	30		None

Save the table as feedback.dbf, and close the table.

Next, create a feedback form. We should let the user add entries and view them, but once the system is live we don't want anybody to be able to delete or edit records. (Changing your boss' entries sounds entirely too tempting, especially with April Fools' Day approaching.) Use the Form Expert to help you create a feedback table, choosing the Feedback table and all the columns in it. Choose the columnar layout this time and any color scheme that suits your fancy. (In real life, I would recommend that you pick one scheme and stick to it, just for the sake of corporate consistency, but use this opportunity to experiment.)

When you get to the data operations dialog, choose only the access and control you want the users to have, as you see in Figure 2.14. Name the form Feedback. (For long term use, you would probably create at least two forms for the Feedback table: this one, that the users access, where you want to provide the maximum data protection, and a second, which allows you, as the database administrator, to clean up the database, eliminate duplicate or tasteless entries, and so on.)

The company Office table is the final piece. This table will describe each office in the Chocolate Conglomerate's cocoa-based empire. It should have a location ID as a key to identifying hotels and comments (have you noticed

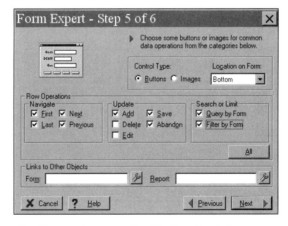

Figure 2.14   Choosing the user's access for the Feedback form.

that we've been using 2 for the Chinese hotels?), ordinary address and telephone contacts, directions from the airport, per diem hotel allowances for that city (New York City and San Francisco cost more than Cleveland), someone to call at the local office if you get lost, and a picture of the building so a traveler can recognize it when he finds it.

Use the Table Designer to create an office structure that looks like Figure 2.15.

The Office table has a fancier data type, a bitmap picture of each company office. IntraBuilder supports photographs and other bitmap images in the standard formats, including:

- Graphics Interchange Format (*.gif)
- Joint Photographic Experts Group (*.jpg, *.jpeg)
- XBitmap (*.xbm)
- Windows bitmap (*.bmp)
- Device Independent Bitmap (*.dib)
- Windows metafile (*.wmf)
- Enhanced Windows metafile (*.emf)
- Tagged Image File (*.tif, *.tiff)
- PC Paintbrush (*.pcx)
- Encapsulated PostScript (*.eps)

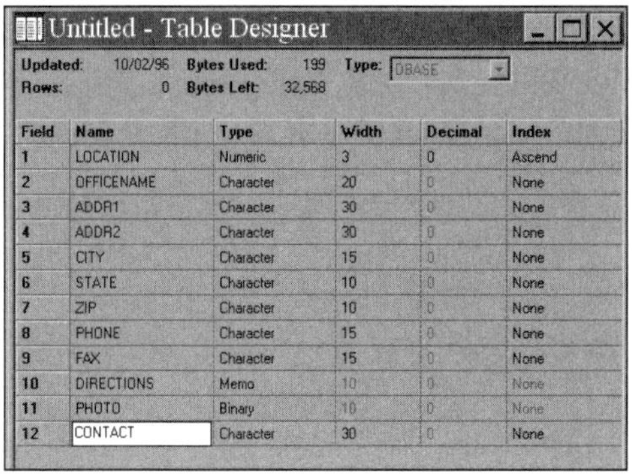

Field	Name	Type	Width	Decimal	Index
1	LOCATION	Numeric	3	0	Ascend
2	OFFICENAME	Character	20	0	None
3	ADDR1	Character	30	0	None
4	ADDR2	Character	30	0	None
5	CITY	Character	15	0	None
6	STATE	Character	10	0	None
7	ZIP	Character	10	0	None
8	PHONE	Character	15	0	None
9	FAX	Character	15	0	None
10	DIRECTIONS	Memo	10	0	None
11	PHOTO	Binary	10	0	None
12	CONTACT	Character	30	0	None

Figure 2.15 The Office table definition.

Pragmatically, use jpg formats whenever you can; it seems to have become the online standard based on both size and quality. Bmp is the next-best choice. Besides, I had trouble displaying database records on forms when they were in other formats. Jpg or bmp will keep your life simple.

Graphic Language

When you design forms (and intranet databases for that matter) always remain cognizant that your users might be accessing the site from a slow modem, over terrible phone lines, and usually in a big rush to get to the content. If you include a 20 MB graphic, they'll have to download that data—and that takes time. While it's instructive to include the graphic format here, don't use large images gratuitously. Remember that the emphasis of your site should be on the content you make accessible; while a picture is worth a thousand words it should never be provided at the expense of the site's content.

If you check the diagram of our online travel guide, at the beginning of this chapter, you'll see that the Office page links to the Feedback form (where people can comment about travel issues) and to the Hotel form. IntraBuilder provides the means for you to add links to other forms manually, but you can also use an Expert to get started.

Use the Form Expert to create a straightforward form for the Office table. Include all the column names, but don't worry too much about layout. We'll edit the form in a few minutes. When you get to the data access page, though, in Links to other objects, add the file name for the Hotel form, as you see in Figure 2.16. We will want to use the Feedback form too, but the IntraBuilder Expert only permits one at a time. Go ahead and finish creating the form, naming it Office.

When you look at the Office form you generated, you'll see a button that says Run Form, which will launch your Hotel form. Since you're working in IntraBuilder, not accessing it from your the Web site, IntraBuilder will open a second window for the Hotel form; on the Web site, the browser will load the Hotel form.

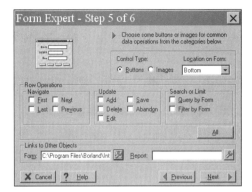

Figure 2.16   The IntraBuilder Form Expert lets you refer to other forms you can reference later.

While you're there, add a record or two to the Office database. To add or change the bitmap image, right-click on the area next to the Photo field; the display area will be hash-marked. Choose Import image and select the bmp or jpg file, as in Figure 2.17. Add a few records (just be sure to add one for China, at location 2), and then close the form.

Introducing The Form Designer

The office form doesn't provide everything we need, so let's change that.

With the Office form highlighted, choose File Design Form (or press Shift+F2) to open the Form Designer. The Form Designer is a grid on

Figure 2.17   Adding a bitmap image to a database table.

which you place text, graphics, data access objects (i.e., instructions for IntraBuilder to retrieve and update data), and controls (telling IntraBuilder what to do with those objects when the user does something with or to them, such as clicking on a button). Because it's a visual environment, it provides plenty of the (possibly familiar) functions that let you move, copy, and resize objects, with layout tools that help you align and position objects correctly.

The Component Palette lets you place controls where you want them, with immediate visual gratification. You can insert HTML codes (such as headings and ordinary links), general text, graphic lines (HTML calls these rules), bitmap images, passwords (hidden text), and selections in various manners including drop-down lists, list boxes, radio buttons, and check boxes, text areas, and buttons. Any object may be hidden. The Component Palette also lets you add Java applets to the form, and view and operate ActiveX applications. (Be aware that using ActiveX will limit the degree to which your site is usable with operating systems other than Microsoft Windows. If one of the reasons you chose an intranet was to minimize cross-platform problems, you should keep this thought in mind before you add ActiveX functionality.)

A Field Palette displays all the columns in the databases you have associated with the form, making it easy to drag-and-drop the appropriate column onto the visual surface. A toolbar gives you short-cuts to frequently used items. The largest item on the screen (next to the form itself) is the tabbed Inspector, which lets you adjust the behavior of the form itself as well as all the objects on it.

Notice the small box, a data retrieval object, at the top right of the Office form, labeled SQL. The boxes associated with databases appear when you're in the Form Designer, but are invisible to the user when she runs the form. IntraBuilder lets you include three kinds of data access, all of which display on the form while you're designing it but invisible to the users who run it. You can run a query on databases, including local DBF (dBase) and DB (Paradox) tables, as well as SQL, ODBC, or other remote tables. To access a table, you must use a **query** object; otherwise, the form won't be able to communicate with a database at all. A database access object lets you give

IntraBuilder forms access to SQL databases, permitting users to enter a login string for access to a SQL database. Session objects control record-locking and security. You can add multiple database access objects, linking the form to multiple tables in multiple ways.

The Form Expert created the SQL query object you see here; if you start with a blank page you will have to add your own. (We won't do it now, but all you have to do is drag the table from the IntraBuilder Explorer and drop it on the form.)

This extremely busy screen will make you yearn for a large monitor. After you fill out the paperwork to requisition a purchase order for your new monitor, get the temporarily-unnecessary parts out of your way. If they're visible, push aside the Field Palette and Component Palette, to make it easier to work with the Inspector, or use the View options in the menu bar to turn off their displays.

First, modify the column descriptions so they sound more English-like, as you did when changing the Hotel table a few pages back. You can also experiment with the Font properties to use any fonts you happen to have on your system.

Not Just A Pretty (Type) Face

Keep in mind that any non-standard fonts you use in your forms will need to be on both the server and the client systems. Minimize the number of fancy fonts, or your users might get annoyed at you because your site won't be legible. That's an important issue when you create an Internet Web site for customers, but it's even more meaningful when you create tools for your own coworkers to use. If nothing else, they know where your desk is, and whoopee cushions are inexpensive nowadays.

Always, always err on the side of usability and responsiveness, even if you have to sacrifice a pretty demeanor.

Use the Visual Properties in the Inspector to change colors for different objects. It's your graphical creation, after all; happily, the only limits in IntraBuilder is your own bad taste.

Move descriptions and text entry fields around to make the page prettier and to highlight information that deserves emphasis. To move a single item, select it and drag-and-drop it where you want it to go. To move more than one item at a time, use the mouse to draw a box around the group; dragging will re-position all of them at once. Resize items by selecting them and grabbing the boxes along the side or at the corners, then dragging the box to the size you prefer. If you move around several fields (such as rearranging the city, state, and ZIP to appear on one line), you might want to use the Layout Align option to reorganize the page's appearance.

You can waste a whole morning fiddling with such things without adding to the functionality of the form, but it will be prettier.

The Form Expert does an excellent job of creating useful forms that help you get started, but it's not very creative at naming objects. When you examine the various options in the Inspector, you'll notice that IntraBuilder calls objects exciting names like button13. Feel free to change these names to something you'd be more apt to remember, especially when you're working in a real-world environment.

At any rate, once you've completed your image enhancements (it sounds better than "messed around with fonts and colors"), it's time to make a few functional changes.

As you already discovered, telling IntraBuilder to link the Hotel form to the Office form added a button that said, simply, Run Form. Look at the Inspector for that button. Switch to the Events page. In the **OnServerClick** field, you'll see something that looks like

```
{;_sys.forms.run("C:\\Program
   Files\\Borland\\IntraBuilder\\APPS\\Travel\\Hotel.jfm")}
```

which tells IntraBuilder to run the Hotel form when you click on this button. On the first page of the Inspector, you can (and probably should) edit the text of that button to Area hotels, or something similar, so your users will know which form will be run when they click on the button; Run Form isn't especially meaningful.

IntraBuilder allowed us to connect the Hotel form automatically, but we need the Feedback table, too. Right-click on the Hotel button, and choose Copy. Paste the copy of the Hotel button onto the page, move it to a pleasing location, and go through the process of renaming the text to "Comment on the area" and updating the **OnServerClick** information (changing the file name), so IntraBuilder will start the Feedback form when that button is clicked. (Another way to add a database table to a form is to drag-and-drop it from the IntraBuilder Explorer; however, I'm a great believer in taking the easy way out. Copying something that works requires even less typing and minimizes typos. I hate typos.)

While you're thinking of it, save the form. IntraBuilder doesn't automatically save your changes; you can turn a form into an awesome work of art, pithy, important and life-changing, and then lose it all because you clicked on the Close button without telling IntraBuilder to save your work first. It's a good idea to get in the habit of doing so manually.

If you like, you can also run the form at this point, to see what changes you've made; your travel guide might look something like Figure 2.18—three forms linked together, however haphazardly.

Cranking Up The Code

This setup is imperfect. As currently implemented, the Office form will call the Hotel form all right, but it will show *all* the hotels in the database

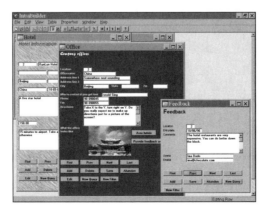

Figure 2.18   The travel guide site, taking shape.

not just the ones associated with the current location (China, for example). To show only the hotels for this area (and feedback too, for that matter), we need to write a few lines of code.

First, we have to tell the Office form to launch the Hotel form with only the records that match the current location; it will be necessary to pass the value in the location field (the "2" for China) to the Hotel form, so the database will know which records to retrieve. Then we have to make the associated changes in the Hotel form, instructing it to look for the location parameter and retrieve only the records matching that value (the "2" for China, again).

Examine the Inspector notebook a little closer. Its three pages (and information kept below each page) lets you control the properties, events, and methods for each object on the form. Later chapters will explore each in depth; at this point, we'll just poke at it to see what we can do.

What's In A Name?

If you're already an experienced object-oriented programmer, note that JavaScript refers to a method as a "function."

Open the design view of the Office table. As mentioned earlier, IntraBuilder generates default variable names that aren't very useful once you start programming with them. Since we'll be referring to it later, use the Inspector to change the field name (not the descriptive text) for the LOCATION column to locationText.

Click on the button you modified earlier that links to the Hotel form to select it. In the Inspector, choose the Events tab and look again at **OnServerClick**; it's the same field we edited earlier when we duplicated the button for the Feedback table. Since we want to override the default behavior that loads the Hotel form, it's necessary to change this. Click on the tool icon. IntraBuilder will ask you if it's okay to overwrite the existing information; say Okay, because that's precisely what we want to do. The Method Editor will be displayed, as you see in Figure 2.19;

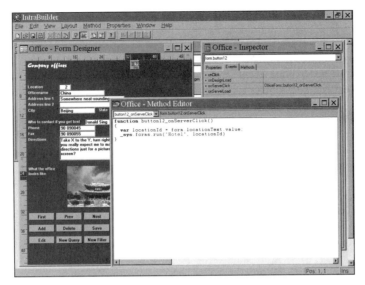

Figure 2.19   Using the Method Editor.

the drop-down list at the top of the Method Editor will identify what you're changing.

Type in the code in Listing 2.3. This is all it takes to tell IntraBuilder to pass the current value as in Location as a parameter when it starts the Hotel form.

LISTING 2.3   METHOD FOR CONNECTING THE OFFICE TO THE HOTEL.

```
function button12_onServerClick()
{
  var locationId = form.locationText.value;
  _sys.forms.run("Hotel", locationId)
}
```

Notice that the method is identified by IntraBuilder as **button12_onServer-Click()**, which would be distressingly unhelpful if we had to maintain this code or figure out what it was up to. It's a good example of why you should immediately change the names of objects in anything but the most trivial projects.

When you looked at the original code for the **onServerClick** field—the one that just ran the Hotel form—you might have noticed that IntraBuilder stuck the entire path name for the form name to be run. Depending on how you've organized your directories, it is probably okay to just use Hotel, as we do in this example, since **_sys.forms.run** defaults to the jfm file in the current directory. This is actually cleaner to deal with, since when you deploy the files over to the live directory you'll really hate cleaning up all the code that refers to temporary work directories.

Some other visual development environments let you drag-and-drop a form field from the visual surface to the editor, and automatically generate code to get the value from that field. The benefit of doing so is that you don't have to remember the name of every field in a big location that way. No such luck with IntraBuilder; neither the Field Palette nor drag-and-drop in the visual surface provides this capability. Stock up on Post-it Notes.

Save your changes in the Office form and close it. Open the Hotel form's design view. We have to make a few changes so this form can retrieve the locationID passed to it by the Office form; if we didn't, the Hotel form would just ignore the information.

Now that you're writing methods, it might help to use the IntraBuilder menu bar to display automatically the Method Editor. Alternatively, you can right-click on the background and tell IntraBuilder to display it. Once the Method Editor is displayed, choose Header from the drop-down menu and add the code in Listing 2.4.

LISTING 2.4 *MAKING CHANGES TO THE HOTEL HEADER.*

```
var f = new HotelForm();
f.argv = HOTEL.arguments;
f.open();
return;
```

This code duplicates IntraBuilder's normal behavior when a form is opened; compare it to the first two lines in Listing 2.2 to see what was duplicated. The only real change is the addition of the second line, which instructs IntraBuilder to get the argument passed to it. (It's actually an array of arguments, though we only have one to worry about.) The argument is made available to the other functions we define in this form. Anytime you pass information from one form to another, you'll have to include code similar to this.

While Hotel is the name of the form we called, **HotelForm** is the object name of the form. We created the new objects and passed the new arguments to the form in the object.

So far we've simply made that "2" for China available to the Hotel form, but we haven't done anything with it.

Now we have to follow the steps for creating a new function. With the general Hotel form selected (no objects, specifically), highlight the **onServerLoad** field in the Inspector, and choose the tool icon to begin working on it in the Method Editor. Add the code you see in Listing 2.5.

LISTING 2.5 *SPECIFYING WHAT INFORMATION IS RETRIEVED.*

```
function Form_onServerLoad()
{
   if ( form.argv.length == 1 )
   {
      if ( form.rowset.applyLocate("location=" + form.argv[0]) )
      {
         form.title = form.title + "s for area " + form.argv[0];
      }
      else
      {
         form.title = "No " + form.title + "s for area " +
            form.argv[0];
      }
   }
}
```

This code is executed whenever the server initially loads the form; it happens only once. If the user does a refresh with his browser, the code will not execute again. In this short program, we check to see if we did, indeed, get the number of arguments we expected. If we did, we call the **applyLocate** method, passing it the SQL constraint. If you're used to SQL programming, you probably would consider this the comparison you would have in a normal SQL when-clause. In English, it simply means "get the data that matches the value of the argument."

The form's real name doesn't limit us. If the retrieval operation finds any matching records for location 2, we set the title to "Hotels for area 2." Otherwise, we set the title to "No hotels for area 2."

If we wanted to make the operation a little spiffier and if no records was found, we could insert the value (2) into the LOCATION field, minimizing the amount of time the user needs to spend entering new data. But let's leave this simple example as it is. To finish up the project, you would also need to perform the same operation with the Feedback table, limiting the feedback information by the location specified—but now you know enough to do so on your own.

Save your work, and then go ahead and run the forms. Once you've satisfied yourself that they work correctly (typos can be deadly), view the forms as JavaScript, and see how much of the generated code you can figure out. It's probably more than you initially expected. Test the system as you've built it so far; it should look something like Figure 2.20 in your browser.

Pulling It All Together

You're probably used to Web home pages, which are the entrance to a larger site, like the foyer in a home or office. IntraBuilder home pages are similar; they, too, are entry pages, though their emphasis is on organizing and presenting IntraBuilder applications as well as ordinary Web pages. For our purposes, we'll create a home page form that Chocolate Conglomerate employees can use to access the travel guide; naturally, you could, and would, add other functionality as it's developed.

IntraBuilder provides a Home Page Form Expert to help you create a home page, although it isn't quite as easy to stumble across as are its other Experts.

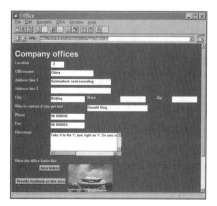

Figure 2.20   Hey, it's working!

In four quick steps, IntraBuilder walks you through the process of choosing a title, logo, Webmaster email address, and links to other forms.

From the menu bar, choose File|New|Home page expert. The by-now familiar dialog asks if you want to use the Designer or the Expert; choose the latter. On the first page of the Expert, type in the name of the company and any description you'd like to include; pick an image file to use as the company logo (see Figure 2.21).

In the second step, you select the forms IntraBuilder should add as links. In this case, the only one we need to add is the Office form (since the other two are connected from within that one). Note that the text you add can include any description you want; you aren't stuck with Office. Select a scheme and finally click on Run Form.

Once you have verified that it works the way you expect in IntraBuilder, you're ready to deploy the files and make it live. Copy the files from the Travel directory to the IntraBuilder Apps directory; when you link to the site from your Web browser, you should be able to use it.

In a more holistic scenario, we would provide a lot more information. The Chocolate Conglomeration's site would probably include several text-based Web pages describing the company's rules about travel expense reporting, overall guidelines about behavior on the road, and so on. If you wanted to

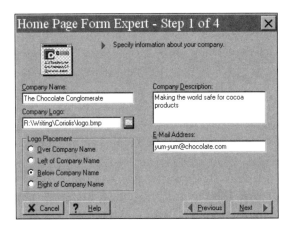

Figure 2.21   Creating a home page form.

get fancy, you could add a travel expense reporting database and forms to this system, which could make the people in charge of reimbursing expenses up-to-date. Perhaps the check would be ready by the time you returned from the business trip.

We haven't done anything throughout this project to check for the validity of data; nothing verifies that a given database record contains a required subset of data, for instance. Doing so would require more programming.

Conclusion

This isn't bad for a first try, is it? We created a Web site based on a few databases linked together by topic. We explored most of the basic functions in IntraBuilder (though you haven't worked with queries or reports yet).

By this point, you should be familiar with what IntraBuilder can do, and ready to dive into meatier topics.

Ingredients For Intranet Development

Esther Schindler

The technological elements that IntraBuilder uses and depends on, and how all those pieces are blended together in an intranet feast.

For seven years, we lived on an island off the coast of Maine. It was a beautiful place if you can stand winter, but in culinary terms it was extremely dull: Most residents considered a sprinkle of paprika to be awfully daring. The nearest pizza place was 20 miles away. The nearest Mexican restaurant an hour and a half away, if the weather was good, which it usually wasn't. If we wanted ethnic food we cooked it ourselves.

We collected cookbooks and learned to order food via mail order; UPS delivered galangal, pasilla chiles, and smokehouse bacon on a regular basis. We became great cooks. To ethnic food novices like our Mainer friends, the ingredients were strange and the dinners we cooked were, uh, exotic. But they always asked for seconds.

Every ethnic cookbook begins with an introduction to the country's cuisine, typical ingredients, and how they are generally combined into a meal. That's the intent of this chapter. I'll explain the basic "ingredients" of IntraBuilder and its cuisine: how to think about developing software for intranets. Then I'll blend together the pieces so you can enjoy a meal of another sort.

Intranet Development Concepts

If you're an experienced programmer with a traditional background, learning to develop software for an intranet will introduce dozens of new ingredients to your kitchen. It's easy (and fun) to distract yourself with the newness of each item, but doing so might not help you get work accomplished. It's faster to get productive when you have a context for each new technology ingredient.

That's especially true if you're comfortable with traditional development technologies; like the frustration of getting into a rental car at midnight in a strange city, you're apt to confuse yourself by (virtually) reaching for a stick shift that isn't there, or turning on the windshield wipers when you intended to adjust the headlights. Be prepared to unload some of your software development assumptions, or you'll trip over them.

Creating an ordinary, traditional application isn't too complicated in terms of the ingredients you work with. You might have a network, and you'd certainly have a user sitting at a workstation. To create your application, you rely on at least one compiler or development environment and at least one database engine (or one type of database), which you access directly. At the end of the project, you wind up with a single exe file that gets executed on a single machine, even if that "running on a single machine" model is repeated in many instances. In that traditional model, you also have some degree of predictability about the nature of the workstation where the application runs. Often, in order to establish that predictability, you set minimum requirements for users: a Pentium with 8 MB of RAM, a particular operating system, and a specified requirement of hard disk space.

Intranet development is somewhat different. For one thing, it requires an awareness of multiple ingredients that work in concert. As a traditional software developer, you'll be tempted to think of a Web server as a network server, but it's not. A Web server isn't simply dishing out files, executable programs, and printer resources to users. Instead, the Web server gets URL requests from the clients and, on the fly (based on what you tell it to do, using IntraBuilder or some other tool), creates an HTML file that (probably) embeds JavaScript in it and sends it back to the client. The client system's Web browser interprets the HTML, interprets and runs the JavaScript code, presumably accomplishing whatever cool stuff you wanted it to do. If a local area network is a digital cafeteria lady with her bun in a hair net dishing out whatever the Tuesday Special happens to be, a Web server (and all the tools associated with it) is a short-order cook who creates custom dinners on request.

Primordial Servers

Back in the bad old days of software development (which I blush to admit that I remember), the mentality was server-centric. (We didn't call them servers in those days. We called them mainframes.) All computations happened at the mainframe. Files were managed by the mainframes. The client was a *very* dumb terminal that might, if you were lucky, have a couple of programmable function keys. On the positive side, because computer services were centralized, work could be managed in a somewhat organized fashion by people who generally understood the technology. The disadvantage was that computer departments didn't necessarily understand what users wanted, and users ended up feeling like they'd rather just do the work themselves. At any rate, in this model, Information Services departments controlled all software development, and they were perpetually behind schedule.

Distributed Chaos

PCs swung the control pendulum fully in the other direction. Whether out of resentment towards turgid IS departments or the joy of controlling one's own data, many adopted a distributed viewpoint where everything— computations, database management, you name it—happened at the PC workstation. Applications might be loaded from the server, but primarily the LAN was used as a data repository, a centralized data safe-deposit box. The upside was that users had power over their own data and a better idea of what they wanted; the downside was that wheels were often reinvented and companies' hardware and software standards became disorganized. Departmental developers controlled whatever software projects they could get their hands on (and shunted off the boring or difficult stuff to another department), and they were perpetually behind schedule.

Naturally, both methodologies have their appropriate venues. Unfortunately, in most companies, the issue of application development management gets tied up with political control, the business equivalent of the battle between chaos (innovation) and order (standards). However, technical issues get involved in the equation as well, such as network through-put and the duplication of data at client workstations.

An intranet server is not a shrink-wrapped package, nor is it what we traditionally consider a server platform. Think of an intranet server as a kit of tools that gives you the ability to deploy information and access applications quickly, without having to worry about client-side capabilities. An intranet application is a client/server application that can reside on the server, the client, or be partitioned judiciously across both.

To many intranet proponents, the "without worrying about client-side issues" is key. In the past, developers had to be excessively concerned with the client workstation; on an intranet, the client's needs and behavior are almost irrelevant. Back in the mainframe era, the terminal attached to the system was irrelevant to the process of designing and writing applications; programmers put all their efforts into building functionality. Arguably, the LAN dragged us down into the morass of client issues.

Obviously, the people who are gung ho at promoting the benefits of intranets will explain that, like Goldilocks discovering the third bowl of porridge, intranet clients are not too thick, not too thin, they're just right. The real-world viability is, like all such things, probably somewhere in between.

Thin Clients

The *thin* client is the basic idea behind the whole thing. A thin client is, quite simply, anything that can run a Web browser, as opposed to an elaborately implemented client-side custom application with built-in Web connectivity (a *fat client*). Of course, any time that the computer industry says you *can* be thin, some people think it means you *should* be thin—rather like computing Weight Watchers, I suppose. That is why computer hardware companies are scurrying to create and sell $500 network computers that can run a browser and not much else.

While you think about the differences and similarities between traditional development and intranet development, contemplate how this changes your concerns about network traffic. Since the server is once again given a lot of work to do, more bandwidth will be needed to support the increased traffic from the server to the client and vice versa. That may change how you write applications. Once you think about the amount of data you have to transport over the network (or worse, over a modem), you might reconsider the wisdom of including some of those pretty but gratuitous background graphics. You must maintain all you've learned about effective user interfaces—users will never accept *less*—but now you face the added responsibility of incorporating your data presentation skills into an environment where through-put is the weak link in the chain.

Writing applications for an intranet means that you have to get used to a whole bunch of foreign ingredients in a hurry. Instead of working with local tools that you access directly, you deal with the tools at arm's length. You'll soon surround yourself with ODBC, Web server API extensions, and other such software aids.

Putting Ingredients Together

It's easy to get overwhelmed when you first look at the various chunks of technology that go into IntraBuilder. It's like looking at a complex recipe for *pollo molé*, which has 28 separate ingredients (including four separate kinds of chiles) and several pages of instructions. The process is confusing, you're not sure what needs to be done when, and some of the ingredients— like, for instance, chocolate, chiles, and turkey—might not seem to go together. (It's delicious. Trust me.)

Let's examine some of the ingredients that IntraBuilder uses, so we can better understand how they work together. Some tools run on the server. Some run on the client. A few use both.

Ingredients On The Server Side

On the server, intranet applications can include interpreted scripts (written in languages such as csh or Perl under UNIX, REXX on OS/2, or various

Basic variants under Windows NT), and compiled binary programs (either standalone or as DLLs). The operating-system specific tools give the Webmaster full access to the resources of the operating system. For instance, a REXX-enabled Web server permits an OS/2 Webmaster to use any REXX-enabled application on the OS/2 Warp computer, such as DB2/2 databases. However, those tools generally have to be hand-constructed and are less portable to other operating systems.

Another important server component, used almost everywhere, is the Common Gateway Interface (CGI). A major benefit of CGI is that it's a *real* standard; the exact same interface is available on *every* Web server regardless of platform, without anyone else's ideas of a "standard plus extensions" thrown in to muddy the waters (which is like a can of ordinary tomatoes, except for the basil and spices we threw in). CGI does a great job at processing forms, but it's slow because CGI stores its data in system environment variables. To do something with the data, you need a separate program (usually written in C) to manipulate it. CGI programs are separate executables that run at the server; every time a page is accessed, the CGI program (and any database access it requires) has to be started, run, and exited.

Options abound. A Web server can use a customized application programming interface (API) instead of CGI or in addition to it, such as Netscape's NSAPI, O'Reilly & Associates' WSAPI, or Microsoft's IIS' ISAPI. These proprietary APIs promise—and deliver—higher performance and greater functionality than CGI.

ISAPI, the Microsoft solution, is in a fierce battle with Netscape's NSAPI. Each of them offers the same basic functionality, providing a high-performance interface to back-end applications with custom functions that interface with the Web server. At heart, each of these is just a DLL that you add to the server's memory space. The API running in the server space is always there so it doesn't get bogged down in a start/exit cycle.

These API extensions are clearly in the market position of "pick a standard, any standard," but all of them really do offer useful proprietary enhancements. For example, NSAPI exposes the server architecture to programmers, allowing access to functions such as authentication and processing forms.

The best part, from your point of view as an IntraBuilder user, is that you don't have to care about the benefits and disadvantages of these various extensions. IntraBuilder will work with nearly all of them (assuming they run on Windows 95 or Windows NT), and you don't have to concern yourself with the details.

Ingredients On The Client Side

The primary client ingredient is, of course, the Web browser. If Java is supported on the operating system where the Web browser runs, the client can also run applets and embedded scripts, code that the server sends to the client and executes on the client. Java (which is far less similar to JavaScript than their names imply) generates platform-independent byte codes that ostensibly run securely on the client. JavaScript is a browser-based scripting language which, as you already saw in Chapter 2, "Cranking It Up," runs on the client system as well. JavaScript is embedded in the HTML that the server sends to the client.

It's also possible to write partitioned Web applications that use both client and server. A Java application might run on the client but access data on the server.

As you can see, the ordinary state of intranet development is a collection of intertwined technologies and tools. So far, so good. But much as I hate to admit it, in order to simplify your access to all of the above, IntraBuilder actually adds more technology to the pot.

Database Foundations

IntraBuilder works the way our family (my parents and four children) used to unload groceries. We lived in a tall, narrow house, blessed with several steep stairways and a food pantry in the basement. After a trip to the grocery store, instead of making many trips up and down the back stairs, my parents organized a passing party: My mother would be stationed in the pantry while my father unloaded grocery bags, and our job as kids was to hand soup cans and pudding mixes downstairs, one kid to the next—Phyllis to Sam, etc.—with occasional forays into the kitchen to put milk in the refrigerator.

The entire enterprise took the effort of six people, but it was remarkably efficient since no one individual had to travel very far. And it sure beat running up and down the basement steps.

Many of IntraBuilder's pieces, as well as the underlying technologies on which it depends, work by the same theory as my parents' grocery-passing scheme. Several software "children" pass information back and forth and exchange data, one item at a time. Eventually, the item reaches its ultimate destination. Just as my brother was expected to decide that cheese should be routed to the kitchen, each broker, server, or library in the interrelated IntraBuilder pantheon has such a job.

If you're used to traditional software development and dive headlong into the innards of IntraBuilder, that degree of indirection—Sam passes the bread to Phyllis, who gives it to Esther to take into the next room—can be enormously frustrating. Why doesn't Sam just take the bread into the kitchen himself? Nonetheless, like my parents' passing parties, the method is truly more efficient.

As you'll learn in Chapter 7, "Database 101," every database vendor has its own storage format and its own interface to that format. Ideally, at least in the opinion of those vendors, the world would standardize on the one perfect format (that is, *theirs*), but this isn't a homogenous world. Applications often need to access different sorts of databases on a variety of hardware platforms and across operating systems. Either programmers would have to write applications specific to each proprietary database interface (which is doubtful) or someone would have to come up with a translation engine to perform that function. Someone did.

ODBC

Microsoft developed Open Database Connectivity (ODBC), a translation API that permits you to abstract a program (that is, separate it conceptually) from a database. Third-party databases provide an interface to the ODBC

Manager through their own ODBC drivers. Your program need only talk to ODBC, and you can access any database for which you have an ODBC driver. You do so in a cross between predefined ODBC APIs and a very plain SQL. The ODBC Manager translates your generic request into the calls necessary to talk to the specific database: Paradox or DB2/2 or Oracle. The driver manager provides the interface to the application. It also dynamically loads the necessary driver for the database server to which the application connects. In ODBC parlance, the database engine is called a data source. (See Figure 3.1.)

You need to install an ODBC driver specific to the type of database you will be using. Not surprisingly, Borland includes ODBC drivers for dBase and Paradox right out of the box. If you need others, you'll need to acquire them from the database vendor. Most database vendors have ODBC drivers available for download from their company Web site.

The good news, of course, is that you don't have to know everything—or even *anything*—about every database that your application needs to access. You need only know ODBC. This is very much a good thing.

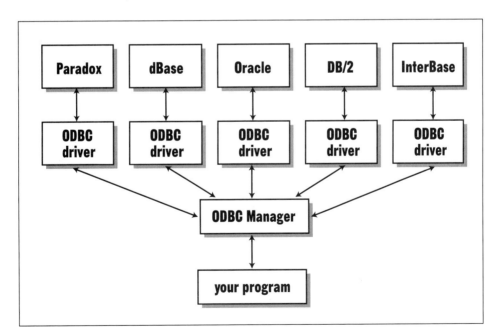

Figure 3.1   How ODBC works.

The disadvantage to ODBC is that it will always be slower than accessing the database directly. (This will, of course, be the case with nearly any translation layer API you could name.) For instance, nearly every database worth its salt has proprietary optimizations that read or sort or what-have-you. Because ODBC is generic in nature, there's no way that it can exploit every database's strengths. If you accessed DB2/2 directly, for instance, you could use DB2/2 extensions that may or may not be supported through ODBC, such as graphics storage, huge text blocks, math on date/time fields, and so on.

Even for operations that are straightforward duplicates of database requests, at best you're wasting CPU time with a call to a call. This is as inefficient as asking Phyllis to hand Sam the spaghetti, when Sam is standing right in front of you. Of course, you'd be wasting a lot more human time by writing routines specific to a database you don't know very well—which is like asking Phyllis to give Sam the spaghetti because he's the tallest and can store it on the highest pantry shelf without getting a step ladder.

Another real-world consideration is that ODBC is defined and controlled by Microsoft, which is practically an API factory. The ODBC specification is thus a moving target. Most vendors (including, presumably, Borland) pick a version of ODBC that they're willing to live with and stick to that one. (Microsoft has its own extensions for ODBC, which seems to circumvent the purpose of having one standard API to talk to.)

ODBC is just one ingredient, however, like the curry paste you assemble before you cook a dish that uses it. (And, like curry paste, ODBC is used with several other Borland and non-Borland products, so it never hurts to have a general understanding.)

The Borland Database Engine

In addition to ODBC, Borland provides its own Borland Database Engine (BDE) with IntraBuilder. The BDE provides a universal translator between the front-end tool (that is, IntraBuilder) and the database. This sounds a lot like ODBC, doesn't it? The BDE, while it resembles ODBC superficially, actually has an agenda quite its own. The BDE is a collection of database access routines defined by Borland to provide a common access mechanism to Borland's own database formats from within Borland's development tools. In a sense, the BDE is a driver manager that allows Borland's development environments like Delphi, IntraBuilder, and the upcoming OPEN JBuilder to use the same compiled code to get at the same Borland databases.

Yes, it's another layer, and another pair of hands at the database passing party. When you're not using a Borland database on the back end, the BDE makes its moves through ODBC. Through ODBC? Yes, as Figure 3.2 shows. When your application wants to communicate with a Microsoft Access database, for example, its request is passed through the BDE, then the ODBC database manager, then the Access ODBC driver, and finally to Access. It sounds awkward, but it's still a heck of a lot better than running up and down the basement steps.

Where you see ODBC in Figure 3.2, you can insert the contents of the ODBC architecture you saw in Figure 3.1; this is where you add the two tablespoons of ODBC curry to the BDE dish.

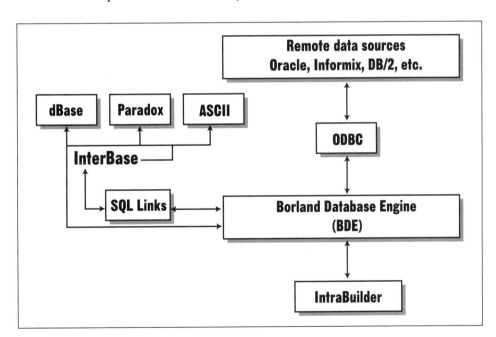

Figure 3.2   The Borland development environment architecture.

Despite the "engine" in its name, the BDE is much more like an API than an engine. It's a DLL full of database access routines. You could think of it as a new standard database access API that Borland is trying to insert into the computing world—though as much for its own benefit as for yours. BDE does offer several technical advantages, including:

◆ A common database query engine, with native access to PC and SQL database servers.

◆ Small memory and disk space footprint.

◆ Transparent connections to ODBC-compliant data sources. Applications can use BDE features even when they're using an ODBC driver, such as cached update transactional models and bi-directional cursors.

◆ Shared system services for data buffering, memory management, and other performance enhancements.

◆ IntraBuilder encapsulates much of the BDE into high-level objects that can be edited and used when you create IntraBuilder applications.

One key BDE concept is database aliases. BDE aliases are shorthand names that you refer to in your application. They're much like a network drive assignment, letting you connect the name (R:) with a specific location (\aloe\writing\coriolis). Later on, you can change the path where the database files are kept without having to edit all the code that refers to those files. Database references within applications can use alias names, making the applications easily portable.

To change an alias, you use a tool named, appropriately, the BDE Configuration Utility, as you see in Figure 3.3. You also use the BDE Configuration Utility to add ODBC drivers to your system.

IntraBuilder supports an automatic optimistic locking scheme, but you can configure pessimistic locking through a variety of methods.

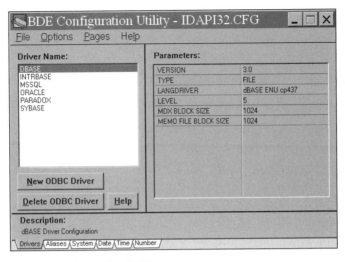

Figure 3.3 The BDE Configuration Utility.

The IntraBuilder Server

That covers how IntraBuilder handles databases. But how does it connect the databases to all those Web server connections we examined earlier?

In addition to the IntraBuilder Designer (the integrated development environment in which you'll spend the bulk of your time), IntraBuilder provides IntraBuilder Server components. These process management tools consist of an IntraBuilder Broker component and one or more agent components. The IntraBuilder Server software works alongside your Web server software, responding to requests from Web browsers.

The Intrabuilder Broker And Its Agents

The Broker is split in two parts on disk: INTRASRV.ISV and INTRASRV.DLL. You'll find one or more IntraBuilder agents, instances of INTRA.EXE, each of which run minimized on the server's desktop. Additional agents can be configured to handle increased network traffic.

The IntraBuilder Broker communicates with the Web server. To be exact, it exchanges information with the httpd server. IntraBuilder Broker, in turn, communicates with each of its agents, whose jobs are to manage

JavaScript server processes, report, and form objects. The IntraBuilder Broker is a CGI broker; if you look at the installation instructions, you'll see that it replaces WinCGI.

Getting the files installed correctly can be awkward, so it helps to understand what IntraBuilder will be looking for, in what place. By default, IntraBuilder expects to find htm, html, jfm, and jrp files in a directory that, as the installation instructions tell you, gets an *ibapps* alias in your Web server setup.

IntraBuilder will look for the tables, bitmaps, and other files you reference in your forms and reports, by default, in the directory relative to the IntraBuilder agent's base directory. So, if your form is in \intrabuilder-\apps\cocoa and it refers to a bitmap cake.jpg, IntraBuilder will look for it in the cocoa directory. This might or might not be what you had in mind. The files that you will need to deploy to make an application work are:

- forms (jfm)
- reports (jrp)
- base forms (jcf)
- custom components (cc)
- scripts (js)
- HTML (htm and html)
- bitmaps (gif, jpg, and others)

The database tables and index files also need to be copied to the correct directories.

The IntraBuilder online help files provide a few guidelines to deal with the where's-my-file directory annoyances, but frankly, deploying files is one of the weak spots in IntraBuilder development.

The Integrated Development Environment (IDE)

By this point, you understand the ingredients and the overall cuisine of IntraBuilder, so you have a context about how they're used. But you *use* them in the IntraBuilder integrated development environment (IDE), the virtual stove on which you prepare your IntraBuilder applications. Some of the documentation refers to this as the IntraBuilder Designer.

As you learned in the hands-on example in Chapter 2, "Cranking It Up," the IDE is arranged in a notebook format with tabs dividing the different tools (Forms, Queries, Reports, etc.). Each notebook has at least one Expert to guide you through the basics of creating just about every object in intranet development. A Home Page Expert is also "hidden" in the menus.

As you already learned, you create applications by placing components on forms and reports. You can modify the properties of those components interactively or by writing JavaScript code. Components specific to data access include Database objects, Query objects, and Session objects. Database objects create a connection to the database server—not as you might be used to from more traditional PC software development—to the database. Query objects are primarily containers for SQL statements and the set of rows that result from the statement. They happen across that IntraBuilder-to-database-server connection. Session objects permit separate handles into the BDE.

While the IntraBuilder application is being executed, the server keeps track of the state of the Database object(s) on every client browser. Its job (among others) is to ensure that whenever a user presses a Next button, the next record in the user's particular result set is displayed.

You'll be working more with the IDE and learning the details of how each piece works in future chapters. For now, however, you have a context of how the whole mechanism works together.

By now you're probably hungry for some exotic food. How far away *is* the nearest restaurant that serves *pollo molé?*

Development System Configuration 4

Terence Goggin

An easy, step-by-step guide to choosing a system, installing Windows NT, and selecting from these three intranet servers: Borland's Web Server, O'Reilly's WebSite, and Netscape's FastTrack.

*I*n this chapter, we'll set up an intranet/IntraBuilder server. By the end of the chapter, you'll have a step-by-step outline of how to choose hardware components, how to determine their compatibility, and how to choose and install Web server software. All of this is based on my own recent experience building a system.

How To Select Your Components

The first decision you have to make is whether to buy or build. The place to start is an informal survey of the market to determine which—if any—off-the-shelf systems would work for you. What we quickly discovered was that ready-made solutions offered either far too much or far too little, and none even came close to meeting our needs.

For example, one company would not install a hard drive larger that 2 gigabytes unless we opted to go with its "server" model. That sounded okay until the rep told us that the server option was an additional $2,000. The only difference between the server option and the machine we were attempting to create was that they'd install the larger drive for us. Many stores and catalogs did not offer any Windows NT machines, and since many of the Windows 95 machines had limited RAM and hard drive capacity, it didn't seem practical to buy one of these systems and then attempt to install NT. Therefore, we concluded that the only way to get what we really wanted was to build the machine ourselves.

Building Your Own

To build your own machine, you'll need to choose hardware components before thinking about software. To do that, start with a thorough analysis of system requirements:

◆ How big must the hard drive be to hold your data?

◆ Will you go SCSI or IDE?

◆ How much RAM will the system require?

◆ Will you need a Pentium or will a 486-class machine do?

◆ Motherboard?

The Unexpected Problem

At first glance, this might seem like a fairly routine component selection. However, because NT is still a relatively new operating system, it is not yet supported by all vendors. This means there's a crucial difference with NT— the question of compatibility. This can come as a real surprise to anyone who has cruised along in Windows 3.x or Windows 95 with virtually no compatibility issues, but when constructing a system specifically for NT, you'll have to deal with those issues before going any farther. So, how do you know if a given product will run acceptably with NT?

There are three ways to determine this. However, since the first two may not be 100 percent reliable, you'll probably want to use a combination of all three.

First, on a semi-regular basis, Microsoft releases a Hardware Compatibility List (or HCL) that contains, as you might guess, a list of hardware devices that are supposed to be compatible with Windows NT. However, this list is not always the best source for compatibility information. Some devices that are 100 percent compatible are not listed. Other devices listed are not officially supported by the manufacturer. Perhaps if enough people have used the device without complaint it is then considered to be compatible. But if you buy it and you can't get it to run properly, you may be stuck. In some cases, the manufacturer's tech support line will not even attempt to help you configure the device.

Next, consult the manufacturers themselves. If the product advertises compatibility with Windows NT, there's a very good chance the device will work just fine. Of course, just as with unsupported devices being listed on the HCL, there are some products that don't advertise compatibility and yet are, in fact, fully compatible with NT.

Which brings us to the third and final method to determine NT compatibility: Use the Internet to ask someone. For example, on CompuServe try both the vendors' forums as well as the Windows NT forums. Usually, the answers you'll receive are based on individuals' experiences, which will tell you more about the product than either the HCL or an advertisement.

Our third and final goal in selecting components was to keep the cost low. While this goal is sometimes contradictory to the first two, a few minor changes here and there can help to keep costs down without a huge loss of either features or compatibility.

SPECIFYING A HARD DRIVE

As you know, the rule of thumb when specifying a hard drive is to get the largest drive you can afford and think you're unlikely to outgrow. In our case, we thought that 2 gigabytes were too small but 9 gigabytes too expensive, so we compromised on 4 gigabytes, which was about half the cost of the larger drive.

SCSI Or IDE

Once the hard drive question was settled, the controller question was—for our machine—answered. Because 4-gigabyte drives are only available in SCSI format, we really didn't have much choice in the matter—it was either SCSI or a smaller drive. SCSI is more expensive than IDE, but it can be worth the extra expense if your requirements include the following:

1. If you're likely to need (now or in the near future) drives larger than 2 to 3 gigabytes, consider SCSI. IDE hard drives are getting larger, but SCSI still dominates the large-drive arena.

2. If you anticipate adding more than two to three hard drives in the future, consider SCSI. Even the Enhanced IDE (EIDE) standard only supports a maximum of four drives. If likely to need more than four drives, SCSI is the way to go.

3. If you'd like to use Iomega's ZIP drive, you'll definitely need SCSI. As of this writing, the ZIP drive parallel port version is still not supported under NT. You should use SCSI if you're even thinking about a ZIP drive.

RAM

The next choice we had to make was how much RAM to put in the machine. Although Microsoft rightly claims that NT will run in 16 or even 12 MB, performance under those figures really isn't acceptable. Conventional wisdom holds that NT needs a minimum of 32 MB of RAM. In addition, *InfoWorld* magazine tested 4.0 and found that 16 MB gave poor performance, 32 MB gave very respectable performance, and 64 MB the best performance. Since 32 MB were adequate and 64 MB were more money than we wanted to spend, we went with the 32 MB.

CPU

We also had to decide on a CPU. In the same test on RAM and NT performance, *InfoWorld* magazine also tested CPUs. The 486 chips performed so poorly on each test that the clear choice was the Pentium. We chose the midrange model—a 133 MHz Pentium—both in terms of performance and price.

Motherboard

Only the motherboard remained to be chosen. We decided on one with an on-board SCSI controller—even though it was a more expensive option. In doing so, we hoped to avoid configuration problems that might surface with a separately purchased SCSI controller card. The requirement of on-board SCSI did increase the cost somewhat. However, as we later learned, the SCSI portion of the setup practically configured itself, which justified the higher cost.

Summary

When it comes to Windows NT, it's always best to play it safe. Consider your goals ahead of time (making sure that compatibility is one of those goals, of course). Then, choose your components according to your goals and you can have an easy and trouble-free NT installation.

Installation Tips For Windows NT Itself

Whether you're upgrading an existing system or building one from scratch, you may have a difficult installation ahead of you. Of course, this is greatly minimized if you've chosen your hardware carefully, but it's still an issue. Based on some of our experiences with previous installations of Windows NT, there are a few things you can do to make it go more smoothly.

First, turn off any hardware level (i.e., BIOS or hard drive controller) disk caching. We've seen some installations where crucial parts of the installation files will not get completely copied from the CD-ROM drive to the hard drive simply because of disk caching.

Second, some newer motherboards can boot from a CD-ROM—provided, of course, that the CD-ROM is bootable. The trouble here is that when you boot from the NT CD-ROM, the set-up program is started again. Clearly, this is not what you want if NT is already installed (or is currently in the process of installing). So make sure that you remove the NT CD once you're finished with it.

Third, as part of its normal installation procedure, NT restarts your machine several times. However, SCSI controllers usually don't reset themselves along with the rest of the machine. If you find that your SCSI controller is locking up as the system reboots, you may want to turn the machine off (for just a few seconds) each time NT tries to restart the machine. The NT set-up program should resume right where it left off without complaint.

Finally, when you install NT you're essentially overwriting any existing operating system, so the set-up program will ask you to make several emergency boot disks. Make sure that you keep these boot disks—they can prove invaluable in completing the installation should it suddenly stall or crash.

Choosing A Web Server

Now that we've got Windows NT set up and ready to go, we'll move on to the Web server software side of things. Specifically, we'll look at choosing, installing, and configuring a Web server to use with IntraBuilder, which you will need in order to publish documents on your intranet. Without it no one could retrieve documents—let alone IntraBuilder forms—from your Web site/host machine.

Background

The term *Web server* refers to the software that manages the retrieval of files from the machine on which it resides (the host) as they are requested by a user at another machine (the client).

Web server software is constantly running in the background on the host machine, listening and waiting for files to be requested. When a user at a client machine opens up, say, Netscape Navigator, and enters the URL of a page on the intranet host, that user is requesting a document from the host machine.

When the request is received by the host, the Web server's job is to find the requested file and send it over the network to the client machine.

Borland has thoughtfully packaged two free Web servers with IntraBuilder—Borland's own plain vanilla Web Server and the high-end Netscape FastTrack server. (For comparison purposes, the popular midrange O'Reilly's WebSite server will also be covered here, although it is not provided with IntraBuilder.)

The Tradeoffs

When you choose your Web server, there are several issues you'll want to consider. The first and most important issue is the time it takes to get the Web server up and running for the first time. If you need to get your intranet started in a hurry, it's a safe bet you're not too concerned about the fancy features a given Web server offers. If that's the case, the Borland Web Server (yes, that's actually its name) is the one for you. It's installed when you install IntraBuilder and requires no configuration at all. Just add it to the startup group in your Start menu (so that it will be started each time you start NT) and you won't have to think about your Web server again. (WebSite server comes in second and FastTrack third in terms of amount of configuration required.)

Next, you'll want to consider the overall ease of administration of the server. In other words, how easy is it for you to change a single aspect of the server's behavior every now and then. As the simplest and plainest of the Web servers, the Borland Web Server has the fewest properties to change, and changing any single property is but a few clicks away. Ditto for O'Reilly's WebSite server—it has quite a bit more functionality than the Borland Web Server, but it's still easy to change any one value or property. Both of these servers' property dialog boxes are only a right-click away. The FastTrack server, on the other hand, uses an HTML interface to manage its properties. This can be disconcerting and may take a bit of getting used to. Of course, this is largely a matter of personal preference and you might even want to try out some additional servers until you find one that suits you.

Third, consider the feature-related issues. For instance, if you need to restrict access to certain files or set up individual user accounts, you'll need to use either the WebSite or FastTrack servers because the Borland Web Server does not offer this functionality. Likewise, if you're going to need Secure Socket Layer (SSL) capability, Netscape's FastTrack server is almost certainly the way to go.

You may find that there are other issues for your applications, but this is a good, general list by which to choose your Web server.

Borland Web Server

Of the three Web server packages, the Borland Web Server is definitely the simplest. While that means that it doesn't offer some of the features of the other two servers covered here, it does mean that the Borland Web Server is the easiest to install, configure, and use.

Installation

When you install IntraBuilder, the Borland Web Server is automatically installed for you. You don't even have to decide where to install it—that's already decided for you as well. Other than about 600 K of free disk space on your C drive, the Borland Web Server has no special requirements beyond IntraBuilder's own requirements. The only sort of install work you might want to do is add a shortcut to it in the Startup group so that it will be started each time you start Windows NT. After all, if your machine is going to be used as a Web server, you should probably start-up the Web server software when the machine is started.

Configuration

Because the Borland Web Server comes pre-configured, one of its clear advantages is that it already knows everything it needs to know about IntraBuilder applications and should be able to run them just fine without any additional tweaking.

Use

The Borland Web Server starts as a taskbar icon, near the clock. By right-clicking it, you can pull up a menu that lists four options: View Connections, Shutdown (or Startup), Properties, and Exit.

VIEW CONNECTIONS

If you select the first option—View Connections—you will see a window like that shown in Figure 4.1.

The main window for the Borland Web Server displays a list of the most recent requests that it has processed. It is instructive to watch this window as documents and IntraBuilder forms are retrieved by users because you

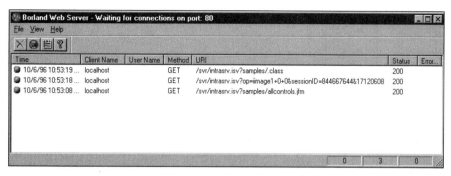

Figure 4.1   The main window of the Borland Web Server.

can see exactly what's involved in displaying a single document. (One simple IntraBuilder form was actually considered to be three requests because it contained a Java applet and an image.)

Of the three servers covered here, the Borland Web Server is by far the best at displaying this information dynamically. While Netscape's FastTrack server does show accesses dynamically, it does not provide anywhere near this level of detail. Similarly, O'Reilly's WebSite displays performance data dynamically via the Windows NT Performance Monitor, but not in great detail. All three servers offer the option to direct this information to a text file.

SHUTDOWN/STARTUP

If you click on the second menu item—usually Shutdown—you will temporarily disable the Borland Web Server, which might be useful whenever you need to restrict access to the server on a short-term basis to change settings or fix a bug in an IntraBuilder form. (When you shut down the Borland Web Server, the second menu item becomes Startup, which, of course, re-enables the server software.)

PROPERTIES

Under the third menu item—Properties—you will see a dialog box like that shown in Figure 4.2. (This dialog box is also accessible via the third button on the main window's toolbar.)

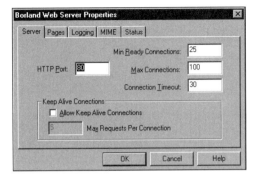

Figure 4.2   The Borland Web Server Properties dialog box.

As you can see, this dialog box has five tabs, each of which has its own property page.

◆ Server—the first property page of the dialog box—contains options relating to how connections are to be handled. For most applications, these settings should be just fine as they are. However, Borland does suggest that if you need to conserve memory, you can lower the Ready Connections value slightly.

◆ Pages—the second property page—contains options about files that the server might need to locate. For instance, "Base path" is the directory where your Web pages are stored. "Default page" is the HTML document that will be displayed when a user visits the server without requesting a specific page. The remaining two options—the Header property page and the Footer property page—can be used dynamically to include an HTML document at the bottom and/or top of each Web page sent out by the Web server. This might be used to display a copyright notice at the bottom, or perhaps a welcome message at the top of each page.

◆ Logging—the third property page—offers the option to display the listings in the main window automatically saved to disk for later viewing.

The MIME property page lists file types and what the server is to do when it receives a request for one of them. Text files, for instance, are to be displayed, while ZIP files are to be treated as objects to be saved to a hard drive.

The Status property page contains miscellaneous options. The Client Name Lookup translates the IP addresses of the users' machines into more meaningful domain names. However, this translation can take time and may negatively impact performance. The remaining options refer to the appearance of the main window and what type of information is displayed there.

EXIT

The fourth and final menu item—Exit—removes the Web server program from memory.

Conclusion

Although the Borland Web Server is limited in its functionality, it is adequate for simple applications. In fact, it is perfect for anyone who wants to get started with IntraBuilder and/or his or her intranet right away without having to learn about strange configuration options and complicated set-up procedures. And, as an added bonus, it is the only server to display all the data regarding requests and connections as they happen.

O'Reilly's WebSite 1.1 Server

The WebSite server is a happy medium between the Borland Web Server and the FastTrack Server. In fact, it probably offers 90 to 95 percent of the FastTrack features. Its great advantage over the FastTrack server is its friendly Windows-based administration program.

Installation

There are no special requirements for installing O'Reilly's WebSite. In fact, WebSite has probably the easiest-to-meet requirements of the three Web servers discussed here.

Configuration

There are a few minor settings you must adjust in order for WebSite to work properly with IntraBuilder. As described in the SERVER.HLP file, you simply have to add two CGI-redirect paths to the WebSite settings.

Use

WebSite can run in a variety of modes as either a standard application or a Windows NT service. For ease of use and configuration purposes, you'll probably want to run it as either an application or service, with a taskbar icon.

When you right-click on this taskbar icon, you will see a menu with three options: WebSite server properties, Pause (or Resume) WebSite server, and Shut down WebSite server.

As with the Borland Web Server, the Pause WebSite server disables the server on a strictly short-term basis. And, just as with the Borland Web Server, the Pause item is changed to Resume if the server is already paused.

The Shut down WebSite server option removes the program from memory; i.e., a more long-term shutdown.

Of course, it is the WebSite server properties tab that interests us with its dialog box with nine tabs/pages worth of options. Figure 4.3 shows the WebSite configuration dialog box.

Those options tabs are labeled General, Identity, Mapping, Dir Listing, Users, Groups, Access Control, Logging, and CGI.

The General property page has some miscellaneous options relating to the working and temporary directories as well as the default email address to be used in HTML documents. It also gives you the option of whether you would like the WebSite program to run in one of four different options.

The Identity property page contains information about the server machine's domain name, IP address, and so on.

The Mapping property page contains information about paths in URLs and to which physical directories they correspond. For instance, the /ibapps/ path might point to D:\IntraBuilder\APPS. (It is this page that is shown in Figure 4.3.)

The Dir Listing property page contains options that tell the server how to respond if the user requests a listing of files in a directory. (Usually, this is

Figure 4.3   The WebSite configuration dialog box.

done when the user simply neglects to specify an actual file and simply ends the URL with a directory; e.g., http://somedomain.com/ibapps/ versus http://somedomain.com/ibapps/sample1.jfm.)

The Users, Groups, and Access Control property pages all deal with the adding, deleting and editing of users, their passwords, and what files they can and can't access.

The Logging property page contains several options of what information the server should save to the log file. It also contains the DNS Reverse Lookup option (also known as Client Name Lookup), which, as mentioned above, translates the IP addresses of the users' machines into more meaningful domain names.

The CGI property page contains options about how data should be passed from Web pages to CGI programs. O'Reilly recommends that you not change these values as they could easily adversely affect the operation of your CGI applications.

Conclusion

O'Reilly's WebSite is a midrange server. It is perhaps the optimal choice based on its ease of use and setup. Its only disadvantage in this context is that it doesn't come with IntraBuilder. (Note: Pricing and availability information for O'Reilly's WebSite server can be found at http://www.ora.com.)

Netscape's FastTrack Server

The FastTrack Server may be easy to install and configure, but using it can be complicated. In fact, it's at the end of this chapter simply because it's so different from the other two servers discussed here.

Installation

The only special installation instructions regarding FastTrack is that Netscape Navigator 3.0 must be installed first.

Configuration

Configuring the FastTrack server to work with IntraBuilder is relatively straightforward. In fact, IntraBuilder may already have made the necessary changes for you when you installed it. If not, all you have to do is manually edit two text files as described in the SERVER.HLP file.

Use

Using the FastTrack server itself, though, is a bit complex. This is because the FastTrack server has absolutely no Windows-based administration program. Instead, all of the server management and use is done through a combination of HTML, JavaScript, and Windows NT Services, which can be quite a shock to anyone who starts with one of the other two servers mentioned in this chapter. And it definitely does take a bit of getting used to. Additionally, this method of administration seems slower than that of the other two servers.

Startup/Shutdown

There are two ways to start up or shut down the FastTrack server. First, you can use NT's Service Manager (found in the Control Panel as Services). As shown in Figure 4.4, you can easily start up or shut down both the Netscape Admin Server or the Netscape FastTrack Server itself.

The Status column indicates that the service is either paused, stopped, or running. Likewise the Startup column indicates whether the service is to be launched on startup (Automatic), manually launched (Manual), or completely disabled (Disabled). By highlighting a particular service, you

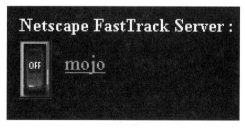

Figure 4.4   Windows NT Service Manager.

can set any of these properties by clicking on any of the buttons to the right of the Services list.

Of course, this is pretty minimal administration, which makes the second startup/shutdown method relevant. Either by selecting the friendly Start menu shortcut or by manually entering the URL in Navigator (usually something like http://localhost:33203/admin-serv/bin/index), you will be taken to the Netscape Server administration home page.

After being prompted for a user name and password, you'll be shown a page that lists the Netscape servers on your system. The machine in Figure 4.5, for example, has only one Netscape server installed—it's a FastTrack Server named mojo.

As you'd expect, clicking the on-off switch starts up or shuts down the server, depending on its current status.

Figure 4.5   Netscape servers.

Clicking on the name of the server (mojo, in Figure 4.5) sends you to another page that allows you to access all of the many properties and features of the FastTrack server. Figure 4.6 shows the clickable bitmap that displays the seven feature areas that you can configure with the FastTrack server: System Settings, Access Control, Encryption, Programs, Server Status, Config Styles, and Content Management.

System Settings

There are six sub-options under System Settings feature area. The first, On/Off, displays two buttons that do exactly the same thing as clicking the light switch pictured in Figure 4.5. The second sub-option, View Server Settings, lists several of the more standard Web server properties. From here you can do things like turn on and off the security features, change the hostname property, and set the document and CGI directories. The Restore Configuration page enables you to backup and restore alternate configurations. The Performance Tuning page allows you to fine-tune a few options concerning domain name lookups. (As noted with the Borland Web Server above, translating domain names to IP address can take time and may negatively impact performance. However, your access logs will be much more readable with domain names instead of IP addresses.) The Network Settings page contains options regarding the port the server should respond to, the name of the machine (www.somename.com), and how to make the server work with multiple IP addresses.

The last sub-option page, Error Responses, lets you set up your own HTML files to show the user in the event of an error. (For example, instead of the standard "Error 401: File not found" you could display your own HTML file that perhaps redirects the user back to your home page.)

Access Control

The Access Control feature area has 11 sub-options, all of which relate to user access and passwords. You can create, delete, list, and edit user profiles

Figure 4.6   FastTrack feature areas.

(Create User, Remove User, List User, and Edit User sub-options, respectively). You can also organize users into groups, so as to be able to set files accessible to groups of users rather than having to enter that information for each user. (Of course, there is also a set of sub-options related to groups: Create Group, Remove Group, List Groups, and Edit Groups.) You can also use the Restrict Access sub-option to hide certain directories and files from users. Lastly, you can create multiple-user databases and even import lists of users from pre-existing text files.

ENCRYPTION

The Encryption feature area contains seven sub-options. The first is simply On/Off, which, as you'd expect, turns the encryption features on and off. The second sub-option, Security Preferences, is where you can configure the types and levels of security you require. You can also generate new public/private keys or change your key passwords via the Generate Key and Change Key Password sub-options. The remaining two options, Request Certificate and Install Certificate, have to do with obtaining and installing an SSL certificate on your server.

PROGRAMS

The Programs feature area lets you tell the server where it should look for various files, as specified by users or via links in HTML documents. Basically, all these sub-options do is redirect a request from a virtual directory (say, http://www.hostname.com/cgi-bin/test.exe) to a specific, physical directory (say, D:\FastTrack\Webfiles\executables\test.exe). The CGI Directory sub-option, for example, allows you to do just this for standard CGI files. The CGI File Type sub-option allows you to decide whether to register CGI files as a separate file type. The Java, Live-Wire, WinCGI Directory, and ShellCGI Directory all contain similar directory and enabled/disabled settings.

SERVER STATUS

The Server Status feature area contains sub-options pertaining to access logs, error logs, and activity logs. The View Access Log and View Error Log sub-options will display as many entries in the access and error log as you choose. The Monitor Current Activity sub-option displays connection information dynamically. (In contrast to the Borland Web Server, however, FastTrack does not show any level of detail—just a very general overview of the current activity.) The Archive Log page allows you to backup log files— either immediately or automatically—on a regular basis. The Log Preferences page tells the server what information to save to the log files. Finally, the Generate Report page will do just that after you have had an opportunity to set what sorts of data you'd like in the report.

CONFIG STYLES

The Config Styles feature area lists five sub-options relating to styles, which are sets of properties that can be applied to, say, a group of files. The idea is that you set up the style and then apply it to a whole group of files or directories rather setting it for each file or directory separately. It follows, then, that you can create, delete, edit, and assign styles via the New Style, Remove Style, Edit Style, and Assign Style sub-options. The List Assignments sub-option displays the currently applied styles.

CONTENT MANAGEMENT

The final feature area, Content Management, contains 10 sub-options, many of which are duplicated elsewhere in the server management pages. For example, you'll first encounter the Additional Document Directories setting under the System Settings|View Server Settings sub-option. Likewise, the Parse HTML sub-option first appears under Config Styles|Edit Style.

Conclusion

Netscape's FastTrack server is clearly a very powerful package judging by its great number of options and settings. However, if you're looking to get started quickly or you don't have a really large intranet, the Borland Web Server is the place to start. Until you're up and running with IntraBuilder and you have a good understanding of some of the more unfamiliar settings and interface presented by FastTrack, you may want to hold off on it for a while. Or, if you prefer, there's O'Reilly's WebSite server, which is very much combination of the two: It's easy to use, like the Borland Web Server, and it has many of the same features that FastTrack does.

JavaScript From Square One 5

Peter Aitken

JavaScript is the "native" language of IntraBuilder. It adds considerable power to your toolkit, and in this chapter you'll get a flavor for language basics and how JavaScript's features work together.

*I*ntraBuilder applications are written in JavaScript—but IntraBuilder does most of the "writing" for you by generating nearly all of the JavaScript code (especially for simple applications) automatically. So while you don't necessarily need to know JavaScript to create effective applications in IntraBuilder, it certainly adds to the power you can bring to bear on any given application development problem. JavaScript is supported in both the Netscape Navigator and Internet Explorer Web browsers, so it's well worth learning, irrespective of how much you may end up using it within IntraBuilder.

Like any programming language, JavaScript has a lot of details. I've heard it said, "The devil is in the details." Then again, I've also heard, "God is in the details." I don't know where these quotations originated, but if either one of them is true—or both!—we're still stuck with learning the details.

If you have experience programming in C or C++, then a lot of JavaScript's details will look familiar to you. JavaScript is, in fact, based on C. There are plenty of differences, however, so you need to pay attention!

JavaScript And HTML

JavaScript code exists only within HTML files—which are what the IntraBuilder server sends down the wire to the Web browser intending to run an IntraBuilder application. Each section of JavaScript code within an HTML file must be set off with special tags that identify it as script:

```
<SCRIPT>
JavaScript statements go here
</SCRIPT>
```

You can include a script language specifier as part of the first script tag:

```
<SCRIPT LANGUAGE="JavaScript">
```

The language specifier is optional, possibly because JavaScript is the only scripting language available in many browsers. I always stick it in, though, just to be safe.

The JavaScript code also needs to be hidden from browsers that don't support it. This is accomplished by placing the code inside HTML comment tags:

```
<!-
JavaScript code goes here
->
```

Without these comment tags, a browser that is not JavaScript-enabled will consider your code to be part of the Web document being displayed and will display the JavaScript code on the user's screen—not a good thing!

These issues are handled automatically in the code generated by IntraBuilder.

The JavaScript Object Model

JavaScript is an *object-based* language. Note that I did not say object *oriented*. There is a distinction between the two that will make a difference to you only if you have some experience programming with a truly object-oriented language such as C++, Object Pascal, or Smalltalk. I'll talk briefly about the differences in a bit, but first we need to deal with the more general question—what's an object?

In truth, that's not an easy question! I could say "an object is a data construct with properties and methods," but I don't think that gives a clear idea of the concept. Perhaps it's easier, rather than trying to explain what an object is, to explain how objects came to be.

In the days before objects, programs had data and programs had functions (also called *procedures*), and the two were totally separate. Data was stored in variables, and all a variable could do was to hold a chunk of data—a string, for example, or a number. If you wanted to do something with the data, you had to write a function yourself or find one in your language's library. If you had some string data and wanted to find out something about the data—its length, for example—you had to pass the string to a function and get the result back as the function's return value. Likewise, to manipulate the string in some way, such as changing it to all upper case, you also needed a function.

This method of programming, called *procedural* programming, works perfectly well and has been used to write thousands of terrific programs. But still, some computer scientists thought that there might be some advantages in doing things differently. The notion of removing the separation between variables and functions seemed promising. What if we had some entity that could do both—contain data like a variable, and manipulate it like a function? Thus, the idea of objects was born.

Programmers create objects based on the needs of the program. Since there are many tasks that are common to most programs, object-based languages such as JavaScript provide a collection of built-in objects. The objects you use in your programs will include some of these built-in objects and may also include objects that you create yourself.

The concept of an object will be easier to understand with an example. I spoke earlier about using variables and functions to work with string data. Let's see how this works with a JavaScript object. Suppose that you have a variable named **X** to which you assign some string data:

```
X = "JavaScript"
```

X is not just a simple variable in JavaScript, but a **String** object (one of JavaScript's built-in object types). If you want to determine the number of characters in the string, you do not need to pass the data to a function. You can use one of the object's properties:

```
Y = X.length
```

After this statement executes, the variable **Y** has the value 10. Likewise, to manipulate the data—say, convert it to upper case—you use one of the object's methods:

```
Z = X.toUpperCase()
```

After this statement, the variable **Z** contains "JAVASCRIPT."

I hope this simple example has given you a feel for what objects are. You can look forward to many more details, but hopefully you will be able to understand them better now that you have at least a faint view of the "big picture." Not all objects have to do with user data—there are some that are related to the document and others to the browser—but they all share the same basic idea.

Data In JavaScript

Almost all of the JavaScript programs you will write are going to deal with data in one form or another. JavaScript can work with four types of data (values):

◆ Numbers such as 123, -0.45, and 0.

◆ Strings, or text, such as "JavaScript" and "Internet."

◆ The boolean (logical) values **true** and **false**.

◆ The special value **null**.

The data you work with in JavaScript will be represented either as a variable or as a literal.

Variables

A *variable* is a named storage container for a value. Once you create a variable, you use its name to refer to it in code. JavaScript variable names must adhere to the following rules:

◆ The first character in the name must be a letter or the underscore (_) character.

◆ Subsequent characters can be letters, numbers, and the underscore.

It's a good idea (a *really* good idea, in fact) to use descriptive variable names. In other words, the name of the variable should describe the value that it holds. If your program uses the prime interest rate in its calculations, for example; you wouldn't get into trouble calling the variable Prime_Rate. You could just as easily call it XY, Bushels_Of_Corn, or Rush_Limbaugh_Is_A_Twit, and JavaScript wouldn't care one bit. When you or someone else reads or modifies the code, however, you'll have a lot better chance of understanding what's going on if you used Prime_Rate.

A Case Of Ease-Sensitivity

For reasons totally beyond me, JavaScript variable names are case-sensitive (as is the language as a whole). Thus, the variable TOTAL is a different variable than TOTAL or TOTAL This is a real pain in the tail lights, but we have to live with it, so be careful. If you select a variable name style, such as all caps or initial cap only, and stick with it, you'll be less likely to have problems.

JavaScript is a *loosely typed* language, which means that it does not have different types of variables for different types of data. If you've ever programmed in C, Pascal, Basic, or another traditional language, I'm sure you're familiar with all the different variable types: one type for integers, another for floating point types, still another for strings. JavaScript makes it so much easier. There's only one type of variable, and you can put any value your heart desires into it. Furthermore, JavaScript is pretty smart when strings and numbers are mixed. Usually what happens is that the number is converted to a string. Thus, if you write

```
X = "The distance is " + 100 + " miles."
```

the result is that the variable **X** contains the string "The distance is 100 miles."

Before you can use a variable, you have to declare it. This is done with the **var** keyword, as follows:

```
var Prime_Rate
```

This statement creates a variable named Prime_Rate. You can optionally initialize a variable to some value when you declare it:

```
var Prime_Rate = .06
```

Multiple variables can be declared with a single **var** keyword:

```
var Prime_Rate = .06, Amount = 5000, Months_To_Pay
```

VAR Be Gone?

Strictly speaking, declaring variables with VAR is required only if the variable is being declared inside a function and another variable of the same name has been declared outside the function. It is good practice, however, and it helps to prevent pesky errors, to use VAR all the time. Even the folks who created JavaScript say it is "good style" to use VAR, and you wouldn't want to be unstylish, would you?

Literals

A *literal* is a "naked" value (that is, a value represented as itself rather than as the contents of a named variable) typed directly into the program's source code. Type numbers just as you normally would:

```
100
0.12
-15.7
```

Number literals can also be entered in floating point notation (sometimes called *scientific* notation). This notation expresses a number as a floating point value multiplied by 10 raised to a power, and is particularly useful for very large and very small numbers. For example, you could write the value 1,234 as follows:

```
1.234E3
```

which means 1.234 times 10 to the third power, or 1.234 times 1,000. Similarly, you can write 0.00000567 as 5.67E7. The "E" can be either upper or lower case.

In addition to the standard decimal (base 10) notation, integer numbers can be expressed in octal (base 8) or hexadecimal (base 16) notation. A leading 0 on an integer literal means octal notation, while a leading 0X means hexadecimal notation. Recall that octal notation uses only the digits 0-7, while hexa-decimal notation uses the standard digits 0-9 as well as the letters A through F.

Hexawhatsis?

Unlike our everyday number system, which expresses numbers in powers of 10, hexadecimal uses powers of 16 and octal uses powers of 8. You can refer to just about any computer encyclopedia or beginner's programming book if you need more details. Hexadecimal is not used much in IntraBuilder development, so don't be alarmed if you don't have the concept down cold.

Strings can be enclosed in either single or double quotes:

```
"Hello, world"
'corned beef'
"100"
```

If a string contains either a single or double quote, you must enclose it in the other type of quotation:

```
"Henry's uncle"
'He said \"hello" to me.'
```

If you must use a quotation mark in text that is enclosed in the same type of mark, precede it with a backslash. This signals JavaScript that the quotation mark is to be treated as part of the text:

```
'He said "That is Henry\'s uncle" to the waiter'
"He said "hello\" to me."
```

For boolean values, use the keywords **true** and **false**. Likewise, for the **null** value, use the **null** keyword:

```
DataSaved = false
Total = null
```

Special Characters In String Literals

JavaScript defines several *escape characters* that can be included in string literals. If you've done any C or C++ programming, these will be familiar to you:

\b	backspace
\f	form feed
\n	new line
\t	tab
\r	carriage return

To be honest, I do not know exactly why these special characters are supported in JavaScript, because they have no effect on the display. Thus, the JavaScript statement

```
document.write("Hello, \t\n there")
```

results in exactly the same display as:

```
document.write("Hello, there")
```

In other words, the escape characters are just ignored. Perhaps they are supported in order to facilitate interactions between JavaScript and C programs, but that's just a guess. In any event, the only practical effect of these characters is that if you want to include a backslash in a string literal, you must precede it with another backslash, thus:

```
MyFolder ="c:\\aitken"
```

Document.write? Wrong!

It's difficult to present JavaScript details without getting ahead of myself, using language features I have not explained yet. The DOCUMENT.WRITE() statement used in the above code is a perfect example. DOCUMENT is one of JavaScript's objects, and WRITE is one of the document object's methods. For now, suffice it to say that this statement displays whatever expression is within the parentheses on the browser screen.

Expressions And Operators

When you manipulate data in a JavaScript program, much of what you do will involve expressions and operators. In this section, I'll show you what they are and how to use them.

Expressions

You've already learned that JavaScript supports three kinds of values: numbers, strings, and logical (boolean) values. An *expression* is anything in JavaScript that evaluates to a value. We have, therefore, three kinds of expressions:

◆ Arithmetic expressions evaluate to a number.

◆ String expressions evaluate to a string.

◆ Logical expressions evaluate to **true** or **false**.

We can see that any literal (number, string, or logical) is an expression. Likewise, any variable that has been assigned a value is also an expression.

Undefined Is Not Null!

If you have declared a variable but not assigned a value to it, its value is undefined. This is not the same as NULL, which must be explicitly assigned to a variable. After the statement

```
var x, y = null
```

the variable x is undefined and y is NULL. If you try to display the value of an undefined variable, you get nothing. In contrast, a null variable displays "NULL". An undefined or NULL variable does not evaluate to a value and is therefore not an expression.

Assignment Statements

Another way to define an expression is to say it is anything that can be placed on the right side of an assignment statement. The equal sign is the assignment operator; when you write the following (called an *assignment statement*)

```
x = expression
```

you are saying, "assign the value of *expression* to x." Note that an assignment statement is itself an expression. Thus, assuming the variables **x** and **y** have already been declared, the statement

```
x = y = 7
```

results in both **x** and **y** being assigned the value 7. The literal 7 is an expression, with the value 7 (of course). The assignment statement y = 7 is also an expression with the value 7.

Arithmetic Operators

The *arithmetic operators* perform arithmetic operations on numerical expressions. The four standard operations are indicated by the usual symbols: addition (+), subtraction (-), multiplication (*), and division (/). The modulus operator, %, returns the remainder when the two integer operands are divided. For example, the expression

```
14 % 5
```

evaluates to 4, and the expression

```
6 % 3
```

evaluates to 0.

String Operators

This section should really have been called "String Operator," because there is really only one. The *concatenation operator* (+) combines two strings into a single string value. If you execute the statement

```
x = "Java" + "Script"
```

the result is that **x** contains "JavaScript." You'll note that the same symbol is used for concatenation as for addition. JavaScript knows what to do based on the difference in the values. If they are both number values, addition is performed. If one or both of them are string values, concatenation is performed.

Increment And Decrement Operators

The increment and decrement operators are used to increase or decrease the value of a variable by 1. They are indicated by ++ and --, respectively. They can be used in two ways: when placed before a variable name, in *prefix* mode, the variable is incremented or decremented and then its value is returned. For example, if the variable **x** holds the value 5, then after executing the statement

```
y = ++x
```

both **y** and **x** are equal to 6. In *postfix* mode, the value is returned before the variable is incremented or decremented. After executing this statement (again starting with **x** equal to 5)

```
y = x++
```

y will be equal to 5 and **x** will be equal to 6. The decrement operator works the same way; with **x** starting with the value of 5

```
y = --x
```

results in both **x** and **y** equal to 4. In contrast

```
y = x--
```

gives **y** equal to 5 and **x** equal to 4.

Table 5.1   The full set of shorthand arithmetic operators.

Shorthand	Means
x += y	x = x + y
x -= y	x = x - y
x *= y	x = x * y
x /= y	x = x/y
x %= y	x = x % y

Assignment Operators

You've already seen the basic assignment operator =, which assigns the value of the expression on the right side of the operator to the variable on the left side. There are also some "shorthand" assignment operators that save you some typing in certain situations shown in Table 5.1. The general form is

```
x <op>= y
```

where **y** is any expression and **<op>** is any one of the standard arithmetic operators (+ - * / or %). This syntax means exactly the same as:

```
x = x <op> y
```

Thus, to add 10 to the value of **x** and store the new value in **x**, you could write

```
x += 10
```

which does the same thing as the long form:

```
x = x + 10
```

Likewise, to divide **x** by (**y+z**) and store the value in **x**, you would write:

```
x /= (y+z)
```

Bitwise Operators

The so-called *bitwise operators* treat their operand as binary numbers—in other words, as a series of 1s and 0s. These operators make sense only for integer operands. The bitwise operators utilize binary representation, but the values they return are standard JavaScript numbers.

Binary Schminary

Binary notation represents a number in terms of powers of 2. The only digits used are 0 and 1. In binary, counting from decimal 1 to 10 goes like this: 1, 10, 11, 100, 101, 110, 111, 1000, 1001, 1010.

The bitwise logical operators compare the digit (0 or 1) in each position of their two operands; the digit in the corresponding position of the result is determined as follows:

◆ Bitwise AND (&): Result is 1 only if both operands are 1. Result is 0 if either or both operands are 0.

◆ Bitwise OR (|): Result is 1 if one of the operands is 1, or if both are 1. Result is 0 only if both operands are 0.

◆ Bitwise exclusive OR (^) Result is 1 if the operands are different (one is 0, the other is 1). Result is 0 if operands are both 0 or both 1.

Here are some examples. JavaScript stores integers with 32 bits, but I've shortened them to 8 bits to make the examples shown below more readable. If **x** is assigned the decimal value 75 and **y** the decimal value 25, we are dealing with these binary numbers:

```
01001011      (decimal 75)
00011001      (decimal 25)
```

Then the three bitwise operators work like this:

```
z = x & y
    01001011
&   00011001
    00001001   (decimal 9)
z = x | y
    01001011
|   00011001
    01011011   (decimal 91)
z = x ^ y
    01001011
^   00011001
    01010010   (decimal 82)
```

The bitwise shift operators have the effect of shifting a binary value's 1s and 0s to the left or to the right. What exactly is shifting? First, you must think of a binary number as having a certain number of *positions*—in JavaScript's case, 32. The first digit on the right is in position 0, the next one is in place 1, and so on up to position 31. Shifting moves digits the specified number of positions either left or right. Shifting left by one, for example, would result in the digit in position 0 moving to position 1, the digit in position 1 moving to position 2, and so on. Digits that "fall off" at one end are discarded. For left shifting, blank spaces that are created at position 1 are filled with 0s. For right shifting, blank spaces that are created at the left-most position are filled with the digit that was there originally. Let's look at some examples. Again, I have shrunk JavaScript's 32 bit format to 8 bits for the sake of clarity:

```
00110100    shifted left 1     01101000
00110100    shifted left 2     11010000
10110100    shifted right 2    11001101
00110100    shifted right 2    00001101
```

The shift operators are written like this:

```
x >> y       Shift x right by y positions
x << y       Shift x left by y positions
```

Why, you may be asking, does left-shift always insert 0s in blank spaces at position 1 while right-shift makes copies of the digit that was originally in position 31 (or, in the above truncated examples, position 7)? The reason is that the highest order bit in a binary representation is the *sign bit*. A 1 in that position indicates a negative number, while a 0 indicates a positive number. By filling blank spaces with the original sign digit, you are assured that the shifted number retains the sign of the original number before shifting. This type of right-shift is known in official parlance as *sign-propagating right shift*.

But wait! Just in case you aren't already confused enough, JavaScript provides a *second* right-shift operation called *zero-fill right-shift*. With this operation, zeros are used to fill blank spaces no matter what the original sign might have been. Zero-fill right-shift is indicated by three right angle brackets:

```
x >>> y
```

As with the arithmetic operators, JavaScript provides shorthand notation for certain uses of the bitwise logical and shift operators shown in Table 5.2.

Logical Operators

The *logical operators* perform operations on logical, or Boolean, values. Recall that there are only two possible logical values, **true** and **false**. In effect, the logical operators allow you to take two or more logical values and combine them to create a single yes/no, true/false answer. You do this every day without realizing it. For example, "I will go to dinner with you, only if it's that fancy French place and you pick up the tab." You are stating two conditions here, and both of them must be **true** for the final answer to be **true**. Congratulations, you've just encountered the AND operator, symbolized in JavaScript by &&. Thus, the expression

```
LogicalExpr1 && LogicalExpr2
```

evaluates as **true** only if both **LogicalExpr1** and **LogicalExpr2** are both **true**. Expressing the original question this way, we have:

```
GoToDinner = FrenchPlace && PickUpTab
```

There's also the OR operator (||) which evaluates as **true** if either one, or both, of its operands are **true**. "I will lend you $50 if you will pay me back by

Table 5.2   Shortcut notations for bitwise operators.

Shortcut notation	Means the same as
x <<= y	x = x << y
x >>= y	x = x >> y
x >>>= y	x = x >>> y
x &= y	x = x & y
x ^= y	x = x ^ y
x |= y	x = x || y

Friday, or if you promise to never ask for a loan again." The expression

```
LogicalExpr1 || LogicalExpr2
```

is false only if both **LogicalExpr1** and **LogicalExpr2** are false; otherwise it is **true**. Again:

```
LendMoney = PayBackByFriday || NeverAskAgain
```

There's one more logical operator, NOT. This operator takes only a single operand, and it simply reverses its value from **true** to **false** or vice versa. Thus,

```
!LogicalExpr1
```

evaluates as true if **LogicalExpr1** is **false**, and evaluates as **false** if **LogicalExpr1** is **true**. For example, "I'll go to dinner with you if it's that fancy French place and you promise not to talk about that stupid JavaScript project." In techie notation:

```
GoToDinner = (FrenchPlace) && !(TalkAboutJavaScript)
```

When would you use these logical operators? They are most frequently used in combination with the comparison operators, to be covered next.

The Truth About True

Computers represent all data internally as numbers. In JavaScript, as in every other programming language I've ever encountered, the logical value FALSE is represented by 0. TRUE is represented by the value 1 (some other languages use -1). JavaScript "knows," however, when a variable is holding a logical value. For example, if you execute these two lines

```
var x = true
document.write(x)
```

you'll get "true" displayed in the document, not "1". If you use a logical value in an arithmetic expression, the internal numerical representation is used. Thus, after these statements

```
var x = true
var y = 10 + x
```

the variable Y will have the value 11.

Comparison Operators

The *comparison operators*, which let you perform comparisons (no kidding!) between values, are shown in Table 5.3. They return logical values: **true** if the comparison is **true**, **false** if not.

You use these operators by placing them between the two expressions you want to compare:

```
Expression1 <op> Expression2
```

This statement is itself an expression that evaluates to **true** or **false** depending on the specific comparison operator used and the values of the two expressions; some examples are shown in Table 5.4.

Table 5.3 Six comparison operators.

Operator	Comparison performed
==	Equal to
!=	Not equal to
>	Greater than
<	Less than
>=	Greater than or equal to
<=	Less than or equal to

Table 5.4 Expressions evaluated.

Expression	Evaluates as
5 < 10	true
6.02 >= 6.0	true
5 != 10/2	false

When comparing string values, "greater than" and "less than" are determined by the ASCII value of the characters in the string. ASCII (American Standard Code for Information Interchange) values are the numbers that the computer uses internally to represent letters, punctuation marks, and other characters. Fortunately, ASCII values follow alphabetical order so comparisons based on ASCII values usually make intuitive sense. I say "usually" because there is one gotcha: Since all the uppercase letters have lower ASCII values, they are considered to be "before" the lowercase letters. Thus

```
Z < a
```

evaluates as **true**. To be exact, the uppercase letters have values 65 through 90 (A through Z), and the lowercase letters are 97 through 122. As long as you are aware of this potential problem, you will have no trouble performing true "alphabetic" string comparisons.

Careless Comparisons

The simplest way to avoid string comparison errors is to be sure that the two strings being compared are both the same case—all upper case or all lower case. Any JavaScript variable that contains a string value has the built-in ability to temporarily convert itself to either all upper case or lower case. You'll learn more about this when we talk about JavaScript objects and methods; for now I'll just show you how to do it. If SV1 and SV2 are the string variables that you want to compare, you would write

```
SV1.toUpperCase() < SV2.toUpperCase()
```

or

```
SV1.toLowerCase() < SV2.toLowerCase()
```

Either way, you are guaranteed a true alphabetical comparison regardless of the case of the original values. Note that using toLowerCase() or toUpperCase() does not actually CHANGE the string stored in the variable—it simply returns a COPY of the string value with the case changed.

Conditional Expressions

A *conditional expression* has one of two values depending on whether a specified condition is **true** or **false**. By **condition** I mean a logical expression—one that evaluates as one of the two values, **true** or **false**. You write a conditional expression like this:

```
(condition) ? val1 : val2
```

If **condition** is **true**, the expression evaluates to the value of **val1**. If **condition** is **false**, the expression evaluates to the value of **val2**. Here's an example of using the conditional expression to compare the values of the variables **x** and **y** and assign the larger one to the variable **z**:

```
z = ( x > y ) ? x : y
```

In the same manner, we could assign the logical value **true** or **false** to the variable **PastDue** depending on whether the balance owed is greater than 0:

```
PastDue = (BalanceOwed > 0) ? true : false
```

Operator Precedence And Parentheses

Funny things can happen sometimes when an expression contains two or more operators. Let me illustrate with this expression:

```
4 + 6 / 2
```

Seems clear, right? Four plus 6 is 10, and 10 divided by 2 is 5. Case closed! But is it really? What if you do the division first. Then we have 6 divided by 2 is 3, and 3 plus 4 is 7. Which answer is correct?

In JavaScript, the second one is correct. Why? Because the division operator has higher *precedence* than the addition operator. When an expression is encountered, JavaScript scans the entire line before doing anything. Operations with the highest precedence are performed first, those with the second highest are performed second, and so on down the precedence hierarchy. From highest to lowest (operators on the same line have the same precedence), this is:

◆ logical NOT (!), increment (++), decrement (--)

◆ multiply (*), divide (/), modulus (%)

◆ addition (+), subtraction (-)

◆ Shift (<<, >>, >>>)

◆ Relational (<, <=, >, >=)

◆ Equality (==, !=)

◆ Bitwise AND (&)

◆ Bitwise exclusive OR (^)

◆ Bitwise OR (|)

◆ Logical AND (&&)

◆ Logical OR (||)

◆ Conditional (?:)

◆ Assignment (all of them)

If the precedence of the operators in an expression does not give the evaluation you desire, you can use parentheses to modify the evaluation order. When an expression contains one or more pairs of parentheses (and they must always be in pairs), JavaScript starts with the innermost parentheses and evaluates its contents first. Then JavaScript works outward until the entire expression has been evaluated. Thus, if you write

```
(4 + 6) / 2
```

you'll get the result 5, because the parentheses force the addition to be performed before the division. Likewise, with the expression

```
(4 * (6 + 3)) / 2
```

the addition is done first, then the multiplication, and finally the division.

You can insert parentheses in an expression even if they are not necessary to change the order of evaluation. This can be useful for complex expressions where parentheses can make the line easier to read.

Statements

A JavaScript statement is simply a way to tell the computer to do something. For the most part, the statements available in JavaScript control the execution of the script—they control which lines of code are executed, when they are executed, and how many times they are executed. If you have any familiarity with C or C++, these statements will look very familiar to you. If you have used another language, such as Basic or Pascal, the actions and logic of the statements will be familiar, even though the precise syntax will be new.

While

The **while** statement executes a group of one or more JavaScript statements, as long as a specified logical condition is **true**. The general syntax is like this:

```
while (condition)
    {
    statements
    }
```

When execution reaches the **while** statement, **condition** is evaluated. If it is **true**, all of the statements within the braces are executed, execution loops back to the **while** statement, and the process starts again. You'll often hear this referred to as a *while loop*, since execution loops back repeatedly. Here's a simple example that counts down from 4 to 1 on the browser screen:

```
var z = 4
while (z > 0)
    {
    document.write(z-- + "<br>")
    }
```

Note that I added the HTML code **
** to the expression being displayed so that each value of **z** would display on a new line. Without this, the output would have been 4321 on a single line.

If **condition** is **false**, execution skips over the statements in the braces and continues with the first statement following the closing brace. A moment's thought about the logic of the **while** statement reveals two things:

1. If **condition** is **false** the first time it is evaluated, then the statements in the braces will not be executed at all.

2. If **condition** is initially **true** and nothing happens inside the loop to change it to **false**, the statements will be executed over and over, endlessly.

To terminate a **while** loop early, you can use either the **break** or the **continue** statement. These are covered later.

For

The **for** statement is another loop that provides the capability to execute a group of statements repeatedly. It is similar in concept to the **while** loop, but has a very different syntax:

```
for (initial ; condition ; update)
    {
    statements
    }
```

The elements **initial**, **condition**, and **update** are all expressions, with **condition** being a logical expression. Here's how a **for** loop works:

1. When execution first reaches the **for** statement, **initial** is evaluated. It is usually used to assign an initial value to a counter variable. You can use var to declare a new variable as part of **initial**.

2. The expression **condition** is evaluated. If **true**, proceed with #3. If **false**, the loop terminates and execution passes to the first statement following the closing brace.

3. All of the statements in the loop are executed.

4. The expression **update** is evaluated.

5. Return to step #2.

To illustrate, here's a **for** loop that does exactly the same thing as the **while** loop presented earlier—count down from 4 to 1 on-screen:

```
for (var z = 4 ; z > 0 ; z--)
    {
    document.write(z + "<br>")
    }
```

The three elements inside the parentheses are optional. You can omit **initial** if the counter variable is assigned its initial value elsewhere in the program.

Similarly, you can omit **update** if the counter is updated by code within the loop. Here's how:

```
var z = 4
...
for (; z > 0 ; )
    {
    document.write(z-- + "<br>")
    }
```

You can even omit **condition**, in which case it is always considered to be **true**. This results in an "infinite" loop and can be used only when a **break** statement within the loop is used to terminate it (more on **break** soon). Note: When one or more of the **for** loop's expressions are omitted, the separating semicolons must still be included.

In these examples, I have included only a single statement inside the loop. JavaScript places no limits on how many statements a loop can contain. Practically speaking, however, I suggest that you avoid overly-large loops because they make the code more difficult to read and debug. It's impossible to assign a precise number to "overly-large." A dozen statements is certainly okay, and a hundred is definitely too many. Use common sense. If a loop is too big to view all at once in your code editor, then it's too big!

if...else

The **if...else** construct is used to execute a group of statements depending on whether one or more conditions are **true** or **false**. You would not use **if...else** to execute statements multiple times. This construct is reserved for those times when you want to execute the statements once or not at all. The syntax is:

```
if (condition)
    {
    block1
    }
else
    {
    block2
    }
```

If **condition** is true, the statements in **block1** are executed (once) and those in **block2** are not executed. If **condition** is **false**, then the reverse holds. The **else** part of the statement is optional; if there are no statements to be executed if **condition** is **false**, then simply omit the **else** statement and its associated block of code.

The braces surrounding the statements following the **if** and **else** are required only for multiple statements. If there is only a single JavaScript statement to be executed, you can (but are not required to) omit the braces. Here's an example:

```
if (z == 4)
    document.write("Z equals 4")
else
    document.write("Z does not equal 4")
```

Break And Continue

Break and **continue** statements can be used only within a **while** or a **for** loop. They are used to terminate the loop entirely (**break**) or to start the next iteration of the loop (**continue**). Expressed another way, when **break** is encountered, execution passes immediately to the first statement following the end of the loop; when **continue** is encountered, execution passes to the first loop statement (the **while** or **for**), skipping any statements between the **continue** and the end of the loop.

Let's look at an example. Remember how earlier we used a **while** loop to print the numbers from 4 to 1 on the screen? This is the method we used before:

```
var z = 4
while (z > 0)
    {
    document.write(z-- + "<br>")
    }
```

Using break, here's how it would look:

```
var z = 4
while (true)
    {
    document.write(z-- + "<br>")
```

```
if (z == 0)
    break
}
```

Note first that we used the logical literal **true** for the **while** statement's condition. This means the **while** loop will execute forever if left to itself. Within the body of the loop, we use an **if** statement to test the value of **z**, exiting the loop with **break** once **z** has reached 0.

The following code illustrates the use of **continue**. Before I tell you, try to figure out what this code will do:

```
var z = 10
while (z > 0)
    {
    z--
    if (z == 6)
        continue
    document.write(z + "<br>")
    }
```

Have you figured it out? It will display the following on the screen:

```
9
8
7
5
4
3
2
1
```

Note that the number 6 is omitted from the sequence. The code in the loop uses an **if** with a **continue** to go back to the start of the loop, skipping the **document.write()** statement, when **z** is equal to 6.

Comments

A comment is not really a statement, since comments are ignored by JavaScript and have no effect on the operation of the program. Comments are used by the programmer to explain what the script does and how it works. You create a single line comment by starting with two slash characters:

```
// This is a comment.
```

Multiple-line comments start with /* and end with */, like this:

```
/* All of this text
is one
big comment. */
```

I suggest that you get in the habit of using comments liberally. Your code may seem perfectly clear to you when you write it, but when you (or worse yet, someone else) need to modify or debug it sometime down the road, you will be glad some plain English explanations of what's going on. You can also use comments as an aid during program development, commenting out program statements to see the effect they are having.

With

With comes in handy when you want to do more than one thing with an object. I know, I know, I haven't discussed objects up to this point, but the concept of the **with** statement is pretty simple, so I'll present it here and then go into more detail later. Actually, you've already been introduced to a JavaScript object, **document**, and one of its methods, **write**. When you want to use one of an object's methods, you write the object name followed by a period and the method name:

```
document.write("Hello, world.")
```

The **with** statement provides a kind of shorthand that is useful when you want to do a number of things with the same object. In effect, the **with** statement specifies a default object for statements within a block. (A block is a group of statements between curly braces.) The syntax is as follows:

```
with (object)
    {
    statements
    }
```

For any statement within the braces that requires an object reference, you can omit the object name and the default object will be used. For example, instead of writing

```
document.write(W)
document.write(X)
```

```
document.write(Y)
document.write(Z)
```

you could write the following:

```
with (document)
{
write(W)
write(X)
write(Y)
write(Z)
}
```

That's all there is to the **with** statement. It's not too helpful for small sets of statements, but if you need to execute a dozen or more methods for a given object, you can save a bit of typing—and make the code easier to read and understand as well.

Other JavaScript Statements

There are several other statements, but I won't be covering them here. You already met the **var** statement, which is used to declare variables, earlier in the chapter. The **for..in** statement is used with object properties, and I'm going to wait to cover that until after you know a bit more about objects. The **function** and **return** statements are used with functions, and they deserve a whole section of their own—coming up next!

Functions

Functions are an important part of JavaScript. In fact, they are central to any programming language used today. A function permits you to create a self-contained section of code that performs a specific action, then assigns that code a name. Whenever you want to execute the code, you refer to it by name in your program—this is referred to as *calling* a function. You can pass data to the function, and the function can return data to the calling program.

There are numerous advantages to using functions. With sections of code that you'll use over and over again in different parts of a program, you can just write the code only instead of repeating it each time you need it. In addition, code inside a function is isolated from the rest of the program, minimizing the chance of errors and other unwanted interactions. Finally, when you encounter JavaScript events, you'll see that functions are the only practical way to connect code to user actions.

Functions And Structured Programming

Functions are such an integral part of programming that it's hard to imagine working without them. In fact, the invention of functions and the associated method of programming, called STRUCTURED PROGRAMMING, is something that happened not all that long ago.

Let's look at an example. Here's the code for a function that adds three numbers and returns the result. Generally, you will not use functions for such simple tasks, but it serves perfectly well as an example of how a function is put together:

```
function SumOf(a, b, c)
{
var sum
sum = a + b + c
return sum
}
```

Let's break this function into its component parts.

1. Every function definition starts with the keyword **function** followed by the name of the function—in this case, **SumOf**. Rules for function names are the same as for variable names, and within a script each function name must be unique.

2. Following the function name is a pair of parentheses enclosing the function's *parameters*. The parameters represent the data that the calling program passes to the function. You can have any number of parameters, separated by commas. Some functions take no parameters, in which case the function name is followed by empty parentheses.

3. The function code is enclosed in braces. A function can contain any JavaScript statements except another function definition.

4. Inside the function code, the **return** keyword is used to specify the value returned by the function to the calling program. Some functions do not return a value, in which case the **return** keyword is simply omitted.

How do you execute (that is, call) a function? A function that returns a value is an expression, so the function can be used anywhere you would use any other expression. When you call a function, you use its name followed by parentheses containing the *arguments*, specific values passed to the function parameters. For example:

```
x = SumOf(1, 2, 3)
```

When this line executes—assuming the **SumOf()** function has been defined as above—here's what happens:

1. Execution passes to the **SumOf()** function.

2. The first argument, in this case 1, is placed in the function's first parameter, **a**. The second and third arguments are placed in the second and third parameters **b** and **c**, respectively.

3. The function code declares a variable named **sum**, adds the values passed in the three parameters, assigns the result to **sum**, then returns the value of **sum** to the calling program.

4. Execution returns to the calling program. The returned value is assigned to the variable **x**.

Argument Versus Parameter

Confusion sometimes arises about the meanings of these two terms. A PARAMETER is a placeholder in a function definition for a value to be passed to the function. In the above definition of SumOf(), A, B, and C are parameters. An ARGUMENT is a specific value passed to a function when a program calls it. Above, 1, 2, and 3 are arguments. Many people aren't aware of this distinction, and use the terms interchangeably.

What about a function that does not return a value? First, let's look at an example. This function takes a single argument, then displays that argument in the document centered and surrounded by asterisks. Here's the code:

```
function FancyDisplay(message)
{
document.write("<Center>*****************************<br>")
document.write("***" + message + " ***<br>")
document.write("*****************************<br></Center>")
}
```

To call it, all that is required is this:

```
FancyDisplay("ANNOUNCEMENT")
```

When using functions, remember that *JavaScript is case-sensitive*. You must use the exact same capitalization when calling a function as you did in the function definition. Also, be sure to pass the correct number of arguments. JavaScript does not require a function call to include the same number of arguments as there are parameters in the function definition. If you pass too many arguments, the extra ones will be ignored. If you pass too few, then the function parameters that did not receive values will be undefined during that execution of the function.

By Value Only

JavaScript function arguments are always passed by value. This means that a copy of the argument is made and passed to the function, and the code inside the function cannot modify the original argument. For example, here's a function that modifies its argument:

```
function foo(x)
{
x = 100
}
Suppose you call it like this:
var num = 5
foo(num)
```

After the call to FOO(), NUM still has the value 5. Because only a copy of NUM was passed to the function, code inside the function could not change the contents of the original variable num. This differs from many other languages, which permit function arguments to be passed by reference, in which case code inside the function can change the argument's value.

Where Do I Put My Functions?

Your function should be placed in the header section of the HTML file; that is, between the **<Head>** and **</Head>** tags. As with any JavaScript code, functions need to be identified as JavaScript with the appropriate tags. Here's an example:

```
<HEAD>
<script language="JavaScript">

function FancyDisplay(message, x)
{
document.write("<Center>*****************************<br>")
document.write("***   " + message + x + "   ***<br>")
document.write("****************************<br></Center>")
}

function AnotherFunction(x, y, z)
{
...
}

function StillAnotherFunction(a, b, c)
{
...
}
</script>
</HEAD>
```

Technically, functions could be placed in the body of the HTML file. This is not a good idea, however, because of the way an HTML file is processed. When a browser loads a file, it processes the contents from the top down as they are loaded. When a call to a function is encountered, the browser can know about the function only if it has already been loaded. The only way to ensure that all function definitions have been loaded before any function calls occur is to place the definitions in the header section.

Conclusion

One of the convenient features of functions is that variables declared inside a function are local. Within a given function, each variable that is declared in the function is separate and distinct from any other variable(s) of the same name that are declared in other functions, or in JavaScript code outside a function (variables declared outside a function are global variables). This independence of variables frees you from having to worry about duplicate variable names, and also prevents unwanted interactions between global and function code. To summarize the relationship between global and local variables:

◆ All variables that you use in global code (code outside of functions) must be declared globally (outside of any function). In global code, variables declared inside functions might as well not exist.

◆ Within a function, a locally declared variable takes precedence over a global variable of the same name. You can access global variables inside a function as long as there is no local variable declared with the same name. Within a given function, variables declared in other functions are not accessible.

UI Creation

Terence Goggin

IntraBuilder's visual design tools are easy to understand and easy to use. Here's what they look like, how they work, and a sample project to show you how to use them.

Most visual programming environments today follow a pretty standard pattern—a design area or form, a toolbar or palette of controls, some sort of list-like view of the controls' properties, and, of course, a code editor. As you might expect, IntraBuilder follows this pattern, too. Figure 6.1 highlights IntraBuilder's major visual design elements.

This chapter introduces you to each of these visual design elements and then shows you how to use them in a sample project.

The Component Palette

The Component Palette is really the heart of any design environment. It's your programming toolbox: All of the available components are neatly arranged and organized according to their function. As you'll notice right away, IntraBuilder's Component Palette is similar to those of Delphi or Visual Basic. There are the 15 standard controls and 3 data access controls followed by any custom controls. The standard controls include basically every sort of control or enhancement that you can put into an HTML document today, everything from a standard Button control to ActiveX and Java Applet controls. Figure 6.2 shows the standard IntraBuilder Component Palette.

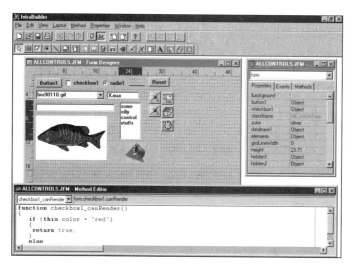

Figure 6.1   IntraBuilder at design time.

Figure 6.2   IntraBuilder's Component Palette.

     Delphi Tip:

If you're wondering what happened to all of the data aware controls—they're all data aware! With IntraBuilder, all controls can be used as standard or data aware controls with no additional coding.

     VB Tip:

Just as in VB, IntraBuilder controls can be used as data aware or non-data aware.

What follows is a description and a brief how-to-use-it introduction to each of the standard controls. (In Chapters 8 and 9 we'll cover the three data access controls in detail.)

The Button

The Button is the very first control on the Component Palette, similar to any button control on any other development environment. As you'd expect, it has a text property that allows you to set the message displayed on its face and a way to respond to mouse clicks. Figure 6.3 shows the Component Palette icon for the Button control.

Figure 6.3   The Button's icon on the Component Palette.

In standard HTML documents, buttons are typically used to submit or reset forms. In IntraBuilder, buttons can be used to process just about any kind of user action, whether it be submitting a form or simply navigating to the next record of a table. The only thing a standard Button control will not do is reset a form. For this task, IntraBuilder provides a special type of button called the Reset control. Figure 6.4 shows a Button control at design time.

Figure 6.4   The Button control at design time.

The CheckBox

IntraBuilder's CheckBox control is like those in any other programming environment. They can be used as standard HTML-style checkboxes, or they can be used as data aware controls. Figure 6.5 shows the Component Palette icon for the checkbox control.

Figure 6.5   The CheckBox's icon on the Component Palette.

The CheckBox control can be used to represent visually a single yes or no option. If you had a Web site that allowed visitors to design a pizza, for instance, you might have a checkbox for each of the possible toppings. Figure 6.6 shows how just such a use of the CheckBox control might look.

Figure 6.6   **Several CheckBox controls at design time.**

The Radio (Button) Control

IntraBuilder's Radio control is the same control most programming environments call a radio button. Other than the name change, there's really nothing different about this Radio control from others you may have used. Figure 6.7 shows the Component Palette icon for the Radio control.

Figure 6.7   **The Radio control's icon on the Component Palette.**

A Radio control is typically used for a situation in which one of three or more choices must be selected by the user, with one Radio control representing each of the possible choices. An example of this would be an order entry form in which the user must choose a method of shipping. One such example is shown in Figure 6.8.

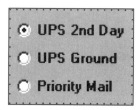

Figure 6.8   **Several Radio controls at design time.**

The Rule Control

The Rule control is IntraBuilder's version of the standard HTML horizontal rule.

Most programming environments support some kind of line or shape control, and that's basically what the Rule control is. However, since most of IntraBuilder's controls are based on standard HTML elements, the Rule control can only be oriented horizontally. Figure 6.9 shows the Component Palette icon for the Rule control.

Figure 6.9   The Rule control's icon on the control palette.

The Rule control can be used whenever you need to separate a single form into multiple areas. An example of this would be separating links by type; i.e., the sites related to music separated from the sites related to dance by a Rule control. Figure 6.10 shows the Rule control at design time.

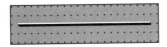

Figure 6.10   The Rule control at design time.

The TextArea Control

The TextArea control is a standard multi-line text entry control. Again, the TextArea control is based on the standard HTML TextArea. Figure 6.11 shows the Component Palette icon for the TextArea control.

Figure 6.11   The TextArea control's icon on the Component Palette.

The TextArea is used any time you're encouraging a user to type as much as he or she needs. For instance, you wouldn't use a TextArea control for a Name or Address field, whereas you would use it for a Notes or Reason for Return field. Figure 6.12 shows a TextArea control at design time.

Figure 6.12 The TextArea control at design time.

The Select Control

A standard drop-down list box control, the Select control can be used to display a list of static data or a list of files in a given directory. Figure 6.13 shows the Component Palette icon for the Select control.

Figure 6.13 The Select control's icon on the Component Palette.

The Select control is useful whenever you need to display a list of several choices from which the user must pick only one. You might use the Select control to display a list of several possible tax rates. Figure 6.14 shows the Select control at runtime.

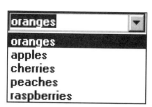

Figure 6.14 The Select control at runtime.

The Text Control

The Text control is a single-line text entry control, again based on the HTML Text control. Figure 6.15 shows the Component Palette icon for the Text control.

Figure 6.15 The Text control's icon on the Component Palette.

It should be used anytime a response of one sentence or less is required. Fields such as Name, Address, and Phone are examples of typical uses for Text controls. Figure 6.16 shows the Text control at design time.

Figure 6.16   The Text control at design time.

The Image Control

The Image control is used to display images of any type. Since Web browsers only display gif and jpeg images, IntraBuilder will automatically convert any other image formats to ones that can be viewed via a browser. Figure 6.17 shows the Component Palette icon for the Image control.

Figure 6.17   The Image control's icon on the Component Palette.

The Image control is used whenever you want to add any sort of picture to your IntraBuilder form. The picture can be a file stored on disk or a graphical image field of a table. Figure 6.18 shows the Image control at design time.

Figure 6.18   The Image control at design time.

The Reset Control

The Reset control is a special kind of Button control that exists only to reset the form. (Resetting a form usually means that the Text/TextArea controls are blanked and the other controls are restored to their default values.) Figure 6.19 shows the Component Palette icon for the Reset control.

Figure 6.19   The Reset control's icon on the Component Palette.

The Reset control is only useful for forms that might need a reset option. For instance, a form that displayed read-only data from a table would not need a reset button, whereas an order entry form almost certainly would. Figure 6.20 shows the Reset control at design time.

Figure 6.20   The Reset control at design time.

The Password Control

The Password control is just like any standard password edit control you've ever seen or worked with—it displays only asterisk characters, no matter what text is entered into it. Of course, it does allow you to retrieve the actual text that was entered. Figure 6.21 shows the Component Palette icon for the Password control.

Figure 6.21   The Password control's icon on the Component Palette.

The Password control is useful wherever a user needs to log onto a system or access password-protected data. Figure 6.22 shows the Password control at runtime.

Figure 6.22   The Password control at runtime.

The Java Applet Control

The Java Applet control allows you to embed Java applets into your IntraBuilder projects. Essentially, it encapsulates the HTML APPLET tag. Figure 6.23 shows the Component Palette icon for the Java Applet control.

Figure 6.23   The Java Applet control's icon on the Component Palette.

While the Java Applet control cannot be easily linked to any of the active data on the form, it may prove useful if you already have applets that you'd rather not discard. Figure 6.24 shows the Java Applet control at design time.

Figure 6.24   The Java Applet control at design time.

The Hidden Control

The Hidden control is an encapsulation of the standard JavaScript hidden object. Figure 6.25 shows the Component Palette icon for the Hidden control.

Figure 6.25   The Hidden control's icon on the Component Palette.

The Hidden control is a way of storing data on a control level so that individual methods may access it. Essentially, it's a scratch pad for your IntraBuilder form. Figure 6.26 shows the Hidden control at design time.

Figure 6.26   The Hidden control at design time.

The ActiveX Control

The ActiveX control allows you to embed ActiveX/OCX controls into your IntraBuilder forms. It is essentially a wrapper around the Microsoft Internet Explorer's OBJECT tag. Figure 6.27 shows the Component Palette icon for the ActiveX control.

Figure 6.27   The ActiveX control's icon on the Component Palette.

The ActiveX control is really only of use if visitors to your site are using the Microsoft Internet Explorer and/or if you've already made an investment in the ActiveX/OCX technology. Figure 6.28 shows the ActiveX control at design time.

Figure 6.28   The ActiveX control at design time.

The SelectList Control

The SelectList control is similar to any listbox control you may have worked with before. It displays several items and, depending on the value of the multiple property, the user can select one or more of those items. Figure 6.29 shows the Component Palette icon for the SelectList control.

Figure 6.29   The SelectList control's icon on the Component Palette.

The SelectList control is useful in forms where you have a long list of items to display; perhaps as a way for a shopping cart application to display a list of items the user has purchased. Additionally, it is useful whenever the user will be allowed to select any number of available choices. Figure 6.30 shows the SelectList control at runtime.

Figure 6.30   The SelectList control at runtime.

The HTML Control

The HTML control provides a way for you to place standard HTML text into your IntraBuilder forms. It supports standard and custom formatting tags, including the FONT COLOR, I(talics), B(old), and HREF tags, just to name a few. Figure 6.31 shows the Component Palette icon for the HTML control.

Figure 6.31   The HTML control's icon on the Component Palette.

The HTML control can be used any place where static text or a link to another Web site are required. It is comparable to the Label component of Visual Basic or the TLabel component of Delphi. Figure 6.32 shows the HTML control at design time.

Figure 6.32   The HTML control at design time.

Those are the standard tools on the palette. We'll now take a look at how a control's properties and events are set and edited at design time.

The Form Design Area

IntraBuilder's Form Designer is much like that of any other environment's form design area. It has the standard dotted grid pattern behind all of the controls so that you can align controls to one another and a ruler-like object at the top of each form that indicates the mouse's current position. As with other environments, the look and feel of the Form Designer can be personalized. By right-clicking the Form Designer and selecting Form Designer Properties from the menu, you can adjust the grid size and several other options. Figure 6.33 shows IntraBuilder's Form Design area.

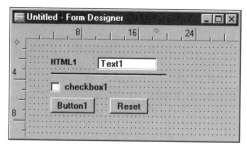

Figure 6.33   IntraBuilder's Form Design area.

If you have experience with Visual Basic or Delphi, you'll find IntraBuilder's Form Designer similar. All controls can be moved about simply by clicking and dragging them to where you want them. Similarly, all of the visual controls can be resized via the black stretch handles (as shown in Figure 6.34) that surround each control at design time.

Figure 6.34   Stretch handles enable you to resize the controls to your liking.

Of course, this really only addresses the visual aspects of the form and its controls. To edit the non-visual properties of a form, you'll need to use the Inspector.

The Inspector

The Inspector is based on a common design found in both Delphi and Visual Basic. It is a window with three tab sheets, each of which has a grid displaying the list of a selected control's properties, events, or methods and their associated values. Any of the controls on the active form can be selected either via a list box at the top of the Inspector window (which lists each of the current form's controls) or by clicking on the control that you want to inspect. Figure 6.35 shows the Inspector.

THE PROPERTIES TAB

IntraBuilder has a slightly different way of editing properties than, say, Delphi. A wrench icon next to a property indicates that there is more editing that can be done for that property. In most cases, this means that there is

Figure 6.35   IntraBuilder's Inspector.

some sort of property editor available. If the property in question is itself another control, clicking the wrench icon causes the Inspector to display that control's properties. (Note: If the wrench icon appears next to an event, this means that clicking it will display the code for that event handler in the Method Editor window.)

 The type icon allows you to select the data type that the control should display. This is used as a way to typecast data. For instance, if your data was stored as a boolean value but for some reason you wanted to display it as a one or a zero, you would click the type icon and select Integer to effect this change.

 The history icon maintains a list of the last two or so values for the property, much like a MRU (most recently used) file list at the end of a File menu.

 The remaining editors are almost self-explanatory: This icon reveals a drop-down list box of possible values (i.e., True and False for boolean properties), and this icon can obviously be used to increment or decrement the value of the selected property.

THE EVENTS TAB

This tab shows the events for the selected control and allows them to be edited and assigned to. Much like in Delphi and other programming environments, if you wanted to write code that was to be triggered on Button1's **onClick** event, you would select button1 (either on the form or via the Inspector's drop-down list box), click on the Events tab, and then locate the **onClick** event. You would then click the wrench button (see the description of the Properties tab, above) to display the Method Editor for that event.

THE METHODS TAB

This tab displays the selected control's methods. IntraBuilder does not permit the methods to be edited or assigned to.

The Method Editor

IntraBuilder's Method Editor is reminiscent of Visual Basic's code editor in that it has drop-down list boxes at the top of the form through which various subroutines and event-triggered code can be selected and/or edited. Figure 6.36 shows the Method Editor.

IntraBuilder's Method Editor, too, has a drop-down list box that displays the routines and events for which code has been entered—but it also has a status bar next to that drop-down list box that shows whether the currently displayed block of code is actually linked to a control or whether it's simply a general procedure.

Again borrowing from Visual Basic's code editor, the IntraBuilder Method Editor provides friendly color-based source formatting: Improperly terminated (a missing quotation mark, for instance) character strings are red, properly terminated (both quotation marks) character strings and numbers are blue, **if** is bolded, and so on.

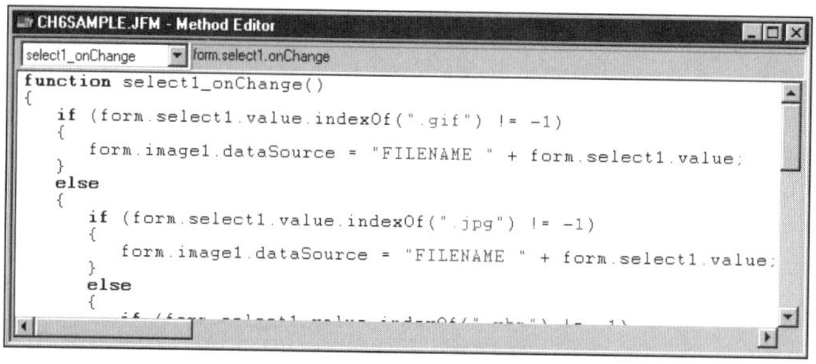

Figure 6.36   The Method Editor.

Putting It All Together

Now we'll use all of this information to create a sample project that uses one HTML control, one SelectList control, and one Image control. When completed, the form will allow you to select an image file via the SelectList. This image file is then displayed in the Image control. The final resulting form is shown in Figure 6.37.

This is by no means a real world application; however, it should help you get familiar with the IntraBuilder environment.

First, select File|New|Form from IntraBuilder's main menu.

Then add the HTML control to the form. This can be done by double-clicking the HTML control's icon on the Component Palette. Repeat this process with a SelectList control and an Image control.

It's now time to put the controls where you'd like them. (This is accomplished by clicking and dragging the controls around.)

Now click the HTML control. Its properties should now be visible in the Inspector window. Using the Inspector window, scroll down until you come to the HTML control's Text property. Highlight this by clicking on it. Click the wrench icon.

This dialog box allows you to edit and format the text that will appear in the HTML control. For this project, the HTML control should say "select a new picture." When you're finished formatting and editing, click the OK button.

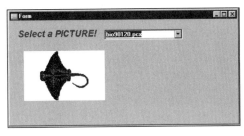

Figure 6.37   The sample project at runtime.

In the same way that you edited the Text property of the HTML control, we'll now edit the **dataSource** property of the SelectList control. Once you have it displayed in the Inspector, click the wrench icon. Set **type** to **Filename** and **dataSource** to *.jif. This tells the SelectList control to display all of the gif image files in the same path as the form file itself is located. It is from this list that the user will be able to select a picture to be displayed.

The only thing left is to tell IntraBuilder to display the new picture as soon as the user selects one. This is done through the SelectList's **onChange** event. To associate code with this event, go to the Events tab for the SelectList control. Highlight the **onChange** event and click the wrench button.

The code editor window should now be visible. In the area between the brackets ({ and }), type the following code:

```
form.image1.dataSource = "FILENAME " + form.select1.value;
```

This code will load the image file the user selected into the Image control. That's all there is to it.

Conclusion

IntraBuilder's visual design tools are easy to get used to—whether or not you have any previous experience. With minimal effort or programming knowledge, you, too, can become an intranet master.

Database 101

Don Taylor

An introduction to database management systems—how they developed, the principles they encompass, and what they can do for you.

***A**s* I write this, it was exactly 20 years ago that my wife Carol and I moved into our present home. By any standards our house is a modest one, but its full basement made it seem like a mansion compared to the small mobile home we left behind. In fact, it seemed so spacious that we developed a special whistle signal to let each other know which room we were in.

The house was so enormous, we thought we could never fill it up. But 20 years of living has proven that theory groundless. Every nook and cranny is now stuffed with, well... *stuff*. The closets. The attic. The garage. Even that little space under the stairs. Stuffed with clothes we never seem to wear. Stuffed with old photographs. Videos. Hundreds of books. Thousands of yards of quilting material. Stuffed with stuff I don't recognize and never knew I had.

One day I whipped into Sears and bought a motorized number two metric Phillips screwdriver—you know, the one with the right-angle pistol-grip handle mounted on a universal flex joint. Later that afternoon I opened a kitchen drawer and discovered three more of them. If I only knew what I own, everything would be just fine. It occurred to me that the solution was to put a complete inventory of everything I own on my computer. After all, I just bought this monster-sized hard drive, one I'll never be able to fill....

Whether it's physically storing items or just storing references to those items as magnetic impulses, it takes resources and some sort of logical system to provide the information we need, while keeping everything in check. In this chapter, we will navigate our way through some of the basics of database systems and how they can help us get a handle on the management of information.

How Did We Get Here?

In the early days of microcomputers, most applications kept data for their exclusive use. This meant programmers were free to create data files in any data format they wished, which was both good and bad. Good because they were free to store information in ways that could optimize how quickly it was read or how much space would be taken to store it—both important considerations in early computer systems. Bad because it was nearly impossible to use the data from one program (a financial spreadsheet, for example) in another (such as a word processor).

Publishers of programs at first liked this situation. Having total control over their data's format not only gave them the flexibility to add powerful features to their products but it also locked their users into those products. As time went on, people began to do more serious work with their computers and demanded the capability of transferring data from one program to another. Other publishers began to create specialized utilities that would exchange data between formats. But new environments like Windows so encouraged data interchange via operations like cut and paste that users came to expect it. Today, most major applications provide data file translation from within the application itself. As we'll see later, techniques used in the database world actually enable the transparent use of numerous data file formats from within a single application.

As microprocessor-based computers matured, they became cheaper, faster, and capable of storing and handling larger amounts of data. It was inevitable they would begin to take on some of the work of large, mainframe computers.

The transition to PC-based business computing brought with it some of the heritage of the world of the so-called big iron—mainframe computers. Databased management systems (DBMS) such as dBASE II began to appear on the scene, storing data in a de facto standard format and giving users an easy means to modify, manipulate, and create reports from their data without needing special applications. As a bonus, DBMS typically enabled programmers to develop applications using features of the DBMS itself.

Today, there are many DBMS along with additional products designed to enhance DBMS and even develop applications that work with them—too many, in fact, even to list them here. Instead, we'll limit ourselves to investigating what a DBMS itself can do for us.

The Common Denominator

One notable exemption to the move toward proprietary data formats is the American Standard Code for Information Interchange (ASCII) format, which enables text to be stored in a format understood by many applications on numerous computing platforms. By representing data as ASCII text, it can be transferred from one application to another. ASCII is usually one of the formats offered by applications to exchange data with other programs.

Databases: Sorting Stuff Into Stacks

Before we delve into the world of the DBMS, it would be helpful to explore what we mean by the term database. For now, we'll describe a database as a sum-total collection of all information needed to perform a set of required tasks. That collection may be broken down in any one of several ways, but the key question is, "What is the task to be performed, and what information do I need to get it done?"

Let's say we wanted to design a database that would document all the stuff in my house. We might drag everything out of the closets, the garage, and that hidey-hole under the stairs and toss it all in one big heap on my living room floor. There it is, the sum-total of my stuff.

We whip out our trusty pencil and a ruled pad and prepare to make a list of the contents of the pile. But what do we say about each item? After a few minutes of thought, we conclude that answering two questions will determine how we might classify any given item in the pile:

1. What specific characteristics does each item share in common with all the other items in the pile?

2. What purpose is the list intended to serve?

In answer to the first question, we come up with the following common characteristics of each item:

◆ It can be given a description that will uniquely identify it

◆ It belongs either to Carol or to me

◆ It was acquired on a specific date

◆ It was acquired from a specific person or business

◆ It was acquired at a specific cost

On our pad we create five columns and begin to pick items out of the pile and record them. After a few entries, our list looks like that in Table 7.1.

Table 7.1   Sample of contents list for the big heap.

Description	Owner	Acquired	Source	Cost
Video, "It's a Gift"	Don	1988	Videos R Us	$10.00
Parka, Med	Carol	1995	Big Eddie's	$87.50
Matl, Med Blue	Carol	1991	Fabriholics Barn	$24.00
Parka, Large	Don	1994	Big Eddie's	$92.75
Video, "Generations"	Carol	1995	Videos R Us	$19.95
Matl, Red Sm Print	Carol	1993	Major Threads	$6.00
Running shoes	Don	1996	If the Shoe Fits	$85.00

It's now time to answer the second question: What purpose is this list to serve?

If it is to be used for tax or insurance purposes, all of the columns might be relevant except the one marked Owner. If we were to use it as a laundry list for a last will and testament, we would be interested mainly in the description and the owner columns. Then again, if its purpose is to serve as a list of items that need to be replaced at some point, we might choose to focus on the Description, Acquired, Source, and Cost columns.

Whew! It was a big job to record all that information, but at least it's done. Or is it?

Divide And Conquer

In looking over the list, I might really like to know more about my videos. The way things are, it's difficult to include much detailed information in a manner it can be easily found. For instance, I might like to record the running time of each film. Of course, I could simply add another column to my list and label it Runtime, but that characteristic would not be in common with any of the other items on the list, so I would have many blank entries.

There is something else. As we stand there admiring our work, we realize it's an awfully big pile. It would be a lot easier to manage the videos if they were all in one place. So we go to work, and soon there are two piles, one a small collection of videos and the other a large heap containing all the remaining items.

We can now view the pile of videos with a different perspective. Sure, they still have the same characteristics as before, but now they have a large set of additional common characteristics: title, studio, release date, category (drama, comedy, documentary, etc.), running time—and possibly several others. I might choose any or all of these characteristics, depending on my intended use for this list.

We look back at the heap. Suddenly a couple of photographs catch our eye, and we decide to separate them out.... Before we know it, we're looking at five distinct piles containing clothes, photos, videos, books, and quilting material. For each pile, we have a list that records the unique characteristics each group has in common. We started by identifying a database that included information on all the stuff. When we finished, we still had a database that contained the same stuff, but instead of just a little information about each item we were able to expand our database from one list to five lists with more detailed information.

So what does all this pencil-and-paper-list jive have to do with a DBMS and its mission of managing data on a computer? Stay tuned.

Putting It All On The Table

To store data, we must have some kind of container to put it in. In the DBMS world, that container is called a table.

Take another peek at Table 7.1. The name says it all: It's a table. It has rows. It has columns. So does a database table. Sure, the information is really being stored in a file located somewhere on the disk in some format only a DBMS could love or understand. But as long as we can rely on the DBMS to store, retrieve, or modify the data that appears in any column in any row, we could care less how the DBMS accomplishes its tasks.

Just as in a table in a book, each row represents an item of the type being recorded in the table, and each column represents a characteristic of that item. As we will soon see, once information has been entered into a table, the table can be searched, sorted, and transmogrified in so many ways it will put our hand-written list to shame!

Legends Of The Database Table

The basis for the database table is actually an extension of the row-and-column model originally developed for financial spreadsheet applications. As these applications matured, they began to offer a subset of data management features available in full-featured DBMS. The DBMS of that day referred to individual characteristics as "fields" and the complete set of data for an individual item as a "record."

Although the data management functions offered by spreadsheets couldn't compare with those of true DBMS, the concept of rows and columns to represent data was a natural. You will occasionally hear the older terms field for column, record for row, and database file for "table." In essence, they're the same things.

Anatomy Of A DBMS

A DBMS, by definition, is a system that manages a database—one or more tables. The typical DBMS can be represented by four primary components. Figure 7.1 identifies these components as Internal Machinery, API, User Interface, and Program Processor. Let's take a look at each.

Internal Machinery

Deep down inside every DBMS lies a murky area full of programmed procedures that accomplish all the real work. These procedures enable the DBMS to create new tables on the disk, modify a single piece of information, delete data, change the order of items—and many other mundane tasks. As illustrated in Figure 7.1, the Internal Machinery interacts with tables resident on the disk both to store and to retrieve information.

API

The Application Programmer Interface (API) is the common connecting point for any program that wishes to call upon the procedures in the Internal

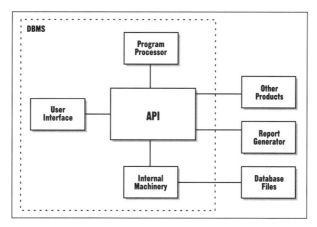

Figure 7.1   Anatomy of a DBMS.

Machinery section. As shown in Figure 7.1, the DBMS's own Program Processor and User Interface both rely on the API to accomplish their work. (Other products can usually connect with the API, as shown in the figure. We'll cover that in just a moment.)

User Interface

This is the visible part of the DBMS. When you run a DBMS, this is what you'll see. Depending on the DBMS you use (see the sidebar "Choose Your Flavor"), the appearance of the interface can vary wildly.

In general, the User Interface (UI) enables you to create new tables, browse through information, and accomplish everyday data management tasks. The UI does its work by invisibly placing calls to the API, which in turn calls the low-level routines in the Internal Machinery section.

Program Processor

If DBMS was made up solely of the Internal Machinery, the API, and the User Interface, it would be a useful tool. But by adding a Program Processor, makes it a powerhouse.

The Program Processor enables a sophisticated DBMS user to create stored programs capable of exercising the DBMS, as if an experienced user was operating the UI. It enables programmers and sophisticated users to develop customized programs (sets of instructions) to accomplish repetitive, everyday tasks without having to perform each operation manually. As can be seen in the diagram, the Program Processor calls on the API to perform the prescribed instructions.

Other Products

The box marked Other Products in Figure 7.1 refers to those products created by companies other than the publishers of the DBMS. These days, just about every DBMS publisher provides access to his or her API, so others can create products that extend the usefulness (and hopefully the sales) of the DBMS.

Report Generator

The final box in Figure 7.1 represents a component included with virtually every DBMS—a Report Generator. This application has the capability of reading (but not modifying) all tables in a database and printing special information reports designed by the user. Like any other program that accesses the database files, the Report Generator works through the API.

Choose Your Flavor

Over the years, several companies have developed DBMS that have gained widespread acceptance—dBASE, Paradox, MS Access, Oracle, Sybase, and Informix, just to name a few. Although each DBMS performs pretty much the same tasks, each has its own user interface, file formats, and API access conventions.

This situation is made a bit more complex because one DBMS may offer features another does not. Paradox, for example, supports referential integrity, while dBASE doesn't. The actual types of information that can be handled by one DBMS may not exactly match that in another. These differences among DBMS carry all the way to the file level; each DBMS has its own proprietary formats, and one DBMS may not be able to operate on tables created by another DBMS.

If you are in a situation where you have to deal with data from a single DBMS, consider yourself lucky. If you find yourself facing tables from two (or more!) DBMS, never fear—today there are slick solutions to nearly every data problem (see "Who *Was* That Masked DBMS?").

Working With Data

Data Typing

So far we've referred to what gets stored in tables as information or data. In reality, the data stored in tables is classified according to *data type*. Is it purely text? Is it numeric? If so, we can perform mathematical operations on it. Is it money? If so, we'll always keep two decimal places. Does it represent a date? In that case we can do math, but the operations and the way we perform them will be quite different from what we do with numbers.

The actual data types available will depend on the DBMS you're using. Table 7.2 lists the data types available in Paradox for Windows.

The overall design of a table is called its *structure*. Each column in a table must have one (and only one) data type associated with it. The data type is specified when the table is created, and is chosen to best correspond with the characteristic recorded in the column. This enables us to make comparisons between items, based on the values in one or more columns, and if the values are numbers, we can even calculate the sum of those values for any or all items.

Table 7.2   Data types for Paradox for Windows.

Type	Description
Alpha	Letters, numerals, and printable symbols
Autoincrement	Long integer values; can't be changed once assigned
BCD	Numeric data in BCD format
Binary	Used for including special code such as sounds
Bytes	Used for including special code such as bar codes
Date	Any valid date up to December 31, 9999
Formatted Memo	Like memo, but text can be formatted
Graphic	Pictures in .BMP format
Logical	Values representing True or False
Long Integer	Whole numbers in the range -2147483648 to 2147483647
Memo	Notes (can be virtually any length)
Money	Same as number, but displayed with '$' and 2 decimals
Number	Numbers from -10^{307} to 10^{308}
OLE	Objects placed in table by programs with OLE server
Short	Whole numbers in the range -32,767 to 32,767
Time	Time of day since midnight
Timestamp	Combined date and time

As you can see in the table, Paradox includes a lot of data types—including several not supported by other DBMS. Fortunately, the most common data types (Alpha, Number, Money, Short, Long Integer, Date, and Time) are supported by most DBMS. In some cases, the data types may in other DBMS be known by different names, and their specifications may vary somewhat. But by and large, at least the most common types are compatible.

For an example of using some of the common types, let's look at a special table that might contain information on my video tapes. The columns and their data types are listed in Table 7.3.

A couple of things need additional explanation. First of all, you'll notice that the first five column names are identical to those in Table 7.1. This was done to keep track of the "core" characteristics of the item in a way compatible with the original list we created for my stuff. To achieve this compatibility, all five of our specialized tables would have these same five columns.

The columns marked Owner and Category use a number (Short) instead of a description. This enables us to represent each of the owners as numbers (0=Carol, 1=Don) and content categories as numbers (0=Drama, 1=Comedy, 2=Documentary, etc.) instead of descriptive text. Since there are a limited number of choices, using a number helps us avoid possible problems caused by typographical errors during data entry.

Table 7.3 Suggested structure for a video table.

Column name	Data type
Description	Alpha
Owner	Short
Acquired	Short
Source	Alpha
Cost	Money
Title	Alpha
Category	Short
Running Time (mins)	Short
Release Date	Alpha

Neither the acquired date nor the release date are of the Date type. That's simply because neither is being used in a situation likely to require date arithmetic (how many days between these dates?). Then why, you might ask, is the acquired date a number (a Short), while the release date is not?

It's accepted practice to use numbers only when you plan to make computations with them. In the case of the acquisition, I may well later decide I want to calculate how long I've had the item by subtracting from the current year. I might be as likely to want to know how long ago the movie was released. It's definitely a judgment call.

Physical Sorts

Left unto its own, the data in a table will be in the same order as it was added to the table. In many cases that is fine. In an accounting system, for instance, it's good to keep an accurate record of the order in which items were entered.

In other situations, it may be desirable to change the order of the items in a table. Consider the video table in Table 7.3. There are times I would like to see my video tapes in order by title, or perhaps by their year of release. One way I can accomplish this is to ask the DBMS to sort the table.

When a DBMS performs a sort, it physically shuffles things around. In the case of a table, the contents are read from the disk, sorted in memory, and then written back to the disk. The changes made to the table are permanent.

Physically sorting a table's rows has some significant drawbacks. For instance, once you've sorted by the values in a column, how do you get the rows back in the order in which they were entered?

There is a simple way to prevent this situation from happening: create an additional column that contains a sequence number (Paradox's Autoincrement data type was designed specifically for this purpose). To get back to sequence order, simply sort on the values in that column. Problem solved.

But sorting has other drawbacks as well. For small tables, sorting is very fast. As the number of rows in a table grows, however, the time it takes to sort them increases rapidly. Depending on the machine running the DBMS, very large tables (we're talking hundreds of thousands of records) can take several hours to sort.

Sorting may be fine if you're the only one accessing your tables, but what if someone else needs to use your data? What order is he or she going to find your rows in? Perhaps more to the point: What order are you going to find your data in once your coworkers finish their tasks?

Indexing

A far more flexible way to order your information is through *indexing*. I suppose if we were to give this process a name today, it might be virtual sorting. Your data appears to be sorted in the order you specify. In reality, it's just a sneaky trick.

How Indexing Works

Imagine we have been asked to create a table containing several pieces of information about registered members of the Greater Poulsbo Lawn and Garden Society. The information can be entered in the table in any order, but we want it to appear as if sorted by last name.

Figure 7.2 shows how this can be done through indexing. (Although greatly oversimplified, it does illustrate the concept.) The piece of the table on the right shows two of the many columns in the table. The table shows the physical order of the rows; we can see that the items have been entered in no particular order.

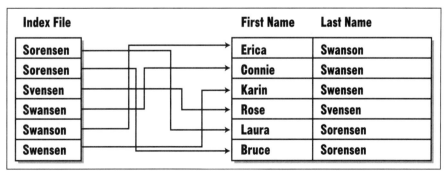

Figure 7.2   Illustration of indexing concept.

The box on the left is a depiction of an additional file (the index file) the DBMS creates to weave its magic. Each time an item is entered, the DBMS adds to the index file a copy of the contents of the column it is tracking, along with information that acts as a pointer to the physical row in the table. Figure 7.3 shows how the table would appear when indexed on the last name.

Because an additional process (going through the index file to get to the table) is required when accessing data, retrieving indexed data is inherently slower than retrieving sorted tables. Even so, indexing is quite fast, and best of all the DBMS does all the work automatically. It is totally transparent to us!

MULTIPLE INDEXES

It's possible to fine-tune this virtual ordering by specifying more than one column for the index. Let's say, for example, we want to add data for a new member named Ann Svensen. Now that we've got more than one person with the same last name, we'd probably like to see the names appear in order by last name, but within that name we would like to see the names appear in order by *first* name.

Fortunately, our trusty DBMS can handle this situation without breaking a sweat. We just tell the DBMS we want to combine the last and first names in our index. When we enter Ann's data, the newly indexed table will appear as shown in Figure 7.4.

First Name	Last Name
Laura	Sorensen
Bruce	Sorensen
Rose	Svensen
Connie	Swansen
Erica	Swanson
Karin	Swensen

Figure 7.3   Table as indexed on last name.

First Name	Last Name
Laura	Sorensen
Bruce	Sorensen
Ann	Svensen
Rose	Svensen
Connie	Swansen
Erica	Swanson
Karin	Swensen

Figure 7.4   Indexed table with new name added.

There is another aspect of indexing that is extremely handy. In addition to specifying multiple columns for an index, it is possible to specify more than one index for a single table. Let's assume our member table contains addresses, and we want to produce a mailing list in ZIP code order. It is not only possible to create a second index based on the ZIP code; we can actually switch back and forth between our indexes at will, giving us entirely different views of our data.

Most DBMS offer the option of "maintaining" indexes, meaning that all indexes for a table are automatically updated whenever data in that table is added or modified. Selecting this option slows down operations involving tables that get modified, but the advantage is having multiple up-to-date views of the data in a table available to us on a nearly instant basis.

Duplicate Indexes

If you were on your toes when I suggested adding Ann Svensen's name to the member table, you might have asked what would have happened had we not decided to extend our index specification.

Depending on the specific DBMS being used, the answer would have ranged from nothing to slightly controlled chaos. Some DBMS will routinely accept duplicate index values. Others will never accept them. The truth is, it's almost never a good idea to permit them, and you should do whatever is necessary to prevent them from happening.

If we were using Paradox as our DBMS and we entered data into our member table for a second person named Ann Svensen, we would cause an error due to the attempt to duplicate an index value. One way around this unhappy situation is to further qualify the index by adding yet another column to the specification. We might try adding the ZIP code column, for instance.

Over the years I have found human beings to be the greatest challenge to any record keeping system. After you have spent months devising an absolutely bullet-proof system, humans will, without even thinking about it, bring your system to its knees—usually on the second or third day your system is operational. They will buy a summer home and move between addresses at will. They will get married and change their name. They will start a commune and invite everyone in the seven neighboring states with the same name to join them. They will establish an alias and make plans to rob the local bank.

It's not a matter of if this will happen to you, it's a matter of when. (I'm told there have been incidents where two people were mistakenly assigned the same Social Security ID number. Can you imagine that confusion?)

Interestingly enough, the solution to this potential problem is the same one we used to restore the original row order after sorting a table: We create an additional column for a unique sequence number for each new row. (The Autoincrement type is ideal for this purpose because it automatically keeps track of the next number in the sequence and doesn't permit deleted sequence numbers to be reused.)

Introduction To Queries

At the outset I said that DBMS enable users to store and to retrieve information. We've now seen how data is stored in tables, and how that information can be physically ordered and indexed so the user can view the information in a table in a desired order.

But what if we want to look at only a portion of our data? What if we were invited to a party and were asked to bring 30 to 45 minutes of comedy on video? How is our DBMS going to help us locate that material?

Descriptive Queries

The answer comes in a very useful process called a query. Queries return to us exactly what we ask about a table. Let's say for example that our video table has been created by the dBASE DBMS, according to the structure listed in Table 7.3. A query entered from the keyboard in dBASE might look like:

```
USE VIDEO
DISPLAY TITLE, RUNTIME FOR RUNTIME > = 30 .AND. RUNTIME <= 45
```

Here, we've asked the DBMS first to make sure it's looking at the video table, and then to display the title and runtime of all videos for which the value in the runtime column is greater than or equal to 30 minutes and less than or equal to 45 minutes.

Query By Example

The main problem with the descriptive query process is that it requires the user to be conversant in an arcane sort of language dictated by the DBMS. The example descriptive query given above is an incredibly simple one. The complexity of queries increases rapidly, and even the most straightforward query description in a real world situation can be difficult to read by anyone not well versed in query language and syntax.

In the visually-oriented computer world we live in today, you'd think there was an easier way, wouldn't you?

Give yourself five points if you agreed. A few years back some astute designers created what they call a *Query by Example* (QBE). The DBMS presents you with what looks like a blank row in the table being queried. You just fill in the criteria you want, and the DBMS returns what appears to be a table containing only those items matching the criteria you specified.

Figure 7.5 shows a QBE filled in for the same query we did on the video table. This time assume we're operating on a Paradox table using the Paradox

Figure 7.5   Paradox QBE example.

DBMS. The check marks indicate in which columns we've chosen to display the result. The criteria have been typed into the RunTime column, separated by a comma. Compared to writing out complex queries, QBE is a breeze.

QBE typically does another helpful thing: It returns what you might call a virtual table. The rows and columns may or may not correspond with the table on which the query was run. You will usually get only a subset of the rows in a table, due to the matching criteria you entered for one or more columns. You will get only the columns you requested. While it exists in memory, the query can even be treated much like a table, and if desired, it can be saved as a table. If the data should change in the table on which the QBE was run, however, it will not be reflected in the table saved from the query. This is best used when you have data that doesn't change often.

Structured Query Language

While the concept of creating queries is very powerful, it suffers because the precise techniques and results vary from DBMS to DBMS. If you are asked to manage a database containing tables created with more than one DBMS, you will likely be required to know the query language for each, right down to its gnarly syntax.

There is an alternative. It's called Structured Query Language (SQL, pronounced "sequel").

Developed in the late 1970s in an IBM laboratory in San Jose, California, the purpose of SQL was to provide a standard query language for use by a number of DBMS. It was structured in a way that described what was wanted from a table, not how it was to be accomplished.

The strategy worked, and it is now promoted by two standards organizations, ANSI (the American National Standards Organization) and ISO (the International Standards Organization). Many DBMS support SQL, some through a special add-on interface and some through special system drivers such as ODBC (see the sidebar, "Who *Was* That Masked DBMS?").

Let's see how the video table query would be written, this time with SQL:

```
select title, runtime
from video
where runtime >= 30 and runtime <=45;
```

This is progress? It looks like the same old descriptive query technique!

That's because it is. But there are some advantages. First, like QBE, SQL is trained to bring back a data set (a virtual table) with rows and columns that can be further manipulated. That in itself is a very powerful capability.

Beyond that, there is more good news. Most of today's SQL-compatible DBMS include a utility that will turn the work of creating SQL queries into child's play. These utilities will typically present you with a QBE-like interface that will enable you to build your queries using a combination of point-and-click and criteria entry. When you're finished, you click on a button and the utility will create the SQL equivalent.

Finally, you will be able to work with tables in multiple DBMS formats, using a single query language. Plus, SQL goes beyond simple queries, actually enabling you to create and manipulate new tables at your command.

Filtering

Several DBMS provide a feature whereby the contents of a table can be filtered temporarily, without modifying the actual data in any way. The technique is accomplished by creating a filter template that specifies the criteria for one or more columns, similar to that done for queries. Those rows containing data not matching the filter in effect become invisible.

The format of the filter template can vary, depending on the DBMS used. Figure 7.6 depicts Paradox's filter dialog, showing a filter specification for the runtime criteria for our video table query example.

When a filter is applied at the table level, all queries will automatically ignore any data that doesn't match the filter specification. When the filter is removed, everything returns to normal.

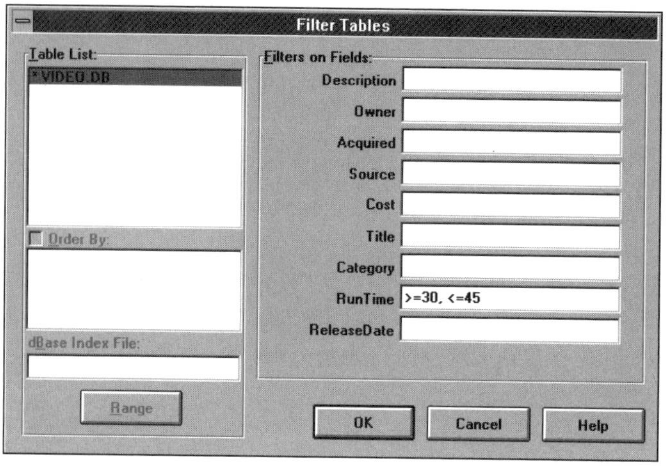

Figure 7.6 Paradox filter dialog.

It's Alive! It's Alive!!

The description of a query we've used to this point implies that a copy of the data from a table is transferred to us for our examination. In this case, which we call a non-live query, we could read the data in the original table, but we could not modify it.

There is another class of queries, however, that do enable the user to edit the data in the table after the query is run. This class of queries is termed live queries.

Query Components

Many of today's visual application development packages (such as Borland's Delphi and IntraBuilder) include queries as software components. These components encapsulate queries in a way that makes working with them easy while providing a large measure of power and flexibility to the application developer.

Many of the concepts discussed here can be found as properties of a query component—properties that can be selected to determine such attributes as these:

◆ Which table will be used?

◆ Will the query data be sorted? By which column(s)?

◆ Will it use a table index? Which one?

◆ Will a filter be applied? If so, what is it?

◆ Will the query be live?

◆ If live, will the query automatically be placed in edit mode?

◆ What SQL statement will be executed to achieve the query?

Who *Was* That Masked DBMS?

The more things are different, the more they are the same—at least when it comes to working with tables. In many cases, enterprise databases used by large companies, universities, and government agencies have evolved over a period of time, frequently without the benefit of careful planning. The result is a database comprising tables created by many people using multiple DBMS and design criteria.

Application development software must be able to bridge the gap, enabling developers to use tables created by several DBMS. Creators of development packages running in the Microsoft Windows environment have been aided by the efforts of DBMS companies themselves, who have developed Open Data Base Connectivity (ODBC) drivers for their packages.

ODBC drivers enable many products to interface with various DBMS through the use of SQL commands. These drivers "connect" with the DBMS' API (see Figure 7.1), translating SQL commands from the user to commands the individual API can process. The result is that any DBMS with an ODBC driver will look like a plain SQL processor to the user.

Borland International carries the process one step further. Its recent data-oriented application development products (such as Delphi and IntraBuilder) include what it calls the Borland Database Engine (BDE), a sophisticated driver that provides a built-in interface with specific codes for dBASE, Paradox, and Interbase tables, with options for extending it with ODBC drivers.

Increasingly, databased applications are being developed with packages like Delphi, IntraBase, and Visual Basic rather than using the programming capabilities built into the DBMS by their creators.

Reports

We've seen that we can browse through a table and see all the items (rows) and their characteristics (columns). We can choose to see the items in the order they were entered, or we can sort them on any characteristic. We can use indexing to view table information in just about any order we wish, without disturbing a hair on its head. We can even filter out any data we don't want to see so the table seems only to contain the information we want.

Beyond that, we can use queries to extract a temporary copy of information from one (or more!) tables. We can limit the characteristics we want to view, and we can limit the items returned by the query to those that meet our criteria.

All this is great. But for my video collection, I want to know the total minutes I have of each category (drama, comedy, etc.). I'd also like to know the total running time of all my videos, and I'd like this all neatly printed out so I can put it in a notebook for reference.

Report Generators

Not a problem. Back in Figure 7.1 we showed a box labeled Report Generator. This application, typically supplied as part of a DBMS, enables users to create even the most sophisticated reports complete with subtotals, group totals, or whatever.

Today's report generators are usually visual in nature, enabling you to use point-and-click techniques to select on which table (or tables) to base your report. You can even create reports based on queries. These visually-oriented applications let you drag logos or other graphics onto the report as you build it on the screen. At the end, the report you create can be displayed on your screen or sent to your printer.

Report Components

With all the emphasis we're seeing in miniaturization, it should not be surprising to find out that some clever programmers, working late at night in their laboratories, have been able to squeeze a report generator down to a size that will easily fit into an icon.

Seriously, most data-oriented visual program development systems now include a report component that performs the major functions (and sometimes *all* the functions) of a full-fledged report generator. As a program developer, you simply drop a report component on a form, and then set its various properties to determine which tables or queries to report on, the order in which to display data, subtotals desired, and so forth.

Relational Database Concepts

Up to this point we have pretty much talked only of working with single tables. But in the real world, multiple table databases are much more common.

Let's consider a classic example. The Stuff Stars Are Made Of is our imaginary mail order business, serving the needs of famous movie actors and actresses. As part of our everyday operations, we must be able to create invoices for the orders we receive.

Now then. Just what information does an invoice contain? A unique number, which should come in handy as a sequence number for a table, a date, customer information, and a list of one or more purchases.

This all seems very straightforward. Just create a table with columns for invoice number, date, customer name and address, first item purchased, quantity of the first item, the second item, and so on.

Wait a minute! If we must have columns for every item on the invoice, just how many columns are we going to allow? Five? Fifty? What if we allow only five items and the customer purchases six? Will we have to start a new invoice? Silly! But if we create a table with enough columns for 50 items and the customer purchases 1, we will be wasting lots of storage space.

Let's take a second run at this. We know the entries for each row in a table must have the same columns. What if each row in the table describes not only one item purchased, but all of the information for the invoice as well? Table 7.4 presents one possible structure for such a table.

Even at a glance, it's obvious that the major part of each row entry would be the invoice information, and only a small part is devoted to the item's data.

But there are even bigger problems hidden within. We must be able to compute and have on file the total for the invoice. Since we have to keep that quantity on file, it's stored in the InvoiceTotal column. But how do we calculate it? Every time we add an item, we have to go back and update this column for every row in the invoice. Not at all good.

A Two Table Approach

Okay. I admit it. I was sandbagging you. This time we'll take a new approach that uses two tables to accomplish the task.

Table 7.4   Structure for a single-table invoicing system.

Column name	Data type
InvNum	Long integer
Date	Date
CustName	Alpha
CustAddr	Alpha
CustCity	Alpha
CustState	Alpha
CustZIP	Alpha
CustPhone	Alpha
ShippedBy	Short
PaidBy	Short
CreditCardNum	Alpha
InvoiceTotal	Money
ItemDesc	Alpha
ItemQty	Short
UnitPrice	Money

Why exactly two tables? What should be in each of them? Good questions, both. Two tables, because it has been pretty obvious that we have been dealing with two different entities. As to the breakdown, it's shown in Table 7.5.

JOINED AT THE HIP

The tables have certainly been broken according to our criteria, with one exception: There is one column (InvNum) that appears in both of the tables. There is still some duplication, but it is very minor compared to the way it was before.

Assuming we're able to keep the two tables in synchronization (that is, the invoice number listed for each item corresponds to the invoice number on which it appears), we have accomplished something significant. Figure 7.7 depicts a simplified version of our tables, showing how each invoice number in the Invoice table corresponds to one or more items in the Items table.

Time for a little dataspeak. We have created a *relation* between the two tables. We say the two tables are related on the InvNum column. The two tables have a *master-detail relationship*, with the Invoice table being the master table and the Item table being the detail table. (Some people also describe this as a parent/child relationship.)

Table 7.5   Breakdown of columns in each invoice table.

Invoices table	Items table
InvNum	InvNum
Date	ItemDesc
CustName	ItemQty
CustAddr	UnitPrice
CustCity	
CustState	
CustZIP	
CustPhone	
ShippedBy	
PaidBy	
CreditCardNum	

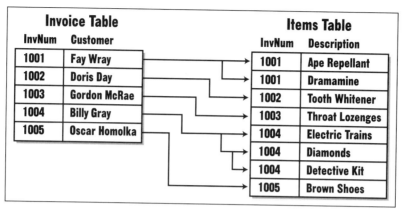

Figure 7.7 Simplified invoice/items relation example.

A Meaningful Relationship

The master-detail relationship is so well accepted and widely used that most visual application development systems provide data components with built-in properties that accommodate it.

When a user *navigates* (moves from row to row) through a table or query, these components automatically move the *cursor* (the imaginary pointer to the currently selected row) in the detail table to the first row that matches the related column in the master table. If you now filter out all rows in the detail table that don't match the related column, you've got a perfect relationship between the two tables (or queries).

USING SQL WITH RELATIONAL TABLES

SQL's greatest application is in working within relational databases. Creating a query that pulls information from two tables with a master-detail relationship is child's play, using a technique called an *equi-join*. Here's an example that will produce an equi-join query for our imaginary invoicing system:

```
select Inv.InvNum, Inv.InvDate, Itm.ItemDesc, Itm.ItemQty,
  Itm.UnitPrice
from Invoice Inv, Items Itm
where Inv.InvNum = Itm.InvNum
```

Although SQL can be used in a standalone fashion to query tables, it is also frequently used from software components to give them more universal access to tables through software links such as the BDE and ODBC drivers.

A True Relational Database

Is it true that only two tables can be related? No way! In a typical relational database, it is not unusual to have several tables share relationships.

Most companies who manage their information on computers do so with several tables that track personnel, customers, inventory, vendors, repair status, and so forth. Relational databases are suited to situations where data processing tasks use information that must come from more than one table.

Consider the invoicing system depicted in Figure 7.8, based on requirements a real-world company might face. Here we have five related tables, each storing specific information, and a single relation between the Invoice table and each of the others.

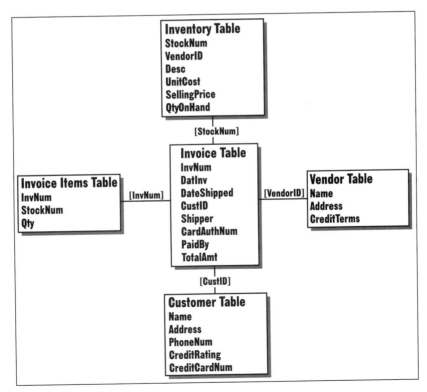

Figure 7.8 "Real World" invoicing model.

Let's say we want to retrieve information from an invoice, using the system in Figure 7.8. Just to make it difficult, we'll gather every bit of detail we can.

As in our simple example, the primary information comes easily because it's stored in the Invoice table: Invoice number, date entered, date shipped, shipper, credit card authorization code, how it was paid, and the total amount.

But notice how we have added some ID codes that enable us to tie into the other tables for more detail. The customer ID brings us the customer's name, address, phone, and credit information from the Customer table. The invoice number retrieves the stock number and quantity of each item ordered, courtesy of the Invoice Items table. That stock number we just got gives us entrance to the Inventory table, which will give us the description, cost, selling price, quantity on hand, and the vendor's ID number. (If we wished, we could use the vendor ID to fetch information from the Vendor table.)

Advantages Of RDBMS

What kind of DBMS handles a relational database? Why, a Relational Database Management System (RDBMS), of course. (You know something is *really* important when it requires a five letter acronym.) Not surprisingly, nearly all popular DBMS are actually RDBMS, and every DBMS-related software component I'm aware of also handles relational databases.

We've seen how powerful a RDBMS is and how easily it can provide us with incredible detail. Let's quickly consider four advantages that RDBMS offer us.

MORE RELIABLE DATA

Have you ever kept two copies of your appointment schedule and tried to keep them in sync? It's nearly impossible! When they don't agree, which one is correct?

That's typical of problems that occur when you're storing redundant data. Using a RDBMS enables you to store a data item only once in a table associated with other closely related items. Through the use of a related column between tables, you can quickly retrieve the item—and you know it's always the only correct copy.

MORE AVAILABLE DATA

By normalizing your data and arranging it in tables that make sense for your overall organization (see the sidebar, "Good Relations"), you make it easier to access and maintain the information.

In the invoicing system in Figure 7.8, we have relegated the various data items to tables that can logically be updated by different people or even different departments within an organization. Dividing the data has also distributed the load on the system. Instead of everyone who needs information making simultaneous hits on a single large table, those requests for information may well be directed to one or two much smaller tables containing the desired data.

MORE COMPATIBLE DATA

SQL was developed to work with relational databases. Even though your database may consist of tables that have been developed with several RDBMS over many years, SQL provides a lowest common denominator approach to accessing that data in a consistent fashion.

REFERENTIAL INTEGRITY

Let's say you had set up a master-detail table pair to handle invoicing, related by an invoice number column in each table. That relationship is dependent upon an exact match between the column values in the two tables. What is to prevent someone accidentally entering slightly different values in each?

The usual answer is this: nothing. And when (not *if*) it happens, your system is toast, because typically an error will be generated when an attempt is made to match the two and nothing happens.

Some RDBMS offer a feature that helps ensure that your relations will be safe from corruption through errors in data entry. That feature is called *referential integrity*. Basically, once you specify that corresponding columns in two tables must have referential integrity, the RDBMS won't allow anyone to enter a value in the detail table unless it matches an existing value in the master table. It's a very useful feature.

Good Relations

The relational database concept is credited to Dr. E. F. Codd from a paper he wrote in 1970 entitled "A Relational Model of Data for Large Shared Data Banks." The model he discussed included 13 rules (referred to strangely as Codd's Twelve Rules, probably because he numbered them from 0 through 12).

Codd's idea for a RDBMS looked at data items as entities that could be grouped into sets and treated with the mathematical techniques of relational algebra to arrange the items into table-like structures.

Codd also defined four levels of what he called normalization, each level reducing both the complexity and the amount of repetition within the database.

The popularity of RDBMS today is due in part to the synergy they share with three other concepts, Structured Query Language (SQL), the Local Area Network (LAN), and client/server architecture, which enables the workload of data storage and retrieval to be allocated between the user's computer and the computer managing the database.

Sharing Data With Others

We have seen how data can be conquered by subdividing it into multiple tables that can be related to one another. But in your working environment, who has access to these tables and for what purpose?

In this final section of this chapter, we'll take a very brief look at some of the aspects of sharing data (including the management of that data) with other users in a company.

Security And Encryption

The first question to be asked regarding data is "Who should have access to it?". Obviously, some data is proprietary to the company—and other data (employee data, for instance) can be highly confidential.

Most RDBMS provide security features. Many SQL servers and ODBC RDBMS require users to log in to the system before gaining access. Beyond this top-level, all-or-nothing protection, many RDBMS provide the capability of encrypting sensitive data. To gain access to the database, a user must be able to specify a valid user name and password. The database administrator is typically charged with assigning names and passwords to authorized users.

Most RDBMS also enable administrators to determine preset access for individual tables. Rather than granting carte blanche access to anyone who has a valid password, it is possible to grant various *levels* of access.

One user may not be allowed any access to a table. Another may be permitted to read information but not edit it. Yet another may be given full read/write privileges. Some RDBMS extend this access capability down to individual columns!

Locking And Unlocking

Let's assume two users have been given full read/write privileges to a table, and they find themselves editing the same row simultaneously. Bob starts his editing but is interrupted by a phone call. As Bob picks up the phone, Jill begins her editing at her desk in another department. She quickly makes her changes to the row and updates the table. Bob then finishes his call and completes his edit, saving his changes to the row.

Whose changes are kept?

Depending on the RDBMS and its settings, both changes may be recorded. In other cases, Bob's edits would take precedence. The potential conflict arises because of the way RDBMS work with users. When a user is editing a row, they are really making changes to a *copy* of that row. When the editing is complete and the table is updated, the existing row is replaced with the edited copy. In cases where there are two copies, the last one recorded wins.

RDBMS vendors have developed some strategies for these situations, some of them quite sophisticated. The most straightforward is that of locking and unlocking rows. Under these conditions, when a user begins an edit on a row the RDBMS marks the "real" version of the row data as being in the editing process. The user who attempts to edit that row will typically receive an error message that asks him or her to try later because an edit is underway. As soon as the first user updates the table with new information, the lock is removed.

Client/Server

Early in this chapter we followed the development of program data from simple, proprietary data files dedicated to a single program up to databases using DBMS, presumably on a single computer. But there's one more installment to this story—the development of systems that can provide information via Local Area Networks (LANs) and intranets to many users within a company, and enterprise systems that provide access to divisions worldwide via wide area networks (WANs).

The concept of client/server architecture was devised to provide data access to a number of users while attempting to minimize the overall workload on the network serving those users. Figure 7.9 depicts a typical client/server system.

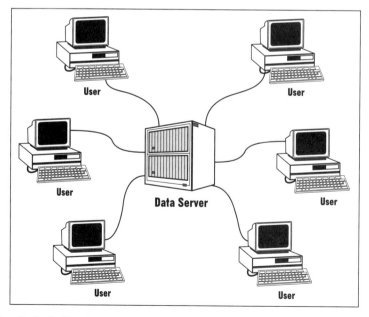

Figure 7.9   Typical client/server system.

The first task was easy enough: Make the data available to others simply by putting it on a single computer and giving people access to that computer through a network. Centralizing the data in this manner also guaranteed there would be one, and only one, copy of the data available to everyone.

Now for the second task: to balance the workload on the data server. The first attempt was to put all the smarts on the user computer. In this model, the server would be solely a repository for data files. Applications running on user machines would download those data files from the server as needed. Dumb server. Dumb approach. Every time a program needed some data, it had to download an entire data file, tying up both the server and the network.

The next attempt was to try it with the model used for years with mainframe systems: Build all the intelligence into the server and turn the user-computers into dumb terminals (basically keyboards and display screens). This time the server didn't need to send data anywhere, but it was tied up tight just processing the keystrokes and controlling the video displays on the dumb terminals.

As they say, the third time was the charm. With the advent of relational databases and SQL, designers were able to build fast servers that would accept queries from applications running on client computers, returning only the data required for the operation at hand.

The result of these efforts is today's client/server system. It's both fast and efficient. Will it meet tomorrow's needs? Likely not. Fortunately, you're in the right place at the right time. You may well help determine the future of data management.

Conclusion

In this chapter you have been introduced to data base management systems on the PC. You've seen the progression from the early days of PC computing to the implementation of enterprise data systems.

You've experienced the analysis of data, and seen how you can group objects (including all the stuff I own) by their characteristics into lists and data tables.

You've taken a peek into the inner workings of a DBMS and seen how the new application development systems can interface with and even emulate many of the functions of a fully featured DBMS, through software components.

You've seen how a DBMS is able to provide different capabilities based on the data types assigned to an individual item's characteristics.

You've explored the concept of data tables, how their information can be physically ordered by sorting or virtually ordered by indexing, and you've seen how entire portions of a table can be made to disappear, through filtering.

You've learned how queries can be used to pull vast amounts of information from several sources, and through the use of SQL you've learned that you can easily access tables of different flavors.

And finally, you witnessed the awesome power of relational databases and relational database management systems and how they can be used to share data within a single company or an entire enterprise.

Congratulations! You've just completed Database 101. Give yourself a pat on the back. Thanks for being here.

Just one more thing before you go: Now that we've got all my stuff arranged in neat little piles all over my living room, who's gonna help me put it all back where it belongs?

Using IntraBuilder's Database Power Tools

8

Don Taylor

After we examine each of the fundamental database tools provided with IntraBuilder, we'll put on our tool belts and learn how to create tables both with the Table Expert and on our own.

*F*or years my parents embarrassed me by telling everyone who would listen that I dismantled the family's only alarm clock when I was four years old. I guess I wanted to know literally what made that clock tick. I'm still like that. When I buy something new, I want to rip open the box and get started with it right away. No manuals. Just plug it in. Let 'er rip. Perhaps you can identify.

It helps to know what a tool is intended to do, and you have to use it properly if you expect to create a good product. And you'll never really know the quality of the tool you have until you take it in hand and use it on something.

In this chapter, we will briefly explore the IntraBuilder database-oriented tools you'll be using the most. You should leave with a working understanding of how to create tables and modify their structures, how to order the information in tables and queries through indexing, and how to use queries to both access and modify information in tables.

We'll accomplish our task by building two simple applications. The first will be a basic address book and the second an invoicing example that incorporates the master-detail concept. Finally, we'll explore the Visual Query Builder and see how it is possible to build SQL statements in a point-and-click environment.

With that said, let's grab a couple of tools and start on a tour that will create some serious sawdust.

Using The Table Expert

It's likely that you already know what you want to accomplish with IntraBuilder. Some of you will be making data in existing tables available to others. Others of you might be building a database from scratch. In either case, there will undoubtedly come a time when you will have to create or modify the structure of tables on your own. Fortunately, with IntraBuilder the process is a simple one.

IntraBuilder's Table Expert will create a table with minimal effort on your part. As with the Form Expert, you make a few selections and a raw product will be created for you. Once you finish, you save your work and you're presented with a running form. In the case of the Table Expert, you will get a default form that contains the fields (columns) specified to the Expert when you created the table.

Create A Working Directory
The sample applications and data we create during our tour will be placed in a single folder. If you intend to try these examples yourself, you should create a folder called datatools within IntraBuilder's APPS folder.

Creating The Table

You have two options for creating a table from within the IntraBuilder designer: You can do all the work manually, or you can put a power tool to work by using the Table Expert. For the moment we'll use the Expert to create a table for a simple address book.

From the IntraBuilder Explorer, select the Tables tab and then double-click on the icon labeled Untitled. The New Table dialog (see Figure 8.1) is where we select the Expert to create our table.

From the Expert's choice of tables, we'll choose the one that is most similar for our purpose. Scanning down the list we find one called Personal Address Book. Clicking on that selection enters seven fields (columns) in the From Sample Table listbox, as shown in Figure 8.2. Since we're demonstrating

Figure 8.1   The New Table dialog.

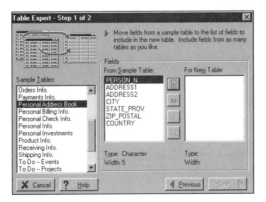

Figure 8.2   Choosing fields for the address book table.

how the Expert works, we'll take everything offered by clicking on the right arrow button. All fields move into the For New Table list. Clicking the Next button moves us to the next page.

We now see the dialog in Figure 8.3, which indicates there is one last choice to make: the format of the table. If we were to create it with an RDBMS, which one would it be? We stay with the default choice, dBASE.

Saving And Leaving

Now that we've created the table, we can save it and enter some data to play with. Clicking the Run Table button brings up a Save Table dialog. We'll save the table in a file called addr.dbf, located in our datatools folder.

IntraBuilder now runs a default form that contains edit controls for each of the columns in the new table. Clicking the right mouse button over the form brings up a shortcut menu, as shown in Figure 8.4.

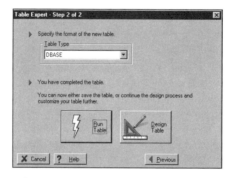

Figure 8.3   Choosing the format of the address book table.

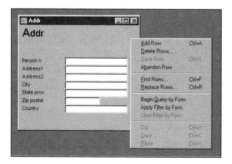

Figure 8.4   Shortcut menu for the table form.

We could perform several of the basic functions from the shortcut menu, but because we're more interested in power tools we'll skip that option and do something that gives us more flexibility and power. Click on the close button for the default Addr form window to put it away.

Manipulating Data From A Form

The default form that appears when running a table may provide some of the basic functions of an RDBMS, but using that functionality is less than convenient. It's time to create a simple form and start using some of the components provided with IntraBuilder—specifically the Query component.

Creating The Form

We'll expand our address book example a bit by creating a form that will make it easier to navigate through the rows and manipulate information.

To create that form we'll use the Form Expert, choosing the addr.dbf table to base the form on, and pretty much taking the default settings. The one exception: We'll include all buttons on the form in Step 5 of the Expert process.

The new form is saved in the datatools folder as addr.jfm. The resulting form is shown running in Figure 8.5

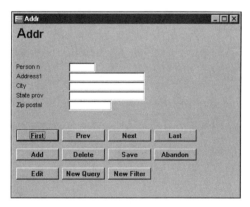

Figure 8.5   Address book form created by the Form Expert.

Adding Data To The Table

A form that enables you to manipulate non-existent data is not an exciting proposition. We'll add to the table some information about a few of our friends, as listed in Table 8.1.

To add this data we first click on the form's Add button to put the form (actually the form's Query component) in append mode. Then enter the data for each person, clicking the Add button again after each entry to save each entry to the table.

While entering the data for Janet, we click the Delete button to see what will happen. Zap! Her data is gone forever, without any warning. We enter the data again, vowing to give a wide berth to that formidable Delete button.

Twice Is Never Too Much

Several of the processes performed on data (queries, filters, and text searches, for example) require two steps for their operation. In the first step, an IntraBuilder component is placed in a certain mode (such as the edit mode) or the user fills in a blank row with information. In the second step, the mode may be returned to the default mode, or the data entered in the blank row is used to perform the requested operation.

Two buttons on the form follow the mode-changing pattern: Add and Edit. The form may be returned to the (default) browse mode without accepting changes by clicking the Abandon button.

The New Query and New Filter buttons follow the second pattern. When they are clicked, their titles change to Apply Query and Apply Filter, and the user is expected to fill in the blanks with information. Clicking the same button that initiated the operation will now carry it to completion.

Exploring The Navigation Controls

When the data entry is finished the form displays the data in the last row, the one containing information about Janet. What if we want to examine the data in other rows?

Table 8.1   Data for the address book table.

PERSON_N	ADDRESS1	CITY	STATE	ZIP_POSTAL
Bill	123 Main St.	Birmingham	AL	35205
Sally	345 Elm St.	Atlanta	GA	30306
Jerry	Box 6532	Medford	OR	97504
Al	8903 Fir Ln.	Seattle	WA	98109
Janet	34 Oak Tower	Hamden	CT	06514

Fortunately, the Form Expert has installed some power tools for us. The first row of buttons on the form are called *navigation* buttons because they help us sail freely through the rows of data.

These four buttons enable us to move to the first or last row, the next row, or the previous row. This affords us a convenient method of moving to any row we desire.

Trying Out The New Query Button

We've been talking a lot about queries—now here's our chance to try one. Let's find Jerry.

First, we move to the first row with the First button. Then we click the New Query button and type "Jerry" in the name control. We click the Run Query button, and up comes Jerry's information!

This is pretty neat. Let's try again, this time searching for Al. Instead of typing in his name, we'll enter "WA" in the control labeled STATE_PROV. Sure enough, there's Al.

Some further experimenting shows us we must enter all the information in a column, exactly as it was originally entered, if we're to get a match. Typing "Wa" or "wa" instead of "WA" won't work. Neither will using "Sal" to find Sally's information. All we get is a blank set of data.

There's a potential source of confusion here. You see, this isn't really a query at all—at least not in the context we have learned about them. When we click the Query button, it is actually performing what IntraBuilder calls a "locate" operation. It doesn't bring back a group of rows; it merely returns the first row that matches the information entered.

The first click of the button begins the location process by accepting a specification for the information to be found; the second click applies this information to accomplish the locate. When no match is found, the data controls become blank, indicating the search went past the last row without finding a match.

We'll see a bit later how we can change the rules used to search for matches.

Fun With Filters

We know that using filters can mask out (or let through, depending on how you look at it) certain rows, based on criteria we can specify. The New Filter button enables us to apply such a filter to our data.

Let's say we want to limit what we see to entries from the state of Connecticut. We click the New Filter button, then type "CT" in the control labeled STATE_PROV. Now we click the Run Filter button.

Up comes Sally's information. Clicking the navigation buttons moves between the rows for Sally and Janet, both living in Connecticut. If we didn't know better, we might think there were only two rows in the table.

What if we try to locate one of the other people? We'll pick Al. We try a New Query, typing "Al" in the name area. When we click Run Query, we get—nothing! Apparently both the navigational controls and the location process honor the filter.

To clear the filter, we click New Filter and then Run Filter (without entering any data). The blank controls we see tell us we're past the last row. We click the First button and we're back in business.

Modifying The Table Structure

After working with this example form, it's obvious that it has some severe limitations. First and foremost, the name area will only accept five characters. It would really be nice if we could expand that capability to, say, 20 characters. That way we could include both first and last names.

The limitation is due to the specification for the table column, which we inherited from the Table Expert's samples list. If we want to expand the length of the column, we have to modify the data table's structure.

Since it could cause some serious confusion if the table columns were to change in size while a program was accessing the table, IntraBuilder rightly insists that no one may use a table—including IntraBuilder forms—during a structural modification.

We close the Addr form and go back to the Tables tab of the IntraBuilder Explorer. We double-click on the addr.dbf icon to run the default form for the table, then we click on the Design Table button on the toolbar (the one with the square and ruler).

Figure 8.6 shows the current structure in tabular format. We have clicked on the Width column and changed the specification from 5 to 20 characters.

To save our work, we tap the Ctrl+S key combination and then close the Table Designer window.

Entering Updated Information

We can now bring up our form and edit the names to reflect our expanded capability.

It is now evident that the Text control that contains the name data is too short to display our longer names. It is perfectly capable of handling those names, however, because the information can scroll beyond the display area.

addr.dbf - Table Designer					
Updated: 10/20/96 **Bytes Used:** 116 **Type:** DBASE					
Rows: 6 **Bytes Left:** 32,651					

Field	Name	Type	Width	Decimal	Index
1	PERSON_N	Character	20	0	None
2	ADDRESS1	Character	20	0	None
3	ADDRESS2	Character	20	0	None
4	CITY	Character	20	0	None
5	STATE_PROV	Character	20	0	None
6	ZIP_POSTAL	Character	10	0	None
7	COUNTRY	Character	20	0	None

Figure 8.6   Address table structure with 20 character name field.

Looking at the status area in the lower-right corner of the IntraBuilder screen, we see it says Editing Row. We are already in the edit mode, so we can merely click in the Text control for the name and start making corrections. When we finish correcting a name, we can click the Save button or just move to another row. The move will automatically cause any changes to be saved.

Let's enter our expanded names in "last name, first name" format. Table 8.2 shows the replacements for each of the five names.

Indexing The Table

With the exception of the limited display of the name, this is much better. Now wouldn't it be nice if we could display the names in order by last name, even though they are in no particular order? And achieve that goal without modifying the data in any way?

That's what we call indexing, and it's really simple to do. Once again, it is done at the table level, and we must change the table's structure to accomplish it.

We again close the Addr form and bring up the Table Designer for the addr.dbf table. This time we click in the Index column for the name field (PERSON_N) so we can select the type of index—ascending, descending, or none (see Figure 8.7). We choose an ascending index and then once again tap Ctrl+S to save the changes. We've completed the task, so we close the Table Designer.

Table 8.2   Changes to the names in the address table.

Original Entry	New Entry
Bill	Williams, Bill
Sally	Gomez, Sally
Jerry	Dunlap, Jerry
Al	Borland, Al
Janet	Switzer, Janet

addr.DBF - Table Designer

Updated:	10/21/96	Bytes Used:	131	Type: DBASE
Rows:	7	Bytes Left:	32,636	

Field	Name	Type	Width	Decimal	Index
1	PERSON_N	Character	20	0	None
2	ADDRESS1	Character	20	0	None / Ascend / Descend
3	ADDRESS2	Character	20	0	
4	CITY	Character	20	0	None
5	STATE_PROV	Character	20	0	None
6	ZIP_POSTAL	Character	10	0	None
7	COUNTRY	Character	20	0	None

Figure 8.7   Address table structure with index on name field.

Trouble In Denmark

When we return to the Addr form, we expect to see the data in order by last name. To our surprise, it is just as we left it. What's going on?

There is another unexplained matter. Why were we able to edit the data earlier, without having to click the Edit button?

Perhaps it's time to dig a little deeper and find out what makes this thing tick.

Getting Under The Hood: The Query Component

To examine the layout of the form, we click the Design Form button on the toolbar, and the familiar grid and rulers appear.

Before going any farther, we click on the Text control associated with the name information and stretch it a bit. One problem solved. The contents of the designer appear in Figure 8.8.

Something grabs our attention. It's the component in the upper-right corner of the form. The one with the characters SQL on it.

It's the Query component, probably the most powerful in the entire IntraBuilder component library. The Query is Communications Central between controls on the form and tables within a database. The Query selects and copies only the rows and columns from a table (or tables) specified by the user into a temporary storage area called the **rowset** object. Changes

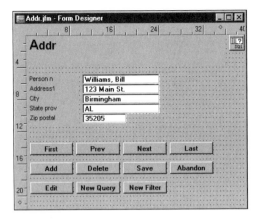

Figure 8.8 Modifying the Addr form.

can be made to the information in a given row in the rowset with no effect on the information in the table. If the Query is live, the changes may then be committed to the table, replacing the table's row with the contents of the corresponding row in the rowset.

Other controls (such as the Text controls used to display and edit data in the Addr table) can connect to a Query through the control's datalink property; it then has access to all information stored in the Query.

Examining The Query's Properties

We click on the Query component and tap the F11 key to make sure the Inspector window is visible. We click on its Properties tab to display properties of the Query. A picture of the Inspector window appears in Figure 8.9.

It would probably be helpful to examine a few key properties more closely.

THE ROWSET PROPERTY

This is easily the most complex of all the Query's properties. As can be seen in Figure 8.9, the **rowset** is itself an object that belongs to the Query. As we've said before, this object is literally a set of rows, which holds the information in columns, as returned from one or more tables.

We'll take a more detailed look at the **rowset** in a moment.

Figure 8.9   Inspector display of Query properties.

THE SQL PROPERTY

This property is a group of one or more SQL statements that specify the table(s) to connect to, which columns to include from those table(s), and any qualifiers that would restrict rows from being included. The rows and columns returned from the table(s) specified in the SQL statement are stored in the Query's rowset.

In Figure 8.9, we can see part of the SQL specification for the Addr form. If we click on that line in the Inspector window, a small button with a wrench icon pops up. Clicking that brings up the SQL Property Builder window (see Figure 8.10), which contains the complete statement.

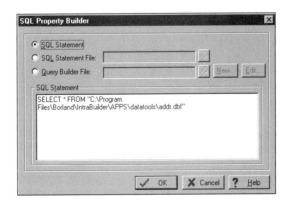

Figure 8.10   The SQL statement for the Query.

This statement, created for us automatically by the Form Expert based on our decisions, selects all columns in all rows of the table addr.dbf. If we wished, we could modify it to include other tables, or we could limit the query to only some of the columns (or rows containing specified values in columns).

We will explore the development of SQL queries in more depth in the final part of this chapter. For now, we'll just close the Property Builder's window.

THE ACTIVE PROPERTY

The value of this property indicates whether the Query is currently linked to a table. If the table does not exist or if the SQL statements have errors in them, the link will not be made.

If a Query is not active, it has no connection to the table associated with it. When not active, it is not able to access information in the table.

THE REQUESTLIVE PROPERTY

This specifies whether we want the query results to be live. As we can see in Figure 8.9, the default value is true, which presumes we want the ability to edit the data returned by the Query.

Note that this is merely a request. The table may have been placed in read-only mode, or the system may have us set up with an access level that will only allow us to read the data in this table. Either of these would override our request.

Examining The Rowset's Properties

The Query component has several other properties, but most of them are beyond the scope of this introduction. Instead, we'll hunker down and investigate one level deeper, examining some of the key properties of the Query's **rowset** object.

To see these properties, we click on the line marked rowset in the Inspector window, then on the wrench button that appears on the line. We see the properties displayed in Figure 8.11.

Figure 8.11   Properties of the rowset object.

THE ENDOFSET PROPERTY

This is one of five properties of the rowset (**endOfSet**, **handle**, **className**, **live**, and **state**) that appear in light gray on the display, indicating they may be read but cannot be changed directly. The **endOfSet** property indicates whether the table's cursor (which points to the currently selected row) is beyond either end of the table.

This property is used most often when a scan is being made of the information in rows. The Locate function (called by the New Query button on the Addr form) makes use of this by examining each row for a match to the specification given. If no match is found and all rows have been examined, **endOfSet** becomes true, signaling the end of the search.

THE STATE PROPERTY

This may sound more like the location of a capitol building, but in this case, it indicates which of the six modal states (Closed, Browse, Edit, Append, Filter, and Locate) the Query is in.

The **state** is currently reported as being in Edit mode, which is in agreement with what the IntraBuilder status display told us about the Addr form.

THE LIVE PROPERTY

Another of the read-only properties, Live lets us know if the Query is a live one. We may have requested a live query; here we can determine if the request was granted.

THE MODIFIED PROPERTY

A read-only property, **Modified** signals us whether data in the Query has been changed but not committed back to the table. **Modified** gets set to false if an editing or appending operation is canceled.

THE MASTERROWSET PROPERTY

This property comes into play when the Query represents the detail part of a master-detail relationship. In this case the value becomes a reference to a row in another Query, which acts as the master data source.

We'll deal with this property in the next section of the chapter.

THE MASTERFIELDS PROPERTY

Like the **MasterRowset** property, **MasterFields** is used in master-detail situations. The **MasterFields** value is set to one or more of the fields (data columns) in the **MasterRowset**.

THE FILTER PROPERTY

This property holds the specification for any filter that is to be applied to the data in the Query's rowset.

THE FILTEROPTIONS PROPERTY

The value of this property determines how the comparison will be made between data in the Query and the specification made in the **Filter** property. There are four options:

- 0 - Match length and case
- 1 - Match partial length
- 2 - Ignore case
- 3 - Match partial length and ignore case

THE LOCATEOPTIONS PROPERTY

Similar to the **filterOptions** property, the **locateOptions** property determines what will be considered a match when a location function is performed. The options are identical to those of **filterOptions**.

Come to think of it, it might be nice to change the locating criteria on the form. We'll select Option 3 and give ourselves the greatest freedom in our searches.

THE INDEXNAME PROPERTY

We have the option of ordering the data in the rowset according to a table index, but we must specify that index here.

Aha! That's why merely indexing the Addr table didn't change the display order of the names on the form. We simply click on the down-arrow button, then select PERSON_N, the only option offered. That should take care of the data-ordering problem.

THE AUTOEDIT PROPERTY

This property determines whether the default state of a Query will be Browse or Edit. If **autoEdit** is set at False, the **state** will be set to Browse. If **autoEdit** is True (its default value), the Query will revert to the Edit state.

We have just discovered why our form's status was Editing Rows, even when we canceled an editing operation. We double-click on the **autoEdit** value to change it to False, and—shazaam! The **state** property changes to Browse, indicating it is now the default state for the form.

Figure 8.12 shows the Inspector window for the **rowset** object, reflecting our recent changes. We tap Ctrl+S to save our work.

Back To The Addr Form

We're ready to find out if the changes we made to the rowset's properties solved the problems we were experiencing. We click the Form button on the toolbar.

The final version of the Addr form appears in Figure 8.13. Sure enough, the names now appear in alphabetical order by last name. The form's status

Figure 8.12   Rowset properties after modifications.

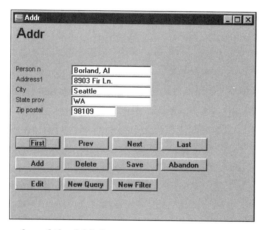

Figure 8.13   Final version of the Addr form.

line now says Viewing Row, and editing with the buttons works as you would expect.

Furthermore, locate operations (using the New Query button) can now take partial-length entries and are no longer case-sensitive. Entering "wi" brings up the information on Bill Williams.

We close the form and sit back. All in all, a good morning's work. But don't remove your tool belt just yet—we've got lots more to do!

Crafting A Master-Detail Relationship

We're now going to develop a second example, one that includes a master-detail relationship between two tables (or as we'll soon see, between two Queries).

We'll use the classic inventory example, where a single row in a table of invoices can relate to any number of rows in a table listing the items on the invoices.

On this tour we'll be traveling pretty fast so we'll keep the tables, form, and expectations as simple as we can. When we finish, our form will have two sets of Text objects and buttons that will enable us to enter and display invoice and item information. The Queries will have referential integrity applied to the relationship between them. When we navigate through invoices, we will be able to see the stock numbers of the items included on them.

Building The Invoices Table

This time we'll build our tables the old fashioned way—by hand, using the Table Designer.

We double-click on the untitled table icon to bring up the New Table dialog. This time we choose the Designer button. Soon we have entered the structure information for our invoices table, as shown in Figure 8.14.

invoices.db - Table Designer					
Updated: 10/22/96 **Bytes Used:** 40 **Type:** PARADOX					
Rows: 0 **Bytes Left:** 32,710					

Field	Name	Type	Width	Decimal	Index
1	InvNum	Alpha	10	0	None
2	InvDate	Date	4	0	None
3	CustNum	Alpha	10	0	None
4	InvTotal	Money	8	0	None

Figure 8.14   Structure of the invoices table.

The InvNum field will hold an alphanumeric value representing the invoice number. Because invoice numbers are sequential and non-repeating, this will provide us with a unique, incrementing value for each invoice. The InvDate field records the date the invoice is written. CustNum identifies the number assigned to the customer purchasing the items. Finally, InvTotal is the total amount of the purchase.

We have chosen the Paradox format for the invoices table. We will do the same for the invoice items table because this format enables us to use referential integrity (which we'll discuss in just a bit).

Each type of table has its idiosyncrasies. While dBASE tables can have several indexes, Paradox tables have a *primary key* that acts as an index. This key must include the first field in the structure, and may include subsequent fields. Paradox permits additional keys, but instead calls them secondary indexes.

We'll use the InvNum field as the primary key for this table (the main reason we have made it the first field in the list). To accomplish this, we call up the Define Primary Key dialog from the Structure menu, then select the field to be the key. The dialog is shown in Figure 8.15.

We'll save the table in the datatools folder as invoices.db, then close the Table Designer window.

Building The Invoice Items Table

Once again, we'll call up the Table Designer to create a new Paradox table. The structure we've chosen appears in Figure 8.16.

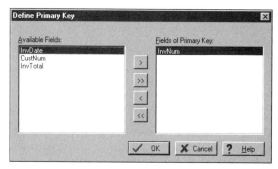

Figure 8.15 **Choosing the primary key for the invoices table.**

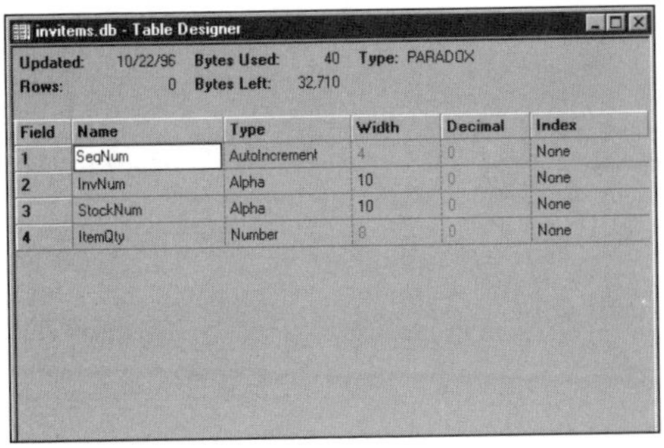

Figure 8.16 **Structure of the invoice items table.**

There can be several items associated with a single invoice, and the same item can appear on any number of invoices. For that reason, we have used an AutoIncrement field as the first (and primary key) field in the structure to ensure that we have a unique sequence number for every row. We have given it the name SeqNum.

InvNum is included to specify the invoice associated with this item entry; note its type and size match that of the InvNum in the invoices table. StockNum is the stock number of the item. ItemQty is the quantity of this item on the specified invoice. It has been declared as a number type, because it will probably be used in arithmetic calculations.

We set SeqNum as the primary key, then save the new table in the datatools folder as invitems.db. We then close the Table Designer window.

Establishing Referential Integrity

Now would be a good time to set up the integrity relationship between the two tables. Under the File menu, we call up the Database Administration dialog. On that dialog we select Paradox as the table type, and the Referential Integrity button becomes enabled. The dialog is shown in Figure 8.17.

We click the Referential Integrity button and the Referential Integrity Rules dialog pops up. On that dialog we click the New button, which brings up the dialog shown in Figure 8.18. Here we have chosen the invoices table as the parent table (the table containing the master reference to a data item) and the invoice items table as the child table (which only refers to the master item). We have chosen the InvNum from the list of Available Child

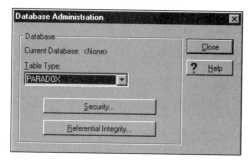

Figure 8.17   Database Administration dialog for Paradox tables.

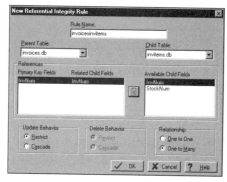

Figure 8.18   New Referential Integrity Rule dialog.

Fields list, and we have chosen the One to Many relationship (one invoice can relate to many rows containing invoice items).

Satisfied with our work, we click the OK button and return to the Referential Integrity Rules dialog shown in Figure 8.19. We click the Close button to put it away, then we close the Database Administration dialog.

Creating An Invoice Display Form

We now need a form that will enable us to enter data in the two tables and to create a display of item stock numbers on each invoice. We use the Form Expert to create a form based on the invoices table, using all fields in the table and accepting all defaults but including only the Prev, Next, and Add buttons to keep things simple. (By leaving the **autoEdit** property in its default state, we can correct errors in our data at any time.)

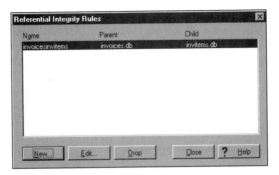

Figure 8.19 **Referential Integrity Rules dialog showing new entry.**

Rather than running the form, we go directly into the Form Designer, where we save the form in the datatools folder under the name invoices.jfm.

Next, we stretch the form to the right and drag the invitems.db icon from the IntraBuilder Explorer Tables page, dropping it onto the form. This creates an additional Query component labeled invitems1. The form in its present state appears in Figure 8.20.

We'll need the same capabilities for the invoice items table, so we Shift+click all the labels, Text controls, and buttons, and then copy them to the right side of the form. These cloned controls not only look identical to the originals, they are—right down to their internal references to the invoices.db table.

We toss the label and Text control for InvDate and readjust the positions of the items on the form. We edit the labels to describe the field (column)

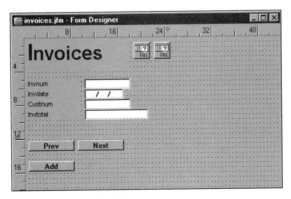

Figure 8.20 **First attempt at the invoices form.**

names for the invoice number, stock number, and item quantity in the invoice items table. We edit the datalink properties in the Text controls so they are tied to the appropriate columns in the invitems.db table.

Now things get a little tricky. Buried within the properties of each of the buttons is a bit of code for its **onServerClick** event. This code performs operations using the Query's **rowset** object. We need to edit that code for each of the cloned buttons, to associate each reference to invitems1 (the Query for the invoice items table).

To accomplish this task, we click on a button, then click the Events tab in the Inspector window. We click on the line marked **onServerClick**, then click inside the right side of that line to un-highlight the text. We can now edit that text, replacing each occurrence of **form.rowset** with **form.invitems1.rowset**. As we finish editing the code for each button, we tap the Enter key to record the change.

Finally, we add a Select List component on the right side of the form. This will be used to display the list of stock numbers that appear on each invoice. In its properties list, we change its name form select1 to ItemsList.

Because we will be displaying numbers with decimal points in the Text control linked to the invoice table's InvTotal column, we need to create a template for that control. We click on the control, then on the property labeled template in the Inspector. For that property, we type in the following specification:

9999.99

The Text control linked to ItemQty in the invoice items table will also be displaying numbers, so it needs a template as well. For its template property we enter the following:

9999

We save it one more time. The final version of the form appears in Figure 8.21.

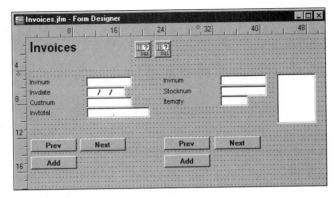

Figure 8.21   Final version of the invoices form.

Filling The Invoices Table

We need to enter data in both tables. We'll start with the master table (invoices) and then take care of the detail table (invoice items).

Using the form we've just created (and the controls on the left side of that form), we enter the data specified in Table 8.3.

One peculiar thing we notice during the data entry is the difficulty entering the InvTotal data. The Text control seems to have a bit of trouble dealing with the decimal point from our template. After a few tries, we realize we can click in the left-most end of the entry area, and the control will then properly accept numbers with decimal points.

Table 8.3   Data for the invoices table.

InvNum	InvDate	CustNum	InvTotal
1001	1/15/97	237	12.50
1002	1/16/97	212	37.85
1003	1/20/97	219	8.20
1004	1/21/97	212	44.75
1005	1/21/97	304	29.90
1006	1/22/97	271	15.55
1007	1/23/97	328	42.00
1008	1/24/97	206	57.80
1009	1/27/97	273	30.25
1010	1/27/97	290	17.65

Filling In The Invoice Items Table

We'll be entering data in the invoice items table, this time using the controls on the right side of the form. Before we get started, however, we decide to try a little experiment.

We try entering data for an invoice with the number 1,000, a bogus number. What happens?

We get the error dialog shown in Figure 8.22. It's telling us we are operating under the rules of referential integrity, and there is no invoice number in the invoices table that matches the one we've tried to enter. Without referential integrity between the two tables, we could turn our data into scrambled eggs and it wouldn't be flagged as an error.

We're now ready to enter data in earnest. We key in the data listed in Table 8.4.

Cementing The Master-Detail Relationship

At this point we are able to navigate independently through each of the tables (actually, the Query rowsets). The navigational controls for each table will move to every row in the table.

We want to create a situation where each time we move to another row in the invoices table, the rows available in the invoice items table become limited to those with an InvNum that matches the InvNum in the invoices table.

Not a problem. We return to the Form Designer. Clicking on the invitems1 Query component, we bring its properties into the Inspector. We move to the **rowset** object, where we will make three small changes.

Figure 8.22   Referential integrity error message.

Table 8.4   Data for the invoice items table.

InvNum	StockNum	ItemQty
1001	3548	1
1002	3235	1
1002	3425	1
1003	3623	1
1004	3832	2
1004	3548	1
1005	3082	2
1006	3253	1
1006	3241	1
1007	3934	2
1007	3827	1
1007	3798	2
1008	3289	1
1008	3235	1
1009	3493	1
1009	3859	3
1010	3078	1

First, we click on the **indexName** property and select the only option, InvNum. This will make the invoice items table appear to be in order by invoice number, which the master-detail relationship requires.

Next, we click on the **MasterRowset** property, and select invoices1, the rowset for the invoices table's Query. Finally, we click on the **MasterFields** property. Here it is possible to select any of the four fields in the invoices table. We select InvNum. We have made the connections we need. The final version of the invitems1 properties page is shown in Figure 8.23.

When we return to the form, we find we have accomplished the goal: When we move between invoices, the controls on the right side change to show us the first item associated with that invoice. Using the controls on the right limit us to examining only the items on the current invoice selection.

Figure 8.23 **Property settings for the master-detail connection.**

Displaying A List Of Invoice Items

Just one more step to go. We're going to hook up the ListBox on the right side of the form to invitems1 so it will list all the items on the current invoice—no having to rummage around with the navigation controls to see what's on a given invoice.

Up to now, we haven't had to write a single line of code. The closest we've come is having to edit the code block in the three buttons we cloned.

To display all the items on an invoice, we must somehow navigate through all the rows in the invoice items table—the ones visible as a result of the master-detail connection. As we navigate, we add each item found to the Select List. That will require a little code.

Once we have the code, we must know when to apply it. Actually, there are three occasions on which we need to perform our procedure:

◆ When the form is first loaded (which fires the form's **onServerLoad** event)

◆ When the invoices table's Prev button is clicked (which fires its **onServerClick** event)

◆ When the invoices table's Next button is clicked (which fires this button's **onServerClick** event)

WRITING AN EVENT HANDLER FOR THE FORM

We'll deal with the form first. Clicking on its **onServerLoad** event and then clicking the edit (wrench) button brings up IntraBuilder's Method Editor, as seen in Figure 8.24. We enter the code in Listing 8.1.

LISTING *8.1* HANDLER FOR THE FORM'S *ONSERVERLOAD* EVENT.

```
function Form_onServerLoad()
{
   this.ItemsArray = new Array();
   form.invitems1.rowset.first();
   while (!form.invitems1.rowset.endOfSet) {
     this.ItemsArray.add(form.invitems1.rowset.fields["StockNum"].value);
     form.invitems1.rowset.next();
}
   form.ItemsList.options = "array this.ItemsArray";
   form.invitems1.rowset.first();
}
```

The code in Listing 8.1 could use a bit of explanation. First, an array (**ItemsArray**) is created. We don't know in advance how many items will be included on an invoice. For that reason we use an array, which will hold any number of data items for us. Next, we make sure the invitem1's rowset is at its first row.

We now perform a loop that will continue until we reach the end of the rowset. Each time through the loop, we first add the contents of the rowset's StockNum column to our array, then skip to the next row.

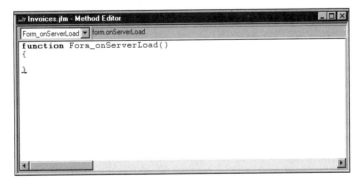

Figure 8.24   Method Editor editing the form's onServerLoad event handler.

When the looping operation is complete, we assign the array to the Select List; it will automatically take care of displaying the list. Finally, we set the Query back to the first row in the rowset.

If this doesn't make total sense at first, don't be concerned. After working with it a while, the clouds will begin to clear. Just be aware that what we have created here is a core routine that will fill the Select List.

WRITING EVENT HANDLERS FOR THE BUTTONS

The buttons already have **onServerClick** events defined in code blocks. We need to replace those code blocks with a true event handler.

Using the same procedure as before, we click on the **onServerClick** event for the invoice table's Prev button. This time, before we enter the Method Editor we are asked if we want to overwrite the code linked to the button. We answer Yes, then we enter the code in Listing 8.2.

LISTING 8.2 HANDLER FOR THE PREV BUTTON'S ONSERVERLOAD EVENT.

```
function button1_onServerClick()
{
if (!form.rowset.next(-1)) form.rowset.next();
this.ItemsArray = new Array();
form.invitems1.rowset.first();
while (!form.invitems1.rowset.endOfSet) {
this.ItemsArray.add(form.invitems1.rowset.fields["StockNum"].value);
form.invitems1.rowset.next();
}
form.ItemsList.options = "array this.ItemsArray";
form.invitems1.rowset.first();
}
```

The first statement in Listing 8.2 performs the action of moving to the previous row (in fact, this is exactly what was in the code block we eliminated). The remainder of the code may look familiar—it's identical to that in Listing 8.1.

If you guessed the code for the **onServerClick** event for the Next button is very similar to that in Listing 8.2, give yourself a gold star. The code appears in Listing 8.3.

LISTING 8.3 HANDLER FOR THE NEXT BUTTON'S onSERVERLOAD EVENT.

```
function button2_onServerClick()
{
if (!form.rowset.next()) form.rowset.next(-1);
this.ItemsArray = new Array();
form.invitems1.rowset.first();
while (!form.invitems1.rowset.endOfSet) {
this.ItemsArray.add(form.invitems1.rowset.fields["StockNum"].value);
form.invitems1.rowset.next();
}
form.ItemsList.options = "array this.ItemsArray";
form.invitems1.rowset.first();
```

Just One Last Look At You

The form now works exactly as planned. The navigation controls work just as before, but the Select List now displays the stock numbers of all the items on each invoice. Figure 8.25 shows the form in operation.

At first, it may seem like it took a lot of work to get to this point. Actually, we did little more than point and click to create a functioning master-detail demo—including the tables.

Before unbuckling your tool belt, there is one more area to cover in this chapter.

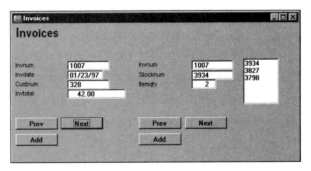

Figure 8.25   Invoices form with item list.

Introducing The Visual Query Builder

SQL may be a universal language for accessing databases, but that doesn't necessarily mean it is easy to learn. The fact is, SQL at its best is more than a little arcane, and queries using SQL in real-life situations can get complex very quickly.

Fortunately, IntraBuilder includes a very serious tool called Visual Query Builder (VQB) that makes composing SQL queries much easier—in some cases, it can be reduced to a point-and-click exercise. In this final section of this chapter, we'll get an overview of VQB and run through several example queries.

The VQB Environment

VQB presents a table's data in a visual format that enables its user to manipulate images to produce a query. The visual query is analyzed by VQB and translated into a block of SQL statements. The user is, at any time, able to run the query and to view the SQL generated.

Figure 8.26 depicts the VQB's environment. The toolbar offers quick access to several of the most-used functions, including creating a new query, loading and saving queries, adding tables to a query, viewing the SQL generated by VQB, and running the current query.

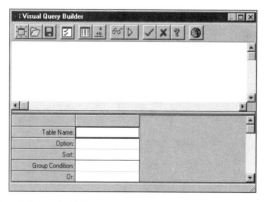

Figure 8.26   The Visual Query Builder environment.

The upper pane of the window is used to hold images of tables, showing each of their fields. The lower pane is where the visual query is built. The visual query consists of one or more columns, each representing a column (field) in a table.

The resulting SQL code can be viewed at any time in the SQL window. This window is non-modal, so it can be kept on screen at all times. This is especially helpful for those learning the SQL language. When queries are run, the results appear in the Result window.

Creating Some Example Queries

Perhaps the best way to explain the operation of the VQB is through a series of simple examples. We'll use the invoices.db and invitems.db tables we built a bit earlier and analyze their contents through some SQL queries.

DISPLAYING THE INVOICES COLUMN DATA

We'll start with something really easy: displaying the contents of the InvNum, InvDate, CustNum, and InvTotal columns in invoices.db.

First, we click the Table button on the toolbar, which brings up the Add Table dialog seen in Figure 8.27. We choose invoices.db and then close the dialog.

Our VQB window now has a list of the fields in the invoices table in its upper half. We click on the InvNum field, drag it down to the blank column,

Figure 8.27   The VQB's Add Table dialog.

and drop it. Labels appear in the blank column, letting us know it is now representing the InvNum field.

We Shift+click on the remaining fields and drag them to the right of the InvNum column in the lower part of the window. VQB instantly creates three more columns to accommodate the new fields. The VQB window as it now appears is shown in Figure 8.28.

By clicking the SQL toolbar button we can see the SQL statements generated by what we've done so far. Figure 8.29 shows those statements.

Our query basically says, "Show me without restriction all column values in all rows of the invoices table." We're ready to see the results of the query. We click the toolbar's Run button, and we get the Result window shown in Figure 8.30.

COUNTING THE NUMBER OF INVOICES

That was pretty simple. But what if there were some criteria associated with the query?

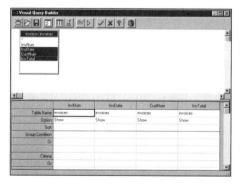

Figure 8.28   VQB window with all columns of invoices.db selected.

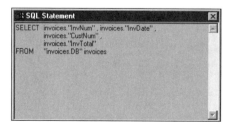

Figure 8.29   SQL generated by the VQB.

	InvNum	InvDate	CustNum	InvTotal
▶ 1	1001	1997-01-15	237	$12.50
2	1002	1997-01-16	212	$37.85
3	1003	1997-01-20	219	$8.20
4	1004	1997-01-21	212	$44.75
5	1005	1997-01-21	304	$29.90
6	1006	1997-01-22	271	$15.55
7	1007	1997-01-23	328	$42.00
8	1008	1997-01-24	206	$57.80
9	1009	1997-01-27	273	$30.25
10	1010	1997-01-27	290	$17.65

Figure 8.30   Result for query on all columns of the invoices table.

Suppose we wanted to know the number of invoices that were written for $30 or more. Everything we would need could be found in InvTotal. We would just have to perform a count and set some criteria to make sure that each row counted has an InvTotal greater than or equal to 30.

We click the New button on the toolbar and refuse the offer to save the old query. Once again we add only the invoices.db file to the upper part of the window.

We drag the InvTotal field from the table image and drop it in the lower pane. If we ran the query now, we would get a list with as many rows as there are invoices, showing the total of each invoice.

We move down to the row labeled Option and right click on that row within the InvTotal column. From the options displayed, we click on Count. If run now, the query would generate a single row answer that would give us a total for all invoices.

Time to add our criteria. We move down to the row marked Criteria: and type in:

> 30

The VQB window is depicted in Figure 8.31. We are ready to run our query. Figure 8.32 contains the result.

INVOICE TOTALS, YEAR TO DATE

Hey—this is kind of fun. Let's say we wanted to know the total dollar amount of all invoices (year to date) for 1997.

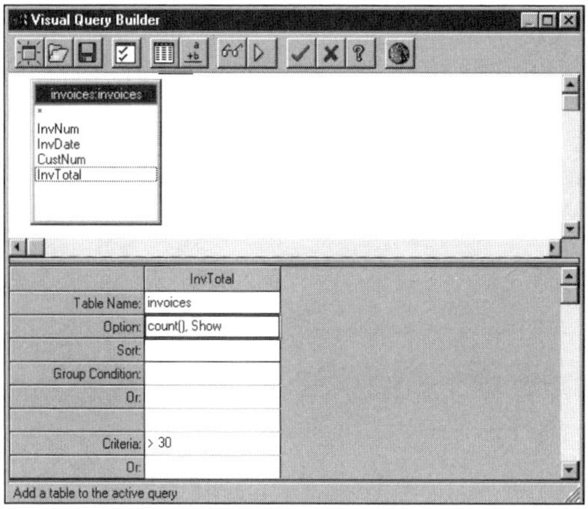

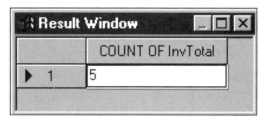

Figure 8.31   VQB window for the invoice count query.

Figure 8.32   Result for the invoice count query.

We'll need two columns from the invoices table to give us the answer. We can add the values in the InvTotal column to get the total, and we can use values in the InvDate column to control which rows we pick to sum.

We start a new query. We drag the InvTotal and InvDate fields into the lower pane, and right-click the box in the InvTotal column and pick Sum. This will give us a single row answer. (If the query were to be run right now, we would get a total for all invoices in the table.)

We now need to set date criteria. We move to the InvDate column and in the box for criteria, we type:

```
>= "01/01/97"
```

This will restrict the consideration to those invoices dated on or after January 1, 1997. But wait. What if we were to run this query a year later? We would be including data from the next year!

We drag down a second copy of the InvDate field from the table image and drop it to the right of the InvDate column in the lower pane. We now have two columns marked "InvDate." In the second column's criteria box we type:

```
<= "12/31/97"
```

The effect of having two columns is that the criteria in each must be met. In other words, we have said, "Restrict the summing operation to invoices written on or after January 1, 1997 *and* on or before December 31, 1997."

Just one more thing. The summing operation will return a single row, but the InvDate rows are still set to display. That means every invoice date will be returned in a row. We can have a result with only one row, or we can have one with lots of rows, but we can't have both. We right-click on the options box in each of the InvDate rows, clicking the Show option to turn it off.

The VQB window for our query appears in Figure 8.33. The results from the query when run are shown in Figure 8.34.

Figure 8.33 **VQB window for the invoices YTD query.**

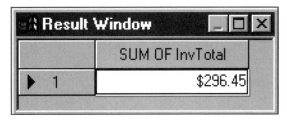

Figure 8.34 **Result for the invoices YTD query.**

This query might well be used many times throughout the year, so we'll save it. We click the Save As button and save the query as YTD97.qry.

QUANTITY OF ITEMS SOLD

This time let's say we wanted to know how many of each item was sold. We would need information only from the invoice items table—the stock numbers and quantities of the items sold.

We start a new query, selecting the invitems.db table and dragging StockNum and ItemQty into the lower pane. Because a stock number will undoubtedly appear on more than one invoice, we need to group these records by stock number so we won't have multiple rows with the same stock number. Then we just perform a summing operation on ItemQty.

In the StockNum options box, we select Group. In the ItemQty options box, we choose Sum. That's all there is to it. The VQB window is shown in Figure 8.35; the query result appears in Figure 8.36.

WHO IS OUR BEST CUSTOMER?

Our best customer has always been Roger Lomax (customer number 212). But is he still better than our newest customers (those with numbers 300 and above)?

Let's find out. We will need the CustNum and InvTotal columns from invoices.db. Once again, there will likely be more than one invoice with the same customer on it, so this time we will group by customer number. We'll sum on the invoice totals, and place some criteria on the customer numbers we'll allow.

Figure 8.35   VQB window for the quantity of items sold query.

	StockNum	SUM OF ItemQty
1	3078	1.00
2	3082	2.00
3	3235	2.00
4	3241	1.00
5	3253	1.00
6	3289	1.00
7	3425	1.00
8	3493	1.00
9	3548	2.00
10	3623	1.00
11	3798	2.00
12	3827	1.00
13	3832	2.00
14	3859	3.00
15	3934	2.00

Figure 8.36   Result for the quantity of items sold query.

We quickly set up the tables and columns for the query. In the InvTotal column we select the sum option. In the CustNum column we choose the Group option.

Now for the criteria. In the CustNum's criteria box we type:

```
>= "300"
```

This will catch the new customers. Now we'll include Roger Lomax. In the box just below the criteria box (labeled Or:) we type:

```
"212"
```

If more than one condition will satisfy our criteria, we enter the additional criteria in the "or" box and (if there are more than two conditions) the boxes below the "or" box. Here we have said, "Limit the rows considered to those with a customer number equal to or greater than 300, *or* with a customer number equal to 212."

Our query is ready to run. The VQB window appears in Figure 8.37. Is Roger still the best? The answer appears in Figure 8.38.

COMPLETE INVOICE INFORMATION

One last example before we quit for the day. This time we want to know all information about each invoice—in other words, we want to run a query and see all data that was displayed on the invoices form in our earlier example.

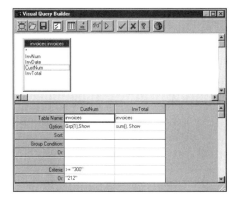

Figure 8.37   The VQB window for the best customer query.

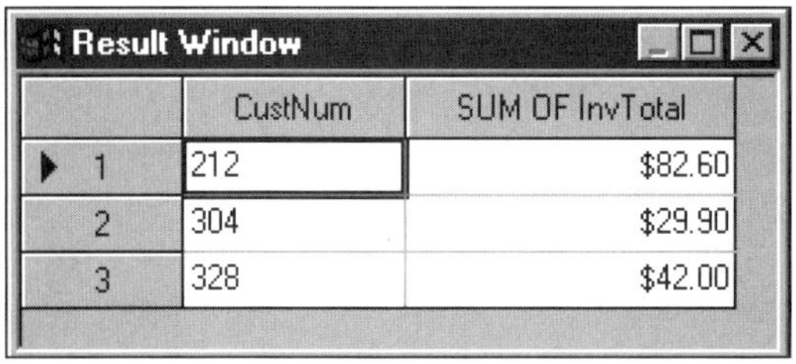

Figure 8.38   Result from the best customer query.

Hmm. To get all this information, we'll have to perform a query across both the invoices and invoice items tables. To accomplish this, we'll be performing what is called an "inner join" on the tables. The effect is much like establishing a master-detail relationship.

Our new query includes both invoices.db and invitems.db in the upper pane. To establish the inner join, we click on the InvItems field in either of the table images, but this time we drag it to the other table image and drop it on that table's InvItems field. A link symbol appears between the two fields, indicating the join has been successful.

From here on out, it's simple. We drag InvNum (from either of the table images), InvDate, InvTotal, StockNum, and ItemQty to the lower pane.

Let's examine the data for invoice number 1007. In the InvNum columns criteria box, we type:

```
"1007"
```

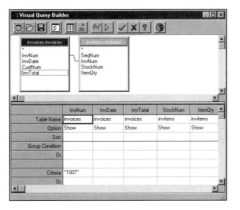

Figure 8.39   VQB window for the invoice information query.

		InvNum	InvDate	InvTotal	StockNum	ItemQty
▶	1	1007	1997-01-23	$42.00	3934	2.00
	2	1007	1997-01-23	$42.00	3827	1.00
	3	1007	1997-01-23	$42.00	3798	2.00

Figure 8.40   Result from the invoice information query.

Believe it or not, that's all we have to do. Figure 8.39 shows the VQB window, Figure 8.40 depicts the result.

As you've seen, the VQB can make easy work of creating SQL queries. Does that mean you'll never have to learn SQL? Likely not. There are occasions where it will come in handy, and there will undoubtedly come a time when you won't be able to get by without it.

Until then, the VQB will do very nicely.

Conclusion

In this chapter you've learned how to create tables, both with the Table Expert and on your own. You've built two forms and experimented with several concepts and techniques, including modifying table structures, indexing, referential integrity, master-detail relationships, writing event handlers that build data lists, and creating SQL queries with a point and a click. Good work!

We can finally remove the tool belt for the day. We've covered a lot of ground and created a big pile of sawdust. Now it's time to jump into the shower and get those pesky wood shavings out of our ears.

Maybe tomorrow we can do something with an old alarm clock....

IntraBuilder Database Connections

Don Taylor

A starting point for creating live data applications on the Web. In this chapter we find out how to tap into IntraBuilder's powerful database connectivity.

In the 80s it was networking. In the 90s it's connectivity. I write this with my tongue planted firmly in my cheek, but there is some truth to the statement. While the term "networking" describes transmission channels that connect one computer with another through a combination of hardware and software, "connectivity" as applied to databases is somewhat more specific—it speaks to the ability of application software to access data sources of many different types in diverse locations.

In this chapter we will examine IntraBuilder's database connectivity. We'll investigate the Borland Database Engine (BDE), Borland's SQL Links, Open Data Base Connectivity (ODBC), and, finally, we'll tie together what we've learned by expanding our invoices example from Chapter 8 to include a table not directly supported by the BDE.

The Borland Database Engine

The BDE is the core product used by Borland in several of its products to provide access to data in tables of various formats. Delphi, Paradox, InterBase, dBASE, and now IntraBuilder all incorporate the BDE.

Software engineers at Borland developed the BDE as a general purpose interface between their DBMS products and applications created with Borland programming languages. With the assistance of the BDE, programs written with Delphi can access tables created with Paradox, dBASE, or InterBase. By the same token, Paradox can access dBASE tables (and vice-versa).

How The BDE Works

Figure 9.1 depicts the BDE's role in data access. An application (such as a running IntraBuilder form) makes a request to the BDE. If that request originates from a Delphi- or IntraBuilder-generated application, the request will be routed through a component layer, which translates the original request into the low-level programming interface to the BDE.

The method used by the BDE to make its dynamic link with a table depends on the type of table.

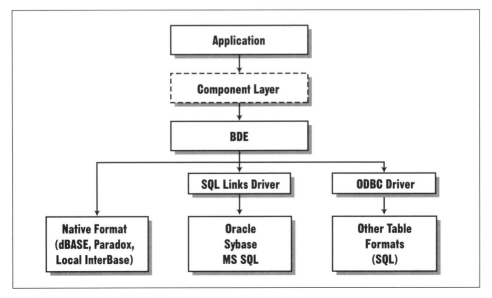

Figure 9.1   BDE-to-table connections.

BUILT-IN CONNECTIONS

If the table is in a native Borland format (dBASE, Paradox, or Local InterBase Server), the BDE is able to make a direct connection through software drivers included in the vanilla version of the BDE.

If you have followed through the examples in Chapter 8, you already know that IntraBuilder Professional has the ability to create tables in three other flavors—Oracle, Sybase, and Microsoft SQL Server. To access these tables, the BDE is equipped with selected portions of what Borland calls SQL Links—special SQL drivers that enable the BDE to communicate with various DBMS table formats used on Windows NT, Netware, and Unix systems.

SQL Links drivers translate standard-form SQL statements generated by an application into the special dialects required by each DBMS.

THE ODBC SOCKET

The BDE has a means of working with other tables as well, through its ODBC socket. This feature enables users to install ODBC drivers for multiple tables, making access to those tables as natural as that provided by the BDE's native and SQL Links drivers.

PUTTING ON THE MASK

In addition to offering DBMS driver management, the BDE provides another valuable function: It enables users to create aliases for database names.

This might at first seem a bit strange. Why on earth would someone want to make up a name for a location when he or she knows the real location? For the same reason people who move or travel a lot use a post office box for their address—even though their physical address might change, their mailing address stays constant and people can still communicate with them.

It's not always a smart idea to use real, live data while you're developing a new application. Believe it or not, things can go wrong—and when they do, it can be disastrous to data.

A much safer technique is to copy a database (or a subset of it) from its actual location to a place on a local hard disk. When the application proves reliable enough to access the real data, all references within the program to database locations are modified to point to that data, and the program is ready to go.

But even that process can be fraught with difficulty. What if just one reference didn't get changed? That means the program will be working with dead data—or worse yet, it will be updating the real database, based on information frozen in time. Yikes!

This is where aliasing comes into play. By creating an alias for each location and by referring to that alias every time you access a database, you need only change the location specified by the alias—all references will now point to the new location.

What's This ODBC Thing?

The purpose of ODBC is to provide SQL access to all kinds of data, from local desktop databases (such as dBASE) to large-scale relational and non-relational systems working across all networks and platforms. The ODBC concept was pioneered by Microsoft, the first version appearing in 1992. Version 3.0, which is supported in the first version of IntraBuilder, was released in the spring of 1996.

ODBC has developed into a standard SQL application programming interface (API) for database access, as well as an architecture that provides a logical separation of an application and the DBMS it uses to access its data.

A DBMS vendor simply writes an ODBC driver that will accept standard SQL commands and translate them into whatever is needed for the operation of the particular DBMS. This means someone who wants to create applications that access a number of different table formats must learn only one set of standard instructions—not multiple sets of instructions specific to each table type. ODBC also makes it feasible for one application to access data from multiple databases.

Installation and management of ODBC drivers are accomplished with Microsoft's ODBC Driver Manager.

Putting It All Together

We've already witnessed IntraBuilder's ability to work with two of its native formats. Our address book example in Chapter 8 used a dBASE table, while the invoices example incorporated a Paradox table.

It's now time to experiment with another table type. In the example that follows, we'll be expanding our invoices example to add the display of customer names, which will be read from a Microsoft Access table we will link to with the cooperative help of the BDE and an ODBC driver for MS Access.

The Invoices Summary Form

While the form we created in Chapter 8 was useful for monitoring the invoice and invoice items data, it's not particularly appropriate for displaying invoices with customer name references.

Figure 9.2 is an updated version of the original form. It has been modified to eliminate redundant displays (used for troubleshooting), to provide navigation controls only for the invoices table, and to include a Text control for the display of the customer name. This more streamlined version will better lend itself to "over-the-wire" use on an intranet.

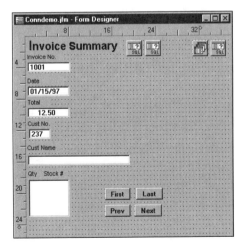

Figure 9.2   Raw form for the Invoices Summary project.

The Customers Table

We have used MS Access version 7.0 to create a database called "company" in the datatools folder. Within that database is a single table called CustTable that will hold information for our customers. The structure for CustTable is depicted in Figure 9.3. The data entered in that table can be seen in Figure 9.4.

Strategy Is Everything

It is our plan to display the name of the customer for each invoice examined. Clicking on the navigation buttons will move from invoice to invoice, each time displaying the name of the customer associated with that invoice.

We are faced with a table not directly supported by the BDE, and for the moment we are not able to establish a link to that table from IntraBuilder.

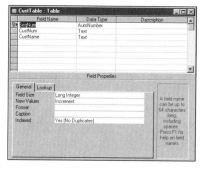

Figure 9.3 **Structure for the customers table.**

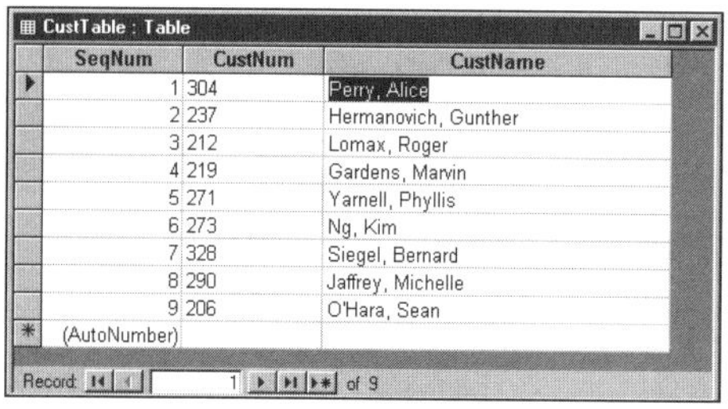

Figure 9.4 **Data entered in the customers table.**

Reaching our goal will require us to accomplish six separate tasks:

◆ Create a custom ODBC driver for the customers table

◆ Install the new driver in the BDE

◆ Create a new alias for the database containing the table

◆ Add components to the form so we can access the database

◆ Develop a SQL statement that will pick the correct name from the table

◆ Connect the Text control displaying the name to the data source

Creating A Custom ODBC Driver

On the Windows 95 Control Panel, we select the icon marked 32 Bit ODBC, which brings up the ODBC Manager for 32-bit systems, as seen in Figure 9.5. The ODBC Manager is displaying all the drivers currently registered within Win95.

We click the Add button to add our new driver, and we are asked to choose between the ODBC drivers already installed on the system, as seen in Figure 9.6.

We select the MS Access driver, which brings up the setup dialog for that driver. We choose a name for the new driver and enter a description of the database. Finally, we click the Select button and navigate our way to the database. The set-up dialog is shown in Figure 9.7.

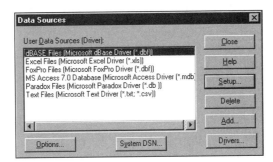

Figure 9.5   The ODBC Manager dialog.

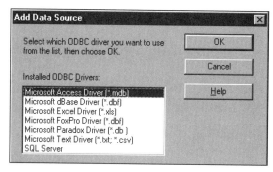

Figure 9.6   The Add Data Source dialog.

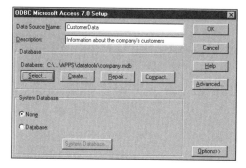

Figure 9.7   Setting up the new ODBC driver.

After closing the dialog, the new driver now shows up on the list of registered drivers. First task accomplished.

Installing The Driver In The BDE

After starting up the BDE Configuration utility in the IntraBuilder folder, we click the button labeled New ODBC Driver. This brings up another dialog that asks us to give the driver a name for the BDE's reference, to specify the default driver (the one for MS Access), and the specific driver to be installed.

For the driver name, we choose ODBC_CUST. After making the other choices, the dialog appears as shown in Figure 9.8. We click the OK button. The new driver appears on the list of BDE drivers. Task number two accomplished.

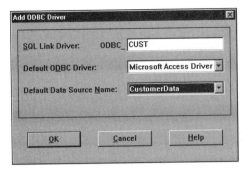

Figure 9.8   Adding the ODBC driver to the BDE.

Creating A New Alias

We click on the tab labeled Aliases and then on the New Alias button. As an alias, we settle on CUSTSTUFF. We then scan through the list of alias types until we come to ODBC_CUST, the driver we just added.

The Add New Alias dialog is shown in Figure 9.9. We click the OK button and see that our CUSTSTUFF alias is now on the list of registered aliases. We save the changes. Task number three accomplished.

Before going further, let's take just a minute to review what has happened so far.

When we created the ODBC driver, we told Win95 the driver type and the database we would be using. By the time we got to the BDE and specified the Access driver as the default, our custom ODBC driver automatically showed up on the list of candidates. By choosing it, the BDE can now link through that driver directly to the customers database in the datatools folder.

Figure 9.9   The AddNewAlias dialog.

Adding Components To The Form

We're going to need a third Query component on our invoice summary form—that's a no-brainer. What isn't quite so obvious is that in order to connect to a table via an ODBC driver, we must do it through a Database component. The Query component will connect to the Database component.

Look again at Figure 9.2. In the upper-right corner of the form you will see a Database-Query component pair. We click on the Database component and then move to the Inspector window, where we choose the alias for the **databaseName** property from the choices provided. Then we set the active status to True. The modified property list is shown in Figure 9.10.

The next step is to hook up the Query component, query1. Its database property has automatically been set to database1, but we can't get it to active status without a valid statement in the SQL property. We click on the wrench button, which brings up the SQL Property Builder dialog. Into that dialog we type the following phrase:

```
select C.CustNum, C.CustName from "CustTable" C
```

This statement will select two of the three columns in the table (the customer number and customer name information), and it will return all rows in the table. This is merely a ploy to provide a valid SQL statement to get started.

Figure 9.10   Property list for the Database component.

We cross our fingers and double-click on query1's active status property. It changes to True. Four tasks down, two to go.

Develop A SQL Statement

This one is a bit more difficult. We need to create a statement that brings in the customer number and customer name from the new table, but we want to retrieve only one row—one for which the customer number matches that contained on the invoice. In SQL lingo, it would read something like this:

```
select C.CustNum, C.CustName from "CustTable"' C where C.CustNum =
  "XX"
```

The problem: The number represented here by "XX" will change every time we click a navigation button and move to another invoice.

The solution: Create this statement dynamically with a short piece of JavaScript code that will provide the correct value for CustNum from the invoices table. Then we must make sure this code is executed when the form gets created and every time one of the navigation buttons is pressed.

If this sounds like the same logic we used to fill the Select control with invoice items, you're right. The resulting code for the **onServerLoad** event handler is detailed in Listing 9.1. Event handlers for the buttons each include this same code.

LISTING 9.1 EVENT HANDLER FOR THE FORM'S onSERVERLOAD EVENT.

```
function Form_onServerLoad()
{
 var s,n;
 // Scan the items table and pick those on this invoice.
 // Combine Qty and Stock # into string and place in array.
  this.ItemsArray = new Array();
  form.invitems1.rowset.first();
  while (!form.invitems1.rowset.endOfSet) {
    n = form.invitems1.rowset.fields["ItemQty"].value;
    s = "" + n;
    n = s.indexOf(".");
    s = s.substring(0, n);
    s = s + " - " + form.invitems1.rowset.fields["StockNum"].value;
    this.ItemsArray.add(s);
```

```
       form.invitems1.rowset.next();
   }
   // Hand array to listbox for display
   form.ItemsList.options = "array this.ItemsArray";
   form.invitems1.rowset.first();
   // Update the customer name display
   s = form.invoices1.rowset.fields["CustNum"].value;
   s = 'select C.CustNum, C.CustName ' +
       'from "CustTable" C ' +
       'where C.CustNum = "' + s + '"';
       form.query1.sql = s;
   }
```

The code in Listing 9.1 has been modified from that developed in Chapter 8 to provide a combination of quantity and stock number in the display of invoice items. Take a look at the code below the line marked "//Update the customer name display." This code reads the value of CustNum from the invoices table and stores it in a variable named **s**, which is then added (between double quote marks) to the part of the SQL statement that doesn't change. The resulting combination is then assigned to query1's SQL property.

It looks like gobbledy-gook, but it works. Only one task left.

Connect The Text Control

On the Text control's property sheet, we click on the **dataLink** property and then click the wrench button. The Choose field dialog appears. We choose the CustName field in query1, as shown in Figure 9.11.

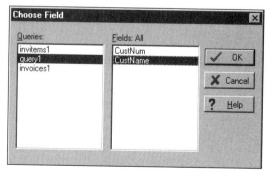

Figure 9.11   **Establishing the data link for the name control.**

We run the form and try out the navigation controls. Everything works perfectly. If only real life were this easy. The running form appears in Figure 9.12.

Conclusion

In this short chapter we have described the powerful database connectivity included with IntraBuilder. In addition to the native capabilities of the BDE to work with dBASE, Paradox, and InterBase tables, it provides for two extensions—SQL Links and ODBC drivers—that enable IntraBuilder applications to dynamically link to virtually any kind of database nearly anywhere on the planet.

In the latter part of this chapter we explored a tiny bit of this connectivity power by melding data from three tables of two different types, one a MS Access database linked through an ODBC driver into the BDE.

It is my fondest hope that you will use the information presented in this chapter as a starting point for many explorations into the exciting world of creating live-data applications for the Web—both in-house and Worldwide. Have fun!

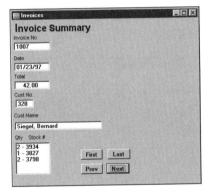

Figure 9.12   Running version of the Invoice Summary form.

JavaScript IntraBuilder Style

10

Matt Telles

Simple examples, simple coding techniques, and simple explanations for creating your own JavaScript programs and extending the power of IntraBuilder.

*T*he single biggest flaw in IntraBuilder is the lack of simple examples for using JavaScript. IntraBuilder comes with several large applications complete with source code. In addition, the tutorial contains a large application that is developed in a step-by-step method. The problem is trying to find out how to do the simple things with IntraBuilder JavaScript.

This chapter presents four separate, simple examples of using IntraBuilder to perform simple tasks. These are not real-world examples, ready to be cloned into your latest Web creations, rather they are intended to show you how to use JavaScript by highlighting one or two important aspects in each example.

The four examples given in this chapter are the Menu program, the Calculator program, the Tic-Tac-Toe game, and a simple database search application called DbSearch. Each will focus on only one or two issues of JavaScript with an eye toward the enhancements that Borland has made to the language for IntraBuilder.

In the Menu example, you will find out how to use the IntraBuilder Form Designer to create a simple menu screen using Button controls. These controls will then be linked to other forms and information screens. In addition, you will see how you can link a button to a simple Exit screen that will close down your IntraBuilder form. Menu applications are common in applications that need to run different forms, reports, or programs during the course of their execution.

The Calculator example shows a simple form that will allow you to enter numerical problems in a calculator style. You will see how to respond to button clicks, modify text displays, and perform simple arithmetic manipulation all within a very simple JavaScript application. Although the Calculator example is quite simple, it shows the power of IntraBuilder and the enhanced JavaScript at its core.

The third example in this chapter is the Tic-Tac-Toe form. This form will allow you to play a simple child's game, Tic-Tac-Toe (also known as three in a row). In this example you will see how IntraBuilder supports graphics, including user interaction with the graphics and on-the-fly modifications to graphic displays. The Tic-Tac-Toe example is a good way to get introduced to JavaScript, while having some fun at the same time.

The final example in the chapter is a database application called DbSearch. Unlike the majority of database forms in IntraBuilder, this one was built entirely from scratch using the Form Designer. You will see how the internals of forms work, how to use loops and decision constructs, and how to use the database functionality of IntraBuilder to build powerful reporting functionality into your applications.

The Menu Program

The Menu program is the first simple JavaScript form we will create. The form for the menu is shown in Figure 10.1. Follow the simple procedure listed below to create the form, then we will discuss how it works.

1. Move to the IntraBuilder samples directory. On a normal installation, this would be \program files\borland\intrabuilder\samples. If you have installed the IntraBuilder system in another directory, replace the

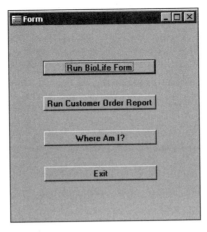

Figure 10.1   The Menu form in IntraBuilder.

\program files\borland\intrabuilder in the above path with the path to your directory. To change your path in IntraBuilder, type in the path in the edit box of IntraBuilder Explorer, or use the path browsing button.

2. Create a new form using the Form Designer. To do this, select the Forms tab from the IntraBuilder Explorer and double-click on the Untitled form listing. When the form creation options dialog comes up, select the Form Designer rather than the Form Expert button. You should now see a blank form staring you in the face.

3. Add four new buttons to the new form in the Form Designer. For the first button, modify the text property to read "Run BioLife Form". To modify the Text property, select the button by clicking on it and select Inspector from the IntraBuilder Edit menu or press F11. Select the Text property by scrolling down to it and double-click on the Button 1 entry to edit it. When the edit box appears, enter the string Run BioLife Form and press Return or Enter. Repeat the above process for the next three buttons and change their text properties to Run Customer Order Form, Where Am I?, and Exit, respectively.

4. At this point your form should now look like the one shown in Figure 10.1. It is now time to enter real JavaScript code to do the job. To begin with, select the first button (Run BioLife Form) from the form and bring up the Inspector window by pressing F11. Select the Events tab from the Inspector window and select the **onClick** method of the

window. Click on the small tool icon that appears on that line and the Method Editor window will appear (as shown in Figure 10.2).

5. Enter the following code into the Method Editor window for the first button:

```
function button1_onClick()
    {
        _sys.forms.run( "biolife.jfm" );
    }
```

6. Select the second button on the form (Run Customer Order Form) and select the Inspector window. Once again, select the Events tab and the **onClick** event. Click on the small tool icon and enter the following code into the Method Editor window when it appears:

```
function button2_onClick()
    {
        _sys.forms.run ("custord.jfm" );
    }
```

7. Select the third button on the form (Where Am I?) and select the Inspector window. Select the Events tab and the **onClick** event for the button. Click on the small tool icon and enter the following code into the Method Editor window when it appears:

```
function button3_onClick()
    {
        alert("You started in " +_sys.env.home() );
    }
```

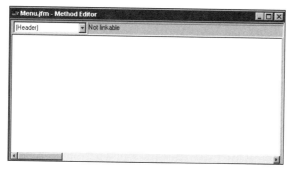

Figure 10.2   The Method Editor window.

8. For the fourth and final button (Exit), select the button as usual and enter the Events tab of the Inspector window. Select the **onClick** event from the events list and click on the small tool icon to bring up the Method Editor. When the window appears, enter the following code into the window:

```
function button4_onClick()
    {
        this.form.close();
    }
```

That is all that is necessary to implement the complete form. To see it run, select the View|Form menu item from the main IntraBuilder menu. Click on the first button (Run BioLife Form) and you will see the BioLife form from the IntraBuilder samples run. Play with it for awhile and experiment a bit. When you are finished, close the form window and the Menu form will once again be visible. Click on the second button (Run Customer Order Form) and the customer order entry form from the IntraBuilder samples will be displayed.

The third button will display a pop-up window with the current path of the IntraBuilder system. If you had installed the IntraBuilder system in the default directory (C:\program files\borland\intrabuilder) and selected the Where Am I? button from the menu form, you would see the alert window as displayed in Figure 10.3.

The fourth and final button will close the form completely and return you to the IntraBuilder IDE. The question is, of course, how does it all work?

Figure 10.3   Alert window showing current IntraBuilder directory.

How Does It Do That?

The first important piece to the IntraBuilder JavaScript puzzle is found in the **onClick** method for the first button (button1). The single line of JavaScript that creates the new form, starts it up, and displays it on the screen is found in this code:

```
_sys.forms.run( "biolife.jfm" );
```

How can one simple line of code do so much work? The answer is that behind that single line of code are hundreds of lines of JavaScript functions, written by Borland and built into the core language. The first part of the line **_sys** represents an object in the IntraBuilder implementation of JavaScript. The **_sys** object encapsulates all of the information and functionality about the running IntraBuilder system. One of the pieces of the **_sys** object is the **forms** object. The **forms** object represents all of the form functionality for the IntraBuilder forms system. The following is a list of all of the functions available for the **forms** object in IntraBuilder:

◆ **forms.design()**   Opens the Form Designer to create or modify a form

◆ **forms.expert()**   Opens the Form Expert to design a new form

◆ **forms.run()**   As shown above, runs another form

As you can see from the above list, the forms object encompasses the entire IntraBuilder system. From within your application you can run scripts that automate the entire form design system.

The second button is quite similar to the first but produces a complete data entry screen when invoked. You will notice, however, that the process to load and display a data entry screen is exactly the same as the one used to produce a simple display screen.

The third button (Where Am I?) shows off another aspect of the JavaScript extensions by Borland, the **env** object. This object has several methods of note, one of which is shown here (**home()**). In addition, the **env** object has the following list of methods:

◆ **env.getEnv()**   Returns the value of a DOS environment variable

◆ **env.home()**   Returns the path of the current home directory for the IntraBuilder setup

◆ **env.id()**   Returns the **id** of the current user on a LAN or other system

◆ **env.memory()**   Returns the total amount of available memory

◆ **env.os()**   Returns the name and version of the current operating system

◆ **env.version()**   Returns the version number of IntraBuilder

The **env** object is quite powerful in its own right. It provides information about the current environment in which your form is running. This information can be useful for debugging purposes, display purposes, or for just showing off your knowledge of the current system. In this example we use the home method of the **env** object to show where the form is currently running.

The final button (Exit) simply closes down the current form. This is done by using yet another built, in object within IntraBuilder, the **form** object. Notice that the actual line of code reads:

```
this.form.close();
```

This is due to the fact that when the **onClick** method is called for the fourth button, the function resides within the application, not within the form itself. The form is simply a piece of the total application and must be referred to specifically. The **this** notation is used to indicate the current object. Our current object is the JavaScript class that represents the running form. To get to the actual **form** object that contains the methods and properties, we use the **this.form** notation. Calling the **close** method of the **form** object closes the form, which removes it from the screen and returns you to the IntraBuilder IDE.

Is everyone clear on how that all works? Not quite? Okay, let's try another example. This time we will focus more on the JavaScript aspects of IntraBuilder and less on the internal objects.

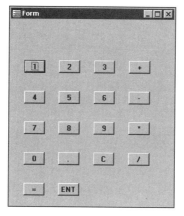

Figure 10.4   The Calculator form in IntraBuilder.

The Calculator Example

The second simple JavaScript form we are going to create will be the Calculator program. The form for the calculator is shown in Figure 10.4. Follow the simple procedure listed below to create the form; then we will discuss how it works.

As with our first example, the steps are quite simple:

1. Add 18 buttons to the form, arranged in 4 rows of 4 buttons and 1 row of 2 buttons. Modify the Text property of each of the buttons by selecting it and pressing F11 to bring up the Inspector window. Once the Inspector window is visible, select the Properties tab and scroll down until the Text property is visible. Double-click on the Text property and enter the text for the button into the field. Press Return to confirm your modification. Table 10.1 lists each of the buttons and the value that should be entered into the Text property for that button.

   Once you have entered all of the text for all of the buttons, go back and check to see that all of the buttons look correct on the form by bringing up the form in Run mode. This is accomplished by selecting View|Form from the main IDE menu in IntraBuilder. If all of the buttons are not correct, go back through and change the text to what it should read to be correct. When you have finished with all of the buttons, go on to the second step.

Table 10.1   Buttons and their values entered into the Text property.

Button Object	Text to Insert
button1	1
button2	2
button3	3
button4	4
button5	5
button6	6
button7	7
button8	8
button9	9
button10	0
button11	. (Period)
button12	C
button13	+
button14	-
button15	*
button16	/
button17	=
button18	ENT

2. Add an HTML component to the top of the form above all of the rows of buttons. Select the HTML component (which should be called html1) and press F11 to bring up the Inspector window. Clear the Text property by double-clicking the Text property in the Properties tab of the Inspector window and pressing the Delete key. Press the Return key to confirm your change.

3. Add another HTML component to the bottom of the form. As with the previous step, remove the text by deleting the text from the Text property in the properties tab on the Inspector window. Additionally, modify the Visible property in the Properties tab of the window to be false. You should be able to do this by selecting the Visible property and selecting false from the resulting combo box that appears.

4. You are now in position to modify each of the buttons **onClick** events to do the job of the calculator. The first batch of buttons we will look at are the numeric buttons. For each of these buttons (0-9), we simply want the status display (the HTML component at the top of the form) to be updated with the current value plus the value of the digit we are adding. For example, if the current status display read "123" and you pressed the "4" key, you would expect to see the status display updated to read "1234". That is exactly what will happen. For each numeric button, do the following: Select the button by clicking on it with the mouse, bring up the Inspector window by pressing F11, move to the Events tab, select the **onClick** event, and click on the small tool icon that appears on the right side of the window. Enter the code for the button in the Method Editor window that now appears.

For button1:

```
function button1_onClick()
    {
        this.form.html1.text += "1";
    }
```

For button2:

```
function button2_onClick()
    {
        this.form.html1.text += "2";
    }
```

For button3:

```
function button3_onClick()
    {
        this.form.html1.text += "3";
    }
```

For button4:

```
function button4_onClick()
    {
        this.form.html1.text += "4";
    }
```

For button5:

```
function button5_onClick()
    {
        this.form.html1.text += "5";
    }
```

For button6:

```
function button6_onClick()
    {
        this.form.html1.text += "6";
    }
```

For button7:

```
function button7_onClick()
    {
        this.form.html1.text += "7";
    }
```

For button8:

```
function button3_onClick()
    {
        this.form.html1.text += "8";
    }
```

For button9:

```
function button9_onClick()
    {
        this.form.html1.text += "9";
    }
```

For button10:

```
function button10_onClick()
    {
        this.form.html1.text += "0";
    }
```

You can now begin to test the form by selecting Form|Run from the IntraBuilder IDE menu. Click on several of the numeric buttons and watch the display HTML control update. When you are satisfied that the buttons are working correctly, return to the designer by selecting Form|Design from the IDE main menu and move on to the next step.

5. Once you have added the new buttons for the numeric entries, it is time to work on some of the other buttons. Let's take the easiest one first, the C (or clear) button. Select the Clear button by clicking on it and bringing up the Inspector window. Select the **onClick** event from the Events tab and bring up the Method Editor. Enter the following code into the **onClick** event for the button:

```
function button12_onClick()
    {
        this.form.html1.text = "";
    }
```

6. Next, let's deal with the missing decimal point key which we overlooked while processing the numeric keys. Select the decimal key and move to the Method Editor for the **onClick** event. Here is the code to add to the new button **onClick** method:

```
function button11_onClick()
    {
        this.form.html1.text += ".";
    }
```

7. Okay, time to move on to the tough stuff. Select the plus (+) button and bring up the Method Editor for the **onClick** event. Here is the complete code for the addition:

```
function button13_onClick()
    {
        var total = parseInt(this.form.html2.text);
        total += parseInt(this.form.html1.text);
        this.form.html2.text = total;
        this.form.html1.text = "";
    }
```

Were you wondering when we were going to get around to using that Hidden HTML control? As you can see from the code above, that Hidden control is used to store the current total for the calculation in progress. This technique, of using Hidden controls as static variables, can be very powerful in IntraBuilder. While you can use class members to store information, you will find that it requires much more work than simply dragging and dropping. After all, IntraBuilder is all about simplicity and visual design, not about grungy editing of scripts.

8. For the minus (-) key, the procedure is almost exactly the same. Select the button, bring up the Inspector window (F11, remember?) and click on the **onClick** method in the Events tab. Enter the following code into the Method Editor for the button **onClick** event:

```
function button14_onClick()
    {
        var total = parseInt(this.form.html2.text);
        total -= parseInt(this.form.html1.text);
        this.form.html2.text = total;
        this.form.html1.text = "";
    }
```

9. The multiply (*) and divide (/) keys are exactly the same way. Select each of them and enter the code below into the Method Editor. In our listing, button15 is the multiply key and button16 is the divide key:

```
function button15_onClick()
    {
        var total = parseInt(this.form.html2.text);
        total *= parseInt(this.form.html1.text);
        this.form.html2.text = total;
        this.form.html1.text = "";
    }

function button16_onClick()
    {
        var total = parseInt(this.form.html2.text);
        total /= parseInt(this.form.html1.text);
        this.form.html2.text = total;
        this.form.html1.text = "";
    }
```

10. That leaves the equal key (=) and the ENTER key (ENT) to deal with. Let's take the easier of the two, the equal key first. This key will simply assign the total value to the display HTML control, thus displaying the new total for the user. Here is the code for the equal key:

```
function button17_onClick()
    {
        this.form.html1.text = this.form.html2.text
    }
```

11. The ENTER key (labeled ENT) is used as a sub-total key in reverse Polish notation (RPN) calculators. Our calculator is not exactly a true RPN calculator, as it also uses the equal key to display values. Here is the code for the ENT key, in any event:

```
function button18_onClick()
    {
        this.form.html2.text = this.form.html1.text;
        this.form.html1.text = "";
    }
```

What Is Really Going On Here?

Now that you have dragged and dropped all of those buttons onto the form and clicked and typed your way through all of those **onClick** handlers, what is it, exactly, that you have created? Basically, the form is a pseudo-reverse notation calculator, such as you might find in a Hewlett Packard style. You enter a value into the calculator by clicking on the appropriate keys (1,2,3, etc) and then clicking the ENT (or ENTER) key. This stores the value in the internal memory of the calculator and prepares it for using the operator keys (+,-,*,/). If, for example, you wanted to enter the equation 1+2+3*4 you would hit the following buttons:

1

ENT

2

+

3

+

4

*

=

If you followed the above procedure with our calculator form, the result would be, as you would expect, 24. This is actually the result you would get with a normal calculator. Note that because our calculator form does not understand parentheses () or handle nested expressions, in the above example you get the result of 1+2+3 before multiplying by 4. If you were solving the above expression by hand you would first multiply 3*4 (to get

12) and then add 1+2 (3) to it to get 15. This is not the expected result in our case.

The calculator form is far from perfect. It is intended, instead, to provide examples of the kinds of things you can do with JavaScript simply and easily without digging deep into the language. It offers examples of the following techniques:

◆ Using hidden fields on a form

◆ Modifying the text shown in HTML controls at runtime

◆ Responding to simple button clicks to produce visible results for the user

◆ Converting text values to numeric values

◆ Converting numeric values to text values

Not bad for a simple form like this, right? IntraBuilder contains many examples of complex forms, but few this simple. This is not a bad thing, really, but it does leave many users feeling overwhelmed by the initial experience of using the system. The entire point to these simple examples is to get you comfortable with using the JavaScript engine in IntraBuilder to accomplish tasks without deluging you with detail.

In our next example, we will begin to delve into the depths of the IntraBuilder graphics engine, by writing a simple Tic-Tac-Toe game that you can really play.

The Tic-Tac-Toe Example

As promised, the third simple JavaScript form we will create is a Tic-Tac-Toe game. The form for the game is shown in Figure 10.5. Follow the simple procedure listed below to create the form, and then we will discuss how it works. If you have never played Tic-Tac-Toe before, the game goes like this. The game begins with nine blank squares. The players alternate placing their symbols (X or O) in squares until either all of the squares are filled or one of the players has completed a row across, up and down, or diagonally.

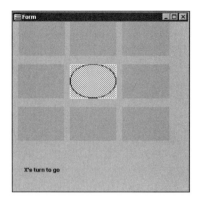

Figure 10.5   The Tic-Tac-Toe form in IntraBuilder.

1. The first thing that is needed for this example is that you will need to create three bitmaps. These bitmaps are used for the "blank" (unselected) state, the "X" state, and the "O" state. As implemented for this example the blank bitmap is simply a blue-green square (Figure 10.6). The X bitmap is a simple X across the diagonals of the square (Figure 10.7) and the O bitmap is a circle that fills the entire square (Figure 10.8). You are not bound by these limitations; feel free to place other bitmaps. Simply follow along with the rest of the instructions and replace the bitmap names with those that you choose.

Figure 10.6   The blank bitmap.

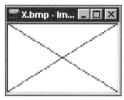

Figure 10.7   The X bitmap for the Tic-Tac-Toe program.

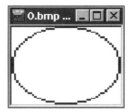

Figure 10.8   The O bitmap for the Tic-Tac-Toe program.

2. Once you have decided on the bitmaps to use in the game, the next step is to create a form with nine squares on it to use as the game board. To do this, create a new form in IntraBuilder. Select the Forms tab of the IntraBuilder Explorer window and double-click on the Untitled form. Select the Form Designer button. You should now see a blank form on the IntraBuilder desktop window.

3. From the Component Palette, select the Image control. Place three rows of three Image controls on the blank form. For each control, select it and bring up the Inspector window by pressing the F11 key. Select the Properties tab from the Inspector window and locate the **dataSource** property. This property is used by the Image control to determine which graphic image to display. In our case we would like the image to come from an external file (rather than a database BLOB field, which is the other alternative). This can be accomplished in one of two ways. First, you can select the file to display by clicking on the tool icon in the **dataSource** property and then navigating to the directory that holds the graphic image file. Do this for your images and set them all to the clear bitmap you selected earlier. We will look at the other way to set this property shortly.

4. Once you have selected all of the images and set the **dataSource** property to be the clear bitmap, it is time to begin writing code to handle the user playing of the game. Select the first Image control (image1) and bring up the Inspector window by pressing F11. Select the Events tab from the Inspector window and click on the **onImageServerClick** method. Select the small tool icon from the window to bring up the Method Editor for the control. Once the Method Editor window is displayed, enter the following code into the editor:

```
function image1_onImageServerClick(nLeft, nTop)
    {
        ChangeSquare(this.form, this.form.image1);
        CheckWinner(this.form);
    }
```

5. Select each of the Image controls in turn and repeat the process of
   selecting the **onImageServerClick** method from the Events tab. Enter
   the following code into the image handler functions.

For image2:

```
function image2_onImageServerClick(nLeft, nTop)
    {
        ChangeSquare(this.form, this.form.image2);
        CheckWinner(this.form);
    }
```

For image3:

```
function image3_onImageServerClick(nLeft, nTop)
    {
        ChangeSquare(this.form, this.form.image3);
        CheckWinner(this.form);
    }
```

For image4:

```
function image4_onImageServerClick(nLeft, nTop)
    {
        ChangeSquare(this.form, this.form.image4);
        CheckWinner(this.form);
    }
```

For image5:

```
function image5_onImageServerClick(nLeft, nTop)
    {
        ChangeSquare(this.form, this.form.image5);
        CheckWinner(this.form);
    }
```

For image6:

```
function image6_onImageServerClick(nLeft, nTop)
    {
       ChangeSquare(this.form, this.form.image6);
       CheckWinner(this.form);
    }
```

For image7:

```
function image7_onImageServerClick(nLeft, nTop)
    {
       ChangeSquare(this.form, this.form.image7);
       CheckWinner(this.form);
    }
```

For image8:

```
function image8_onImageServerClick(nLeft, nTop)
    {
       ChangeSquare(this.form, this.form.image8);
       CheckWinner(this.form);
    }
```

For image9:

```
function image9_onImageServerClick(nLeft, nTop)
    {
       ChangeSquare(this.form, this.form.image9);
       CheckWinner(this.form);
    }
```

6. The last thing we need to add to the form are two HTML controls at the bottom of the form to display status information for the user and keep track of whose turn it is to place a square. Place a single HTML control on the bottom of the form and set the Text property initially to "O's Turn To Go." Leave the name of this HTML control at html1. Place a second HTML control on the bottom right corner of the form. Set the visible property to FALSE and the Name property to "mode". This control will be used to keep track of whose turn it is to place a square.

7. That certainly wasn't too bad, was it? The only problem is that we have these mysterious calls to some functions called **ChangeSquare** and **CheckWinner**. What, exactly, are these functions and how do they work? As you might have guessed, neither of these functions is a part of JavaScript, enhanced by Borland or not. We need to write these functions in order to make the program work. Don't panic; adding new functions to a form is almost as easy as adding controls. First, bring up the Method Editor for the form by selecting the form itself and clicking on it with the right mouse button. This will display a small pop-up menu. Select Method Editor from the pop-up menu and the Method Editor window will be displayed with the first method (probably **image1_ onImageServerClick**) displayed in the editor window.

8. At the top of the Method Editor window you will see a combo box that displays the current method being edited. Select the General entry from this combo box. Your window should now display a blank screen, indicating that you can enter a new JavaScript method into the window. Enter the following code for the new **ChangeSquare** method for the form:

```
function ChangeSquare(whichForm, whichImage)
{
   // Only let the user change the field if it
   // hasn't been claimed yet.
   if ( whichImage.dataSource == "filename CLEAR.BMP" )
   {
      // Who's turn is it?
      if ( whichForm.mode.text == 'X' )
      {
         // Reset the image.
         whichImage.dataSource = "filename " + _sys.env.home() +
            "Samples\\X.BMP";
         // Reset the player.
         whichForm.mode.text = '0';
         // And show the player's turn.
         whichForm.html1.text = whichForm.mode.text + "'s turn to
            go";
      }
      else
      {
         // Reset the image.
         whichImage.dataSource = "filename " + _sys.env.home() +
            "Samples\\0.BMP";
         // Reset the player.
```

```
        whichForm.mode.text = 'X';
        // And show the player's turn
        whichForm.html1.text = whichForm.mode.text + "'s turn to
          go";
      }
    }
}
```

9. After the **ChangeSquare** method, the next method to add is the **CheckWinner** method. This method goes through all of the squares looking for winning positions. Enter the following code into the Method editor immediately below the **ChangeSquare** method code you just entered:

```
function CheckWinner(whichForm)
{
    var so1 = 0;
    var sx1 = 0;
    var so2 = 0;
    var sx2 = 0;
    var so3 = 0;
    var sx3 = 0;
    var so4 = 0;
    var sx4 = 0;
    var so5 = 0;
    var sx5 = 0;
    var so6 = 0;
    var sx6 = 0;
    var so7 = 0;
    var sx7 = 0;
    var so8 = 0;
    var sx8 = 0;
    var so9 = 0;
    var sx9 = 0;
    if ( whichForm.image1.dataSource == "filename O.BMP" )
        so1 = 1;
    if ( whichForm.image1.dataSource == "filename X.BMP" )
        sx1 = 1;
    if ( whichForm.image2.dataSource == "filename O.BMP" )
        so2 = 1;
    if ( whichForm.image2.dataSource == "filename X.BMP" )
        sx2 = 1;
    if ( whichForm.image3.dataSource == "filename O.BMP" )
        so3 = 1;
    if ( whichForm.image3.dataSource == "filename X.BMP" )
        sx3 = 1;
    if ( whichForm.image4.dataSource == "filename O.BMP" )
        so4 = 1;
```

```
if ( whichForm.image4.dataSource == "filename X.BMP" )
   sx4 = 1;
if ( whichForm.image5.dataSource == "filename O.BMP" )
   so5 = 1;
if ( whichForm.image5.dataSource == "filename X.BMP" )
   sx5 = 1;
if ( whichForm.image6.dataSource == "filename O.BMP" )
   so6 = 1;
if ( whichForm.image6.dataSource == "filename X.BMP" )
   sx6 = 1;
if ( whichForm.image7.dataSource == "filename O.BMP" )
   so7 = 1;
if ( whichForm.image7.dataSource == "filename X.BMP" )
   sx7 = 1;
if ( whichForm.image8.dataSource == "filename O.BMP" )
   so8 = 1;
if ( whichForm.image8.dataSource == "filename X.BMP" )
   sx8 = 1;
if ( whichForm.image9.dataSource == "filename O.BMP" )
   so9 = 1;
if ( whichForm.image9.dataSource == "filename X.BMP" )
   sx9 = 1;
// Check for winning positions by O
if ( so1 == 1 && so2 == 1 && so3 == 1 )
{
   alert("O Wins!");
   whichForm.close();
}
if ( so1 == 1 && so4 == 1 && so7 == 1 )
{
   alert("O Wins!");
   whichForm.close();
}
if ( so4 == 1 && so5 == 1 && so6 == 1 )
{
   alert("O Wins!");
   whichForm.close();
}
if ( so7 == 1 && so8 == 1 && so9 == 1 )
{
   alert("O Wins!");
   whichForm.close();
}
if ( so2 == 1 && so5 == 1 && so8 == 1 )
{
   alert("O Wins!");
   whichForm.close();
}
```

```
if ( so3 == 1 && so6 == 1 && so9 == 1 )
{
   alert("O Wins!");
   whichForm.close();
}
if ( so3 == 1 && so5 == 1 && so7 == 1 )
{
   alert("O Wins!");
   whichForm.close();
}
if ( so1 == 1 && so5 == 1 && so9 == 1 )
{
   alert("O Wins!");
   whichForm.close();
}
// Check for winning positions by O
if ( sx1 == 1 && sx2 == 1 && sx3 == 1 )
{
   alert("X Wins!");
   whichForm.close();
}
if ( sx1 == 1 && sx4 == 1 && sx7 == 1 )
{
   alert("X Wins!");
   whichForm.close();
}
if ( sx4 == 1 && sx5 == 1 && sx6 == 1 )
{
   alert("X Wins!");
   whichForm.close();
}
if ( sx7 == 1 && sx8 == 1 && sx9 == 1 )
{
   alert("X Wins!");
   whichForm.close();
}
if ( sx2 == 1 && sx5 == 1 && sx8 == 1 )
{
   alert("X Wins!");
   whichForm.close();
}
if ( sx3 == 1 && sx6 == 1 && sx9 == 1 )
{
   alert("X Wins!");
   whichForm.close();
}
if ( sx3 == 1 && sx5 == 1 && sx7 == 1 )
{
   alert("X Wins!");
```

```
        whichForm.close();
    }
    if ( sx1 == 1 && sx5 == 1 && sx9 == 1 )
    {
        alert("X Wins!");
        whichForm.close();
    }
}
```

What Did We Just Do?

Most of the work of this program takes place in the two functions, **CheckWinner** and **ChangeSquare**. Besides illustrating how to use your own functions in JavaScript, these functions are a wealth of information about how to use JavaScript to accomplish tasks.

In the **ChangeSquare** function we check to see whether or not the current image (which was passed into the function) has already been selected. This is done by verifying that the **dataSource** property of the image is the clear bitmap. If it is the clear bitmap, we set the new bitmap for the Image control based on the setting in our Hidden HTML control. This if-then-else logic is essential to most JavaScript applications. Once we have determined which one (if any) of the bitmaps is to be used for this image, we assign it. This is done in the code which reads:

```
whichImage.dataSource = "filename " + _sys.env.home() +
  "Samples\\X.BMP";
```

This line of code sets the image control dataSource to read "filename C:\program files\borland\intrabuilder\samples\X.BMP". If you have stored your bitmap files somewhere else, simply modify the directory portion of the string. The image control looks at the **dataSource** property to determine from where to load the image. In this case, because the first part of the property string reads filename, it knows that the image to display is an external file containing the data. It could just as easily have loaded the image from another Image control or from a database BLOB field.

Following the Image control set, the function then updates the visible HTML control to indicate to the players whose turn it is. The Hidden HTML control is also updated at the same time to indicate to the application whose turn it is to go.

The **CheckWinner** function is used to determine whether the current board position is a winning one. Winning positions are any positions in which there are three of the same type of image (X or O, not Clear) in any horizontal, vertical, or diagonal line. To do this, we first determine what image is displayed in each of the Image controls and store that information in two blocks of variables (labeled **sx?** and **s0?** where **?** is a number from 1 to 9). These variables are then checked in sequences that are known to be valid winning positions. If one of the positions is found to be true, the **Alert** function of JavaScript is used to notify the players that someone has won.

The Tic-Tac-Toe form is a simple yet powerful example of what is possible with the functionality of IntraBuilder JavaScript. It offers examples of the following techniques:

◆ Using hidden fields on a form

◆ Modifying the Image control at run time to display different images

◆ Responding to simple button clicks to produce visible results for the user

◆ Using if-then-else logic to reach conclusions

◆ Using the **Alert** function to notify users

◆ Closing a form when a certain state (winning position) is reached

The DbSearch Example

The fourth and final simple JavaScript form we are going to create will be a simple database search form. The form for the example is shown in Figure 10.9. Rather than the complicated forms shown in the IntraBuilder samples and applications, this form will be quite easy and will be built from scratch. The purpose of the form is to show you how to find the fields in a given IntraBuilder database table, iterate through the fields to display them, and change the display based on user criteria. IntraBuilder comes with a host of examples of how to change the filters for specific fields, so rather than do yet another example of this we will concentrate on changing the fields displayed for the user. To create the form, follow the simple directions below. After the form is built and running, we will concentrate on how it all works.

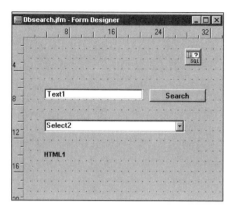

Figure 10.9   The DbSearch form in IntraBuilder.

1. Create a new form in the IntraBuilder samples directory. If you have installed the IntraBuilder system in the default directory, this will be \program files\borland\intrabuilder\samples. If you have installed IntraBuilder in a different directory or drive, replace the \program files\borland\intrabuilder with the drive and directory of your choice. Change the path in IntraBuilder Explorer to be this directory. Select the Forms tab from the Explorer window and double-click on the Untitled form. From the next screen, select the Form Designer option rather than the Form Expert. This will allow us to build the new form from scratch rather than having the expert design one for us.

2. Drag a **query** object (**Query**) from the Component Palette and place it into the new form. Select the **query** object and press F11 to bring up the Inspector window. Move to the Properties tab of the Inspector window and modify the SQL property to read "select * from customer.db". Press Return or Enter to complete your modification of the property.

3. Add a new text edit component to the form. Place it toward the top of the form, below the **query** object. Do not modify any properties for this object.

4. Add a new button component to the form, placing it next to the text edit component. Modify the Text property of the button to read "Search".

5. Add a new select component to the form, placing it below the text edit and button components. Do not modify any of the properties for this component.

6. Add a new HTML component to the form below the select and edit/ button lines. Modify the Text property of the HTML component to be blank. To do this, select the HTML component and press F11 to bring up the Inspector window. Move to the Properties tab and select the Text property for the component. Select the text with the mouse and press the Delete (Del) key. Press Enter or Return to confirm your modification.

7. At this point we have all of the components needed for the form. It is time to load the form with the information we need to display for the user. The first, default, property that will be displayed from the database when the form starts up will be the **name** field. Here is how you will display the **name** fields. Select the form by clicking on it (outside of any components) with the mouse. Press the F11 key to bring up the Inspector window. Move to the Methods tab of the Inspector window and select the **onServerLoad** method from the list displayed. Click on the small tool icon that appears on the **onServerLoad** line and enter the following code into the Method Editor window when it appears:

```
function Form_onServerLoad()
    {
        var name;
        // fill customer array
        this.custArray = new Array();
        while (!this.query1.rowset.endOfSet) {
            name = new
        StringEx(this.query1.rowset.fields["name"].value);
            name = name.rightTrim();
            this.custArray.add(name);
            this.query1.rowset.next();
        }
        this.query1.rowset.first();
        // assign options and value
        this.custArray.sort();
        this.select1.options="array this.custArray";
        this.select1.value = this.custArray[0];
        this.html1.text = "";
    }
```

8. When the form is displayed, it will now have a select component with a list of all of the names for all of the rows found in the database. The next step is to change what is displayed when the user enters a new value (such as city, country, or name) in the text edit field. To deal with this modification, we need to deal with the user clicking on the Search button of the form. Select the Search button and bring up the Inspector Window by pressing F11 again. Move to the Methods tab and select the **onClick** method. Click on the small tool icon to bring up the Method Editor window.

> *Note: If you want a quicker way to bring up the Method Editor for the button, simply double-click on the button itself in the form. This will automatically load the Method editor for the default button event, which happens to be* **onClick***.*

Enter the following code into the **onClick** event for the button:

```
function button1_onClick()
    {
      var name;
      // Check input
      if ( IsValidField(this.form.query1, this.form.text1.value )
        == 0 )
      {
        alert("Invalid Field Name!");
        return;
      }
      // fill customer array
      this.form.custArray = new Array();
      while (!this.form.query1.rowset.endOfSet) {
        name = new
        StringEx(this.form.query1.rowset.fields[this.form.text1.value].value);
        name = name.rightTrim();
        this.form.custArray.add(name);
        this.form.query1.rowset.next();
      }
      this.form.query1.rowset.first();
      // assign options and value
      this.form.custArray.sort();
      this.form.select1.options="array this.form.custArray";
      this.form.select1.value = this.form.custArray[0];
      this.form.html1.text = "";
    }
```

9. Now we're in the home stretch. The next thing that we need to do is to create the **IsValidField** method that was called in the previous block of code. IntraBuilder will complain bitterly (as it should) if you call a function that doesn't exist while running the form. Select the form with the mouse and right-click on it. Select the Method Editor menu option from the resulting pop-up menu. When the Method Editor appears, select the General category from the combo box on the top-left corner of the editor window. A blank window will be displayed in the Method Editor window. Enter the following code into the window:

```
function IsValidField(obj, fieldName)
{
   for ( i=0; i<obj.rowset.fields.length; ++i )
   {
      if ( obj.rowset.fields[i].fieldName ==
         fieldName.toUpperCase() )
         return 1;
   }
   return 0;
}
```

You have just created a "generic function," which can be called from anywhere in your IntraBuilder setup because it does not belong to any specific form. In this case we are passing it a query object (**obj**) and the name of a field (**fieldName**). The function loops through all of the fields in the **rowset** of the **query** object comparing the name that was passed in to the name in the **rowset** field to see if they match. Because field names are in upper case in dBASE databases and the name typed in by the user could be in upper, lower, or mixed case, we use the **toUpperCase** function of the **String** class to make sure that they match.

10. The last thing that we need to do for this form is to change the HTML display when the user actually selects one of the displayed entries in the Select component on the form. This is how it is done: Select the Select component on the form and press F11 to bring up the Inspector window. Select the Methods tab from the Inspector window and select the **onChange** method from the list. Click on the small tool icon to bring

up the Method Editor and enter the following code into the **onChange** method of the editor:

```
function select1_onChange()
   {
      this.form.html1.text = "You have selected " +
         this.form.select1.value;
}
```

When the user makes a selection from the select combo box, the HTML component text will be updated to read "You have selected" and the selected entry. This visual result makes it easy for the user to know that something is happening.

What's Going On?

The program breaks down into two major components: initial loading and handling changes. The initial loading portion is done in the **onServerLoad** method of the form that is called when the form is initially loaded from the server (as you might have guessed). This segment loads the database and then iterates through the records in the database, loading the **name** field into the **select** object. This will all be seen in the block that reads:

```
this.custArray = new Array();
while (!this.query1.rowset.endOfSet) {
   name = new
   StringEx(this.query1.rowset.fields["name"].value);
   name = name.rightTrim();
   this.custArray.add(name);
   this.query1.rowset.next();
}
this.query1.rowset.first();
// assign options and value
this.custArray.sort();
this.select1.options="array this.custArray";
```

As you can see, the code first allocates a new **Array** object (used to hold the names that are retrieved) and then loops through the rows retrieved by the database (through the *rowset* object). Notice the **endOfSet** member of the **rowset** object. This is used to determine when you have reached the end of the database. The next thing that happens is that a new **String** object (actually a **StringEx** object, a Borland Extended String) is allocated and assigned to the name found in the **Name** property of the database record. The trailing spaces are removed using the **rightTrim** method of **StringEx** and the name added to the array.

Following the loop, the **recordset** is reset to point at the beginning again (so we can reuse it later) and the array sorted (using the sort method of the **Array** class). The **select** object is then assigned the new array by using the **options** member variable.

For the second part of the process, the entire sequence is quite similar. The only real differences to be found are the call to check the validity of the column name and the use of that column name to assign values. The validity is found by looping through all of the columns available in the **rowset** and checking to see if the name given to us matches one of the ones in the **rowset** array. This all happens in the **IsValidField** function. This function can be extracted from this form and used in any general purpose application that requires field name checking.

The DbSearch form is a simple, yet powerful example of what is possible with the functionality of IntraBuilder JavaScript and its database extension. It offers examples of the following techniques:

◆ Using a database query "by hand" without requiring the use of the Form Expert

◆ Reading records sequentially from an IntraBuilder database **query** object

◆ Determining whether fields exist in a database

◆ Using if-then-else logic to reach conclusions

◆ Using looping structures to perform a task multiple times

◆ Creating and using **Array** objects

Conclusion

Throughout this chapter, we have stressed the simple: simple examples, simple coding techniques, and simple explanations (we hope). The purpose of this chapter was to expose you to as many examples and techniques of IntraBuilder JavaScript as possible, without overloading you. We hope that is what was accomplished.

In this chapter you learned about simple JavaScript elements, like HTML controls, Edit Text controls, Select (combo box) controls, and Image controls. You learned about simple event handling like user button clicks, form loading events, selection events, and form closing events. Finally, you learned a little bit about the internals of JavaScript, from the simple if-then-else logic through the complexities of Image control and database manipulations.

From here, you can start to create your own JavaScript programs, and to extend the power of IntraBuilder with your own controls and databases. Good luck!

IntraBuilder Reporting

11

Matt Telles

Report writing for real world applications. Here's how to create simple reports, restrict the information in them, and link them together.

*U*sers come to know and expect certain core elements from any database system, such as adding, modifying, and deleting records, using audit trails, and administrative utilities. They recognize form-based entries with triggers for field and record change validations as standard pieces of the database equation.

No piece, however, is more important than reporting, the process of giving users back information they have entered into the database. More systems are chosen for their reporting capabilities than for any other single feature. Reports are the lifeblood of most organizations, allowing them to view and analyze data generated by day-to-day operations of the company.

Most Web pages display a static set of data based on information supplied by the page designer. The idea of being able to view corporate information culled from an internal database is new to the Web, but it won't be for long as the use of intranets and corporate Web pages takes off. When it does, IntraBuilder will be there to help. No longer will users be forced to plow through voluminous documents generated infrequently by MIS departments to find information relevant to their needs or use proprietary software that may only be available on systems at corporate headquarters. IntraBuilder will enable them to access data they need when, where, and how they need it.

IntraBuilder And Reporting

IntraBuilder is a simple, powerful solution to reporting in a Web environment. Built into it is a Report Designer module that creates new reports with a simple point-and-click operation from virtually any database table. To the user, this means the end of the proprietary software running only at the home office or reams of paper-based reports. Getting corporate information can be as simple as dialing in to a local Internet provider (or using a corporate intranet), connecting to the company Web page, and viewing the selected report from a favorite Web browser.

Report Designer is even better news to the programmer. It means an end to patching yet another report into an already too long menu of choices and then writing more code to generate the report.

In IntraBuilder, a report is a specialized form. Report files have different extensions (.JRP) than the normal IntraBuilder forms (which have the extension .JFM), but most of the differences end there. (We'll discuss the differences later.) Like forms, reports can have labels and even event handlers. Reports are generally tied to databases, as are forms. In short, a report *is* a form. The major difference between them is that forms can have multiple tables associated with them, but reports only support single tables. This is really not very much of a limitation, and besides it's likely to change in subsequent IntraBuilder versions.

The general flow of a report in IntraBuilder is as follows:

◆ Select a database table for which you wish to generate a report.

◆ Use the Report Expert to generate a simple report design for the table.

◆ Modify the report design to fit your own criteria or preferences.

◆ Run the report.

Let's discuss each of these steps in more detail before we actually generate some reports.

Select A Database Table For The Report

IntraBuilder supports only a single table for each report, which isn't as much of a limitation as it might seem. While each report can only contain fields from a single table, reports can be linked to other reports so that a detail/summary relationship can be maintained. We will look at an example of such a relationship later in the chapter.

Reports can be made from any database residing on any directory on any machine to which you have legal access on either the client or the server. The usual implementation of reports in IntraBuilder stores the database in a relative sub-directory from the application (for example, apps/database when the application is in the apps directory) on the server, but feel free to ignore this convention if you like. Database tables for different reports could reside on different machines, but this would be an unusual operation and probably slow. IntraBuilder tables normally reside on the server in the directory (or a sub-directory) of the application forms.

To view the available databases for a report, select the Tables tab in IntraBuilder Explorer. You will see all of the known database formats found in the given directory. IntraBuilder speaks Paradox and dBase formats, although any ODBC- or SQL Server-compliant database can be used. You can look at the structure of any table in the Tables tab by right-clicking on the table and selecting View Design from the resulting pop-up menu.

Once you have decided on the table for which you wish to create a report, you will move to the second step of the process, using the built-in tools of IntraBuilder to automate as big a piece of the design process as possible. Reuse is extremely important in today's get-it-done-yesterday world, so you should try to maximize the use of the code given to you for free.

Use The Report Expert To Generate A Simple Report

The whole purpose of the IntraBuilder system is to streamline and simplify the process of building complex Web pages. To this end, Borland has supplied numerous Experts (often called Wizards in other applications) to do most of the work in generating a skeleton application. Building reports is no exception to this rule.

When you select the Reports tab from the IntraBuilder Explorer window for a new application, you will see a single icon displayed in the view, labeled Untitled. Double-clicking on this icon will bring up a dialog box for selecting between Report Expert and Report Designer modes.

The Report Designer, which we will examine in more detail a little later in the chapter, will allow you to design a complete report from scratch, which is to say that you get to do all of the work yourself. Not so with Report Expert. It will lead you quickly and easily through the process of designing a fairly complex report. Once the skeleton report is designed using the Report Expert, you will be presented with two options:

1. Run the report

2. View the current report in the Report Designer

If you have changes to make or are just curious about how the report design will look, you can move on to the next step, modifying the report template in the Report Designer.

Modify The Report Criteria In The Designer

The Report Expert does an admirable job of creating a skeleton report that accomplishes the assigned task. It occasionally falls down in the area of report heading and column widths, but is rescued by IntraBuilder's Report Designer.

Once the Report Expert has done its work, the result is a form. Yes, this form is a report, but it is nonetheless a form. To you that means all of the wonderful things that you have learned during the form development process are all applicable here—with a few minor exceptions. You will need to learn some new terms—page and band—but nothing that you will have to forget, thanks to the wonders of reusability.

The Report Designer application is really just a clone of the Form Designer that was so studiously examined earlier in the book. The unique part of the Report Designer is the ability to view reports on multiple rows of the active table for the report. Unlike forms, which generally work on a single row of a table or tables, reports display multiple rows from a table at a given time. We will go into some detail on how this is implemented when we examine examples using the report system in IntraBuilder.

Once your Report Expert-generated report screen is built, use the Report Designer to tweak it into its final shape. This might involve modifying the static text fields, such as the report title or column headers, or moving and resizing report fields. In any case, the process is exactly like the Form Designer.

When you have finished polishing your report, it is time for the real test: running the report. Like all of IntraBuilder's functions, reports offer two-way modifications. Changes made in design are reflected at runtime, and problems fixed at runtime are automatically reflected in design.

Running The Report

Like all of IntraBuilder's functionality, running a report can be done either directly from within the IDE or programmatically through a form. Actually, because reports are simply forms, you can run reports from other reports. This power makes it extremely easy to build different versions of reports and only run the one appropriate to a given situation.

In our examples, we will look at running reports from within the IDE, running reports from forms, and running reports from other reports.

Example 1: Creating A Simple Report

In our first example, we are going to use one of the sample databases that ships with the IntraBuilder system to get used to the concepts and the flow of the system from one end to the other. When we are finished you should feel comfortable in starting simple reports using IntraBuilder.

The first step to creating a new report in IntraBuilder is to start the IDE. (We will assume that your IntraBuilder setup is configured correctly and that your Web site connection is up and running. Please see the chapter on configuring and initializing your IntraBuilder for more information.) Once IntraBuilder is running, the first thing you will need is access to the

IntraBuilder Explorer window. If the window is not already visible, bring it up by selecting the View|IntraBuilder Explorer from the main IntraBuilder IDE menu.

In the Look In Edit field at the top of the Explorer window, enter the following directory:

```
C:\program files\borland\intrabuilder\samples
```

Note: This directory assumes that you accepted the default path for the installation of IntraBuilder on your system. If you placed IntraBuilder in another drive or directory, replace the C:\programfiles\borland\ intrabuilder segment of the above string with your installation path. For example, if the root path to your IntraBuilder installation was D:\ib, then you would enter D:\ib\samples in the edit box of the Explorer window.

At this point, we begin the real work of creating a new report.

Step 1

Select the Reports tab from the IntraBuilder Explorer window. You will see one or more icons, depending on how many reports have already been defined in this directory. There will always be at least one icon visible in this tab with the caption Untitled, which is used to create new reports. Double-click on the Untitled icon and you will see the dialog displayed in Figure 11.1.

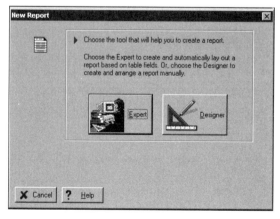

Figure 11.1   Report definition dialog showing Report Expert and Designer buttons.

Choosing the Report Designer button at this point will result in a blank report form. Clicking on the Report Expert button will give you the first page of the Report Expert dialog (similar to the one shown in Figure 11.2).

Step 2

The first page of the Report Expert lists tables available for selection. If there is no tables visible, first check to be sure you entered the correct drive and directory in the path edit box of the IntraBuilder Explorer window. If the drive and directory are correct, you either neglected to install the samples or have since deleted them. In either case, you will need to re-install the samples to continue.

Now select the customer.dbf file, a Dbase file, from the database list labeled Table or Query and click on the Next button to continue.

Step 3

You should now see the next page, shown in Figure 11.3, Report Expert Step 2 of 7. This page asks you to select fields from the database to be included on this report.

In many databases, there are fields—such as flags and status bytes—that need not be displayed to the user and would be left out of the list.

For our purposes, select all of the fields on the left side of the page and click on the button labeled >. Or click on the button labeled >> and all of the

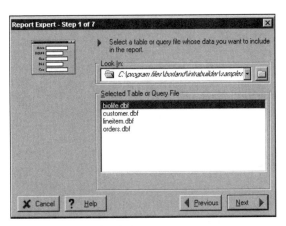

Figure 11.2   Report Expert Step 1 of 7 dialog.

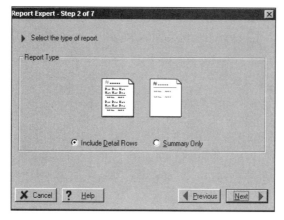

Figure 11.3   Report Expert Step 2 of 7 dialog.

fields on the left side of the page will automatically be moved over to the right side of the page. When you have finished moving fields back and forth, click the Next button to move on to the next step.

Step 4

You should now see the page displayed in Figure 11.4, Report Expert Step 4 of 7 dialog. This dialog will allow you to select the criteria for summarizing your report. These criteria are often known as break criteria, because they indicate when a break should occur for a summary line in the report display. We are going to list our customers by the state or province in which they reside, so click on the STATE_PROV field and then the > button. Leave the Ascending sort order on.

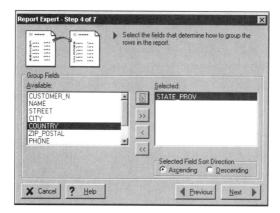

Figure 11.4   Report Expert Step 4 of 7 dialog.

IntraBuilder Reports lets you break on changes to a single field or collections of fields. In addition, you may select different summary options and information for each break. This is a powerful reporting technique that you may need to use a few times before you feel comfortable with it.

When you are finished, click on the Next button to move on to the next dialog.

Step 5

You should now be looking at the Report Expert Step 5 of 7 dialog as shown in Figure 11.5, a rather daunting page that we will not be using in this example. It is worth taking a moment, however, to discuss what is going on in this page of the dialog, which, in combination with the page before, defines the summary line information for the generated report.

When a report is generated, the IntraBuilder reporting engine can be made to sort, count, total, and determine the maximum or minimum value of the fields as the lines of the report are written. The information generated on these summary lines is a reflection of the block that ended with the summary line. In the previous page of the Report Expert Step 4, we defined what field or fields should appear on the summary line. In this page of the Report Expert Step 5, we now define how that information is displayed for the user to view.

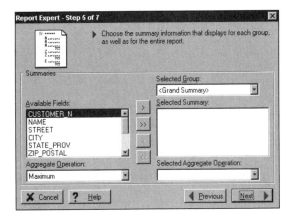

Figure 11.5   Report Expert Step 5 of 7 dialog.

Summary lines are defined by selecting a given database field from the tables selected for the report. You may then apply any of the supported operations to that field. The supported operations in the current release of IntraBuilder are max (maximum value of the field), min (minimum value of the field), and count (the total number of entries in this field).

In addition to the field itself, you can also display aggregate information on the summary lines. In cases where multiple summary lines are displayed, aggregate information totals the totals, as it were. In this case, the summary lines themselves become report lines and can have the same operations (max, min, and count) applied to them.

For our first, simple report, we are not going to worry about the whole issue of summary lines, aggregate information, or operations. Click on the Next button to move to the next page of the Report Expert.

Step 6

You should now see the Report Expert page labeled Report Expert Step 6 of 7, as shown in Figure 11.6. In this page, you are asked to determine the fundamental layout criteria of your report. Although you can go back and change some of these settings by modifying the generated JavaScript code, this can be difficult and extensive. It's easier to accept most of these decisions as givens for a report.

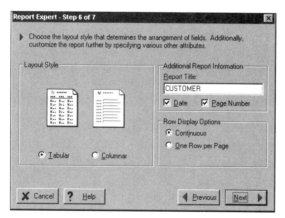

Figure 11.6   Report Expert Step 6 of 7.

The decisions to make here concern the following information:

◆ Tabular vs. columnar format

◆ Title of the report

◆ Display format (continuous or one per page)

Let's take a look at each option and what it means to the final display of your generated report.

TABULAR VS. COLUMNAR REPORTS

A tabular report is one in which the data is arranged in the form of a table, each header describing the data displayed below it. Most reports you have seen in the business world are in a tabular format. In a tabular report, the space between the column headers and the bottom—or footer—is filled with one or more records. Each record in the report table represents a single row from the table that was selected for that report. The row consists of fields, which are generally arranged on a single line of the report. As we will see, this behavior, coupled with the way IntraBuilder creates field widths, can lead to problems in the final generation of the report.

Figure 11.7 shows the default version of our Customer report in the tabular format.

Columnar reports, on the other hand, are displayed more in the fashion of input forms than reports. Each record in the selected set of the table will be displayed in a field name—field value format. In the continuous

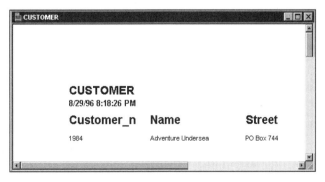

Figure 11.7   Customer report in tabular format.

format, columnar reports are more like data dumps than anything else. In non-continuous mode (that is, one record per page), columnar reports can be used to print forms for mailing, mailing lists, and other kinds of record-oriented reports.

Figure 11.8 shows our Customer report (again with no changes to any of the default selections in the Report Expert) in the columnar format.

Because most business reports are presented in a tabular format, and because the tabular format is the default report format setting in IntraBuilder, we are going to use the tabular format for this version of the Customer report.

TITLE OF THE REPORT

The field entitled Report Title is also important for the final generation of our completed report. Because the report title appears at the top of each page of the report, you should therefore select a report title that clearly communicates its purpose.

In our case, we are going to be displaying a list of the customers in our database, breaking them down on the summary lines on any change in the state or province field. For this reason, we will give our report the title Customers By State.

ROW DISPLAY OPTIONS

The final option on this page is a set of two radio buttons under the title Row Display Options. The two options in this section are Continuous or

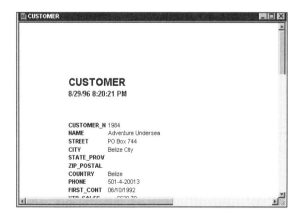

Figure 11.8   Customer report in columnar format.

One Per Page. This is an important distinction, so you should pay attention to the differences between the two options and how they affect your choice of a report format.

A continuous report is one in which each record in the table is displayed immediately after the previous record until the end of the page is reached. Continuous format is generally preferable for tabular format because it allows the user to easily compare and contrast records in order on the report. Continuous format is generally not a good idea in the case of columnar reports, as it tends to lead to a cluttered, hard-to-read display.

A one-per-page format is one in which, as its name implies, records are displayed one to a page. There is not a direct one-to-one correspondence between the displayed version of the report and a printed version, so one per page doesn't always look exactly the way you might think on the monitor display. One-per-page format is generally preferable for columnar reports because it displays a clean separation between records in the table, but it is usually not a good idea for tabular reports because it leads to wide expanses of empty screen or paper.

This can be summarized in a simple rule: Use continuous reports for printing with tabular format and one-per-page report printing for columnar reports.

When you finish reading through all of that and make the appropriate selections on the Report Expert dialog, click on the Next button to move to the next and final page of the Report Expert.

Step 7

You should now be looking at the final page of the Report Expert (shown in Figure 11.9), Report Expert Step 7 of 7. You should see two buttons, Run Report and Design Report.

Selecting Design Report will take you directly into the Report Designer for this report. If you knew what changes you wanted to make to the report, this is what you would do. But because we haven't even seen the report up to this point, we need to run the report to see what it is going to look like to the end user. Click the Run Report button. You might expect to see the report running, but instead a File Save As dialog is displayed. This is

Figure 11.9   Report Expert Step 7 of 7 dialog.

necessary because IntraBuilder expects to run a script (report or form) from a script file. You will need to save the generated report scripts to disk before IntraBuilder will let you compile the script or run the report. It's a good idea to save the report script anyway, since a program crash or machine lockup would wipe out all of your hard work to this point.

Enter CustomerReport for the file name and click the Save button. Since no extension is specified for the report file, it will use the default extension .jrp. All IntraBuilder report script files should have this extension to work properly.

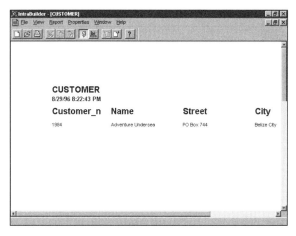

Figure 11.10   The Customers-By-State report—first cut.

Finally, once the report script is saved, the report will run and, barring any unforeseen circumstances, you should see the report shown in Figure 11.10. Take a moment to scroll the report horizontally and vertically to view the whole thing, examining it with a critical eye toward the things you will need to change. We will take that step up next.

Before we begin the process of actually modifying the report, it would be interesting to see the script file the IntraBuilder has generated for you to create this report. A portion of this script file is shown in Listing 11.1. Remember, if you were doing this by yourself, by hand, you would need to write all of this code, not to mention the underlying database functionality.

LISTING 11.1 *THE GENERATED JAVASCRIPT FOR THE CUSTOMER-BY-STATE REPORT.*

```
//
// Generated on 08/19/1996
//
var r = new CUSTOMERSTATEReport();
if (CUSTOMERSTATE.arguments.length == 2) {
    r.startPage = CUSTOMERSTATE.arguments[0];
    r.endPage = CUSTOMERSTATE.arguments[1];
}
r.render();
class CUSTOMERSTATEReport extends Report {
    with (this) {
        title = "CUSTOMER";
        linkText = "Next Page";
    }


    with (this.customer1 = new Query()){
        left = 0;
        top = 0;
        sql = 'SELECT * FROM "C:\\program files\\borland\\intrabuilder
            \\samples\\customer.dbf" ORDER BY STATE_PROV';
        active = true;
    }


    with (this.customer1.rowset) {

    }
```

```
with (this.printer) {
   orientation = 1;
   paperSize = 1;
   resolution = 4;
}


with (this.pageTemplate1 = new PageTemplate(this)){
   height = 15840;
   width = 12240;
   marginTop = 1080;
   marginLeft = 1080;
   marginBottom = 1080;
   marginRight = 1080;
   gridLineWidth = 1;
}

// Code omitted for space

with (this.pageTemplate1.HTML15 = new HTML(this.pageTemplate1)){
   height = 360;
   left = 20619;
   top = 1080;
   width = 1560;
   color = "black";
   fontPointSize = 10;
   text = "<H2>Signature</H2>";
}


with (this.pageTemplate1.HTML16 = new HTML(this.pageTemplate1)){
   height = 360;
   left = 22323;
   top = 1080;
   width = 5760;
   color = "black";
   fontPointSize = 10;
   text = "<H2>Notes</H2>";
}


with (this.streamSource1 = new StreamSource(this)){

}


with (this.streamSource1.group1 = new Group(this.streamSource1)){
   groupBy = "STATE_PROV";
}
```

```
// Code omitted for space

with (this.streamSource1.detailBand.HTML1 = new
   HTML(this.streamSource1.detailBand)){
   height = 1;
   width = 1920;
   variableHeight = true;
   color = "black";
   fontBold = false;
   text = {||this.form.customer1.rowset.fields["CUSTOMER_N"].
     value};
}


with (this.streamSource1.detailBand.HTML2 = new
   HTML(this.streamSource1.detailBand)){
   height = 1;
   left = 2064;
   width = 2325;
   variableHeight = true;
   color = "black";
   fontBold = false;
   text = {||this.form.customer1.rowset.fields["NAME"].value};
}

// Code omitted for space.


with (this.streamSource1.detailBand.HTML10 = new
   HTML(this.streamSource1.detailBand)){
   height = 1;
   left = 16836;
   width = 1575;
   variableHeight = true;
   color = "black";
   fontBold = false;
   text = {||this.form.customer1.rowset.fields["YTD_SALES"].
     value};
}


with (this.streamSource1.detailBand.HTML11 = new
   HTML(this.streamSource1.detailBand)){
   height = 1;
   left = 18555;
   width = 1560;
   variableHeight = true;
   color = "black";
   fontBold = false;
```

```
      text =
{||this.form.customer1.rowset.fields["CREDIT_OK"].value};
   }


   with (this.streamSource1.detailBand.image1 = new
      Image(this.streamSource1.detailBand)){
      height = 720;
      left = 20259;
      width = 1560;
      dataSource = parent.parent.parent.customer1.rowset.fields
         ["SIGNATURE"];
   }


   with (this.streamSource1.detailBand.HTML12 = new
      HTML(this.streamSource1.detailBand)){
      height = 1;
      left = 21963;
      width = 5760;
      variableHeight = true;
      color = "black";
      fontBold = false;
      text = {||this.form.customer1.rowset.fields["NOTES"].value};
   }


   with (this.reportGroup) {
      groupBy = "";
   }


   with (this.reportGroup.headerBand) {
      height = 0;
   }


   with (this.reportGroup.footerBand) {
      height = 0;
   }


   with (this.reportGroup.footerBand.HTML1 = new
      HTML(this.reportGroup.footerBand)){
      height = 200;
      width = 9360;
      variableHeight = true;
      color = "red";
      fontBold = false;
```

```
    fontItalic = true;
    text = {||"Maximum of NAME: " +
this.parent.parent.agMax({||this.parent.streamSource1.rowset.fields
  ["NAME"].value})};
  }

  this.firstPageTemplate = this.form.pageTemplate1
  this.form.pageTemplate1.nextPageTemplate = this.form.pageTemplate1
  this.form.pageTemplate1.streamFrame1.streamSource =
     this.form.streamSource1
  this.form.streamSource1.rowset = this.form.customer1.rowset
}
```

Step 8

The final step in the report creation process is the iterative process of getting the report to look and work exactly the way you want. To accomplish this, we need to learn a little about the Report Designer and the pieces of a report form. Let's first put the report into design mode so we can begin to make the exact changes we want. To move into design mode, select View|Report Design from the IntraBuilder main menu.

Short Cuts

You can move into Report Design mode directly by pressing Shift+F2 (hold down the Shift key while pressing the F2 key). Alternatively, you can move to Report (or Run) mode by pressing the F2 key while in design mode.

You should now notice a collection of windows on the screen. The largest of these is the Report Design window. You will notice that even in design mode, the IntraBuilder report form still shows data from the table. This convenient feature allows you to see what effect your design changes have on real data without the need to switch back and forth between design and run modes.

The first two changes we are going to make to the report form will involve only the Report Designer window and another window not currently on the screen, the Inspector window. Our first change is to modify the column header for the customer number field so that it makes sense. As it is presently, the customer number field (which is the very first column of our tabular report) displays with the column header CUSTOMER_N, which may be confusing to the viewer of the report. We will change it to read CUSTOMER #. To modify the text of any field you find on the report, follow this procedure.

1. Right Click on the field by moving the mouse cursor over the field and pressing the right mouse button.

2. In the resulting pop-up menu, select Inspector. The Inspector window will appear (or be brought to the top of the desktop if it is already open).

3. Select the Properties tab on the Inspector window. Scroll down through the properties until you reach the Text property entry. It should currently read <H2>CUSTOMER_N</H2>.

4. Modify the entry by selecting the text and entering new text for the field. In this case, change the field text to read <H2>Customer #</H2>.

5. The text will now appear, in its modified form, in the Inspector window and in the Report Designer window.

   Note: Do not remove the <H2> or </H2> tags from the text unless you want the text to appear in a different format from all of the other field column headers. These tags, which are HTML (hypertext markup language) tags, indicate that this text should be displayed using the second level header format.

If you now run the report, you will see the change is immediately reflected in the report shown. To test it, select View|Report from the IDE menu in IntraBuilder or press the F2 key. When you have verified that your change worked, select View|Report Designer or press the Shift+F2 key to return to the Report Designer window for more modifications.

You should then follow the same procedure to change the following column headers (as listed in Table 11.1).

So, now all we need to do is to move all of these fields around. There is only one problem. Not all of those fields appear to be in our report. Go back

Table 11.1   Modified column header tags for Customer-By-State report.

Current Setting	Modified Setting
STATE_PROV	State
ZIP_POSTAL	Zip Code
CUSTOMER_N	Customer #
YTD_SALES	Sales (Year To Date)
FIRST_CONT	Contact

and scroll around the report again. If you move to the extreme right side of the Report Viewer window, you will find the STATE_PROV and ZIP_POSTAL fields. Where are the rest of them? That depends on the current release of IntraBuilder. The beta release appears to have a bug that places these fields outside the viewable (and editable) range of the report form. These fields exist, as you can verify by checking the JavaScript listing we looked at earlier. Some browsers will show the fields; others will not.

Before we solve the problem of displaying large amounts of data, let's continue our examination of the IntraBuilder Report Designer environment. We have already seen the actual Report Designer Editor window and the Inspector window. The next pieces of the environment are the palettes.

Reporting Palettes

The first palette (shown in Figure 11.11) is the Field Palette. The Field Palette contains information about the fields for the table(s) in the current report. Because each report may have a different table associated with it, the actual layout of the Field Palette can vary from report to report.

Assuming that you are working with the customer.dbf table as we are for our report, Figure 11.11 should show you all of the available fields in the customer table. You can add specific fields to the report from the table the same way that you would add any other kind of component to the form. Click on the field you want to add to the report and then click on the report at the spot you want the field to appear in the finished product. Moving and resizing of fields within the report form is also the same as any other kind of form.

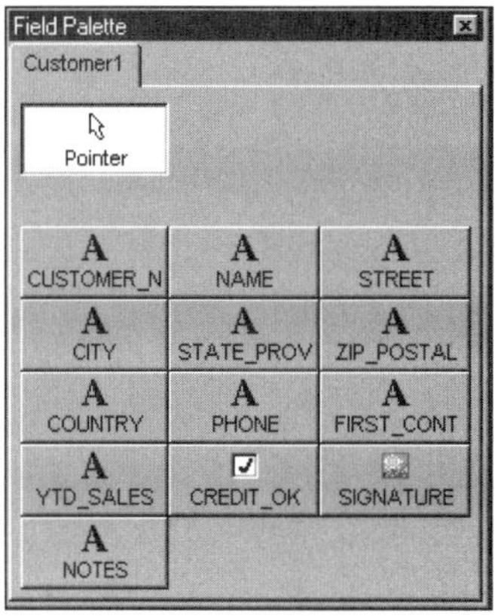

Figure 11.11   The Field Palette.

Note: You do not usually add fields via the Field Palette. It is generally easier to go into Report Expert and generate a report that contains the fields you want from a table. You might use the Field Palette if a table changes and the report must be updated.

This brings us to an important area of report design within the IntraBuilder reporting workshop: banding. IntraBuilder reports have bands of data where different kinds of information are displayed. The header for a report contains generalized information about the report, such as title, short description perhaps, and so forth.

The header area is the next band that usually appears on the report form. In tabular reports this is the area that contains the static text fields labeled with the descriptions of the data below them. In the case of our first cut at the Customer report, we had header titles like CUSTOMER_N, STATE_PROV, and others.

Use English

IntraBuilder creates column headers by changing the case of the database field name to all lower case and then capitalizing the first letter of the word. You can save yourself a lot of time in the report design process if you give your table fields meaningful English (or whatever language you are working with) names.

Following the headers comes the actual data area of the report, the dynamic section that is really the most important area of the report from the perspective of both the user and the programmer. To see what the actual band of the data looks like, bring up the Customer report in design mode. Click below the first column header on the first data element you see. First, notice the large box surrounding the data element and extending to the bottom of the screen. This is the actual data handling area. To see what is going on, right-click on this area and select Inspector from the resulting pop-up menu. The text field shows how this field is associated with the underlying database table. If you click on the top box in the Inspector window (the field name) you will see the hierarchy of objects that create this field. This hierarchy is shown in Figure 11.12.

The second palette that appears on the Report Designer is the Component Palette. Shown in Figure 11.13, it contains all of the standard JavaScript components that can be added to a report form. Here is a breakdown of the available components (the function of these components is the same as forms, so please refer to the form design chapter for more detailed information):

◆ Pointer Tool

◆ Check Box Tool

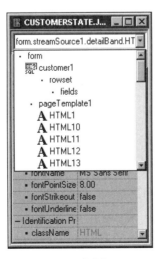

Figure 11.12 Object hierarchy for a report field.

Figure 11.13   **The Component Palette for reports.**

◆ Radio Button Tool

◆ Image Tool

◆ Label Tool

On the Data Objects tab, you will find the following:

◆ Pointer Tool

◆ Query Tool

◆ Database Tool

◆ Group Tool

And finally, on the Reports tab you will find:

◆ Pointer Tool

◆ Group Tool

◆ Report Menu Changes

When you run the Report Designer, you will notice that the menus for the IDE change reflect the functionality of the designer. Here is a list of the changes to the menus and what the commands do in the designer environment:

◆ Report—Changes the report from Design mode to Run mode

◆ Report Design—Changes the report from Run mode to Design mode

◆ Inspector—Brings up (or brings to the front) the IntraBuilder Inspector window

◆ Method Editor—Brings up the Method Editor window

◆ Zoom—Allows viewing in Normal, Enlarged, or Reduced modes

◆ Component Palette—Displays or hides the Component Palette window

◆ Field Palette—Displays or hides the Field Palette window

◆ Toolbars—Allows you to configure which toolbars are visible on the desktop

◆ Status Bar—Displays or hides the status bar

◆ IntraBuilder Explorer—Displays or brings the Explorer window to the top

◆ Script Pad—Displays or brings the Script Pad window to the top

In addition to the changes to the View menu, the Report Designer adds a new menu, the Layout menu. This menu will contain the following choices, used for modifying the physical positions of components on the report form:

◆ Align—This allows you to align multiple fields by one of the following rules:

    ◆ Left

    ◆ Right

    ◆ Top

    ◆ Bottom

    ◆ Absolute Horizontal Center

    ◆ Relative Horizontal Center

    ◆ Absolute Vertical Center

    ◆ Relative Vertical Center

◆ Size—Allows you to resize multiple fields by one of the following rules:

    ◆ Grow to largest width

- ◆ Shrink to smallest width

- ◆ Grow to largest height

- ◆ Shrink to smallest height

- ◆ Bring To Front—Brings the selected object to the front level of the report

- ◆ Send To Back—Sends the selected object to the bottom level of the report

- ◆ Bring Closer—Moves the selected object up one level in the report

- ◆ Send Farther—Moves the selected object down one level in the report

- ◆ Add Groups and Summaries—Displays Groups and Summaries dialog for:

  - ◆ Groups Tab—Changes report field groupings

  - ◆ Summaries Tab—Changes report field summary information

Note: The entries marked with an asterisk (*) are also available on the toolbar within the Report Designer IDE.

Finally, the Report menu adds the following entries in the Report Designer:

- ◆ New Method

- ◆ Edit Event

To demonstrate these tools, let's create another example report.

Example 2: Customer Report By State, Take Two

As you will recall from our last example report, we were unable to see all database fields in the Report Viewer.

Fortunately, there is an alternative to the tabular format for reports: the column report, which can be used to solve the problem of creating a report with many detail fields. Along the way, we will also examine how to display only the records that you want it to display.

Run the Report Expert in IntraBuilder by once again double-clicking on the Untitled icon in the Reports tab of the Explorer window. For each of the seven steps of the Expert, do the following:

Step 1—Select the customer.dbf file. If it doesn't appear, make sure that you are looking in the SAMPLES directory of the IntraBuilder setup.

Step 2—Select the Include Detail Rows radio button.

Step 3—Select the >> button to select all of the fields to include the field list box.

Step 4—Select the STATE_PROV field and click the > button to group by the state field.

Step 5—Skip this step to exclude summary information on the report. Click Next to continue.

Step 6—Click on the columnar radio button. Enter Customer Detail Report for the title of the report. Select the One-Per-Page radio button.

Step 7—Click on the Design Report button.

At this point, you have a complete, record-oriented (rather than table-oriented) report for the Customer table. You can run the report if you want to see what it looks like. When you are finished, close the report window and bring the IntraBuilder Explorer window back up. When you close the report window, give the new report the name CustomerDetailReport2.jrp.

Click on the Reports tab in IntraBuilder Explorer. Right-click the CustomerDetailReport2.JRP entry in the window and select Edit As Script from the resulting pop-up menu. We are now going to modify the script for the report so that we can us this report to view either all of the detail records or only one record representing a customer number passed to us. Why would we want such a report? You will see that in a few minutes, and in the process you are learning how to modify the script for a report, how to capture arguments to the report, and how to modify the selection process for a report.

When the Script Editor window comes up, make the following modifications. Note that only a small portion of the top of the script is shown, because the complete file is rather large. The modifications are shown in Listing 11.2.

LISTING 11.2 MODIFICATIONS TO THE CUSTOMERBY-STATE2.JRP SCRIPT.

```
// {End Header} Do not remove this comment//
// Generated on 08/20/1996
//
var r = new CUSTOMERBYSTATE2Report();
if (CUSTOMERBYSTATE2.arguments.length == 2) {
    r.startPage = CUSTOMERBYSTATE2.arguments[0];
    r.endPage = CUSTOMERBYSTATE2.arguments[1];
}

// Check for passed in restriction on customer number

if (CUSTOMERBYSTATE2.arguments.length == 1) {
    var s = 'SELECT * FROM "C:\\program
        files\\borland\\intrabuilder\\samples\\customer.dbf" ';
    s += 'where customer_n = ';
    s += "'" + CUSTOMERBYSTATE2.arguments[0] + "'";
    r.customer1.sql = s;
}

r.render();
class CUSTOMERBYSTATE2Report extends Report {
    with (this) {
        title = "Customer By State (2)";
        linkText = "Next Page";
}
```

Remarkably little needs to be done to add more functionality to the generated report. The above JavaScript code checks to see whether or not any arguments were passed to the script. If there were any arguments—and there was only one such argument—then the argument is considered to be the customer number for the report to display. In this case, we assign a new SQL statement to the query object in the report form. From that point on, the normal IntraBuilder database functionality takes over, selects the appropriate record(s), and then the report form takes over to display the records one at a time (one per page).

Testing The Report

We now have the report that displays the complete details (that is to say, all of the fields in the database) for one or all records in the table. We can easily test the complete set of records case by simply running the report in the IDE. Since we are not passing through any arguments to the report, no modifications will be made to the SQL string and all of the records are selected. What we need to do now is test the more restrictive case of displaying only a single record. After that, we will understand why we implemented a single-record detail report in the first place.

CREATING THE FORM

The first step in the testing process is to create a simple IntraBuilder form that will allow us to test the detail report. The form itself is shown in Figure 11.14. As you can see, the form consists of only three simple components: text entry field, HTML display field, and button.

Figure 11.14   The test form for the report.

To create this form, do the following:

1. Open the IntraBuilder Explorer window, if it is not already open, by selecting View|Explorer from the main IntraBuilder IDE menu.

2. Select the Forms tab from the Explorer view window and double-click on the first icon labeled Untitled I in the tab view.

3. Select the Designer button to go directly into the form designer, since we are not hooking this form into a table.

4. If the Component Palette is not already visible, select the View| Component Palette menu item from the IDE menu.

5. On the Component Palette, select the HTML component and place it on the form. Right-click the new HTML component and modify the Text Property to read Enter Customer Number: in the Inspector window.

6. On the Component Palette, select the text entry component and place it on the form. Right-click the new HTML control and remove the existing text in the Text property using the Inspector.

7. On the Component Palette, select the button component and place it on the form. Right-click the new button component and change the Text property to read View Report in the Inspector.

8. Still in Inspector, select the Events tab of the view window. Click on the **onClick** event and select the Tool icon in the tab to bring up the Method Editor.

9. Enter the following code into the new event handler for the **onClick** method:

```
function button1_onClick()
   {
      if ( this.form.text1.value != "" ) {
        _sys.scripts.run("CustomerByState2.jrp",
           this.form.text1.value);
      }
   }
```

10. Close the Method Editor.

You have just finished creating a complete form to test the new report.

RUNNING THE TEST FORM

To run the test form, select View|Form from the main IDE menu in IntraBuilder. The form should come up in Run mode. Enter one of the valid customer numbers and click on the View Report button. The speed at which the report window will come up depends on the speed of your computer or network connection, but eventually you should see a screen very much like the one shown in Figure 11.15.

The important things to look at in your version are to make sure the answers to the following questions are both yes.

◆ Does the customer number shown on the report match the one entered in the test form?

◆ Are the next-page and top-page menu items under the View menu disabled?

If both of these answers are yes, then you can be assured that the form and detail report are working as advertised. You have just learned how to write a report that does all of the following:

◆ Accepts parameters

◆ Modifies its selection string where appropriate

◆ Displays records in a columnar format

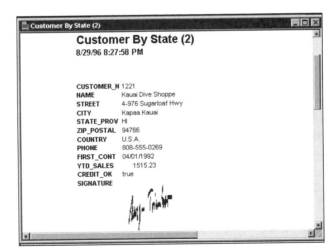

Figure 11.15   The detail report run from our test form.

The Last Step Of Example 2: Making It Pretty

Before we close out the second example of reporting, let's examine some other functionality provided by the IntraBuilder Report Designer system by taking one more step in form building—making it look the way we want it to look.

Bring up the CustomerDetailReport2 in Design mode by right-clicking the CustomerDetailReport2.JRP entry in the Reports tab of IntraBuilder Explorer. Select Design Report from the resulting pop-up menu. The Report Designer window should now appear on your desktop.

Make the following simple changes to the report display:

1. Change the title CUSTOMER_N to Customer Number:

2. Change the title STATE_PROV to State:

3. Change the title ZIP_POSTAL to ZIP Code:

4. Change the title FIRST_CONT to Contact Name:

5. Change the title YTD_SALES to Sales (Ytd):

6. Change the title CREDIT_OK to Ok Credit?:

In each case, the process is exactly the same. Right-click on the field title in question and select Inspector from the resulting pop-up menu. In the Inspector window, select the Properties tab for the view. Scroll through the list until you find the one labeled Text on the left-hand side. Modify the entry of text on the right-hand side from what it presently reads (for example, ZIP_POSTAL) to the new text that you would like it to read (for example ZIP Code:). Press Enter or Return to commit the changes. Before you commit your changes, you can use the usual edit control key sequences (Ctrl+C to copy, Ctrl+Z to undo, Ctrl+X to cut, and Ctrl+V to paste) or you can select a change from the Edit menu.

Once you have modified the text fields in the HTML controls, you will probably discover that you have created a new problem. The text for some of the fields is now too wide for the control windows. Our next job is to make the fields the correct size of the text they hold, a process called control resizing.

In our case, the problem would appear to be the Contact Name string. We could simply shorten the string, of course, and in a production environment you might do that. Since we're trying to learn more about the tools, we will do things the hard way.

The first thing we need to do is to move all of those pesky fields (the ones that display table data, not the HTML controls) to make more room for resizing the other controls. To accomplish this, click on the first data field (the one containing the customer number) and drag it to the right (about a quarter of an inch by the ruler above it). Move down to the next field and repeat the process. Don't worry about making sure they are exactly the same on the left edge; we will fix that very soon.

> *Note: You may notice that the fields do not move immediately when you click on them and try to move them. If this happens to you, try the following. Click once on the field to select it. Press the left mouse button again with the mouse cursor in the field selected. Hold down the mouse button for a full second, then move the mouse in the direction you want it to go. You will find that the field then moves quite easily.*

Next, select the Contact Name field with the left mouse button. Move to the bottom right corner of the selection box for the field. The mouse cursor will then turn into a slanted two-headed arrow. Move the cursor slightly to the right to make the box bigger. Release the left mouse button and the field will be resized to the new, larger, size. You may need to repeat this process to get the field to the size you want.

Now it's time to go back and adjust field sizes on the right side of the report form. Move to the top field and select it by clicking on it with the left mouse button. Hold down the Shift key on the keyboard and select each of the other fields on the right side of the report by clicking on them using the left mouse button. When all of the fields on the right-hand side of the report are selected, select Align from the Layout menu of the IDE. Select Left from the drop-down menu of the Align menu and watch as the report fields are magically aligned along the left edge.

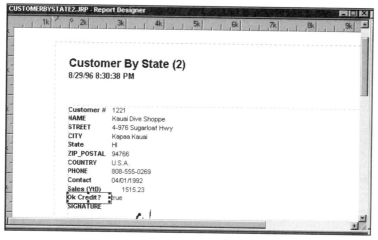

Figure 11.16   The completed Customer-By-State report form.

When you are finished, your new report design should look like the one shown in Figure 11.16.

Views, Views, Who's Got The Views?

Group View is an entirely different way to look at your report. It is always present on the Report Designer window, although you normally will not see it unless you really want to. The entire Report Designer window is actually a split window. The right side (or pane) of the window is the usual designer pane, showing the report as it will appear. It allows you to select individual fields, modify their properties, move them around, and so forth. In short, the right side of the window is what we have been talking about throughout this entire chapter when we have referred to the Report Designer window.

To see the Group View, select the thick bar on the left-most edge of the Report Designer window. The mouse cursor will turn into a two-sided horizontal arrow. While still holding the left mouse button down, move the mouse cursor to the right, toward the center of the window and an entirely new view—the Group View—will be revealed under the old one. This new view is shown in Figure 11.17.

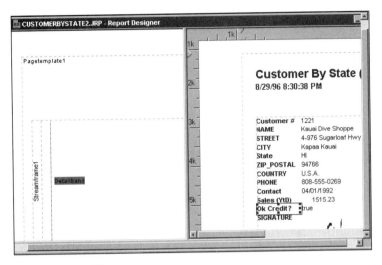

Figure 11.17   The Group View.

What good is a Group View, you might ask. From an editing standpoint, the Group View is not useful. You can't make changes in it, nor can you select items. What you can do is see how the report is structured, what elements overlay other elements, and where things need to be moved in order to make them fit. The Group View is best for situations where you need to know where something should go and where something already is. It uses the element types as labels, so you can quickly identify what a given element on the Report Designer window is really supposed to be.

The Final Example: A Master Detail Report

For our final example of the reporting section in IntraBuilder, we are going to implement a master detail report that will allow users to simply point and click their way from one report to another.

The purpose of this example is two fold. First, it is nice to know how to display records in both detail and summary versions, and how to call one from another. The second reason is that this report will show you how to use the built-in reporting capabilities of IntraBuilder to augment the capabilities of HTML and JavaScript to make your Web pages more powerful.

The problem we are trying to solve here is simple: how to link two reports together without using an intermediary form (as we did in the previous example). Reports are just like regular forms, so we could use a button on the report to link it to another report. The only problem is deciding which entry on the report to link to the detail report. The top line of the report? The middle line? The user needs to be able to get from any line on the summary report to a detail report showing only that record. Here's how to accomplish this in IntraBuilder.

First, remember the underlying medium for IntraBuilder. At its heart, regardless of what the user sees, IntraBuilder reports are still running in a Web browser using HTML. Normally, you tie HTML forms together by establishing a link. By clicking on a given link, the user can then jump to another form to view more information about that item. How can we use this information to help us with IntraBuilder, which doesn't have a link object in its repertoire?

The simple answer is that IntraBuilder does not have a link object that you will find on the Component Palette. Nor will IntraBuilder directly show you links. But in the following example you'll see how to get the IntraBuilder reporting system to generate HTML calls that will create static links to your report.

Generating The Skeleton Report

In order to be able to accomplish this task, we first need a report to work with. That means a trip through the Report Expert to generate a skeleton report.

Run the Report Expert in IntraBuilder by once again double-clicking on the Untitled icon in the Reports tab of the Explorer window. For each of the seven steps of the Expert, do the following:

Step 1—Select the customer.dbf file. If it doesn't appear, make sure that you are looking in the SAMPLES directory of the IntraBuilder setup.

Step 2—Select the Include Detail Rows radio button.

Step 3—Select the following fields to add to the report:

- ◆ CUSTOMER_N
- ◆ NAME
- ◆ STREET
- ◆ CITY
- ◆ STATE_PROV

Step 4—Select the STATE_PROV field and click the > button to group by the state field.

Step 5—If you don't do anything on this step, there will be no summary information on the report. Click Next to continue.

Step 6—Click on the tabular radio button. Enter Customer Summary Report for the title of the report. Select the continuous radio button.

Step 7—Click on the Design Report button.

At this point you have a complete report that shows five fields for each of the records in the database. The next challenge is to link each record in the report link to a detail record that shows the remaining fields for the record.

Linking The Records Together

In order to link the records in our report to another report, we need to modify the actual text that appears in the report, which may seem strange given the fact that we have already generated the fields we want to appear in the report.

But the only modification that will appear to the user is that the fields will become links. In most browsers, that means that the customer number field in the browser will appear as an underlined blue value rather than the standard black text on a white background. The mouse cursor will change when it is placed over such a field, usually into a pointing finger, to indicate that this is a link. None of this, however, is important to you as the programmer. All that you care about is that when the user clicks on this field (the customer number) a sub-report is run.

Select the customer number (CUSTOMER_N) field in the report and right-click on it. Select Inspector from the resulting pop-up menu. In the Inspector, modify the Text property of the field to be as follows:

```
text = {||'<A HREF="CustomerReport2.jrp(' +
 parseInt(this.parent.parent.rowset.fields["CUSTOMER_N"].value) +
 ')">' + this.parent.parent.rowset.fields["CUSTOMER_N"].value + '</
A>'};
```

That's it. That's the only change we need to make to the IntraBuilder generated report in order to make this field link directly to the Customer report to show details for this record. The text for the field sets up a link (using the HTML **<A HREF>** tag) for the customer number field. This indicates to the browser that this field should go somewhere when the user clicks on it. Where does it go? The browser looks at the remainder of the line (the call to CustomerReport2.jrp) and has no idea what to do with it. As a result, it calls back to the IntraBuilder server and asks it what to do with it. The server recognizes the call as a request to run a script (in this case a report, due to the .jrp extension) and will bring up the report form. Within the call to the report form, the customer number is passed as the only argument, which indicates to the detail report that it is supposed to use this customer number only. You will recall that we created that in the last example.

Conclusion

In this chapter we learned about the IntraBuilder reporting system. You saw how to create simple reports, restrict the information that is shown in the report, and link reports together. While this is certainly not the end of what can be done in a reporting system, it covers most of the basics for use in the real world. There is a lot more that can be done with reports in IntraBuilder, which you can learn by playing with the system and looking at other people's code. You will find that the system is flexible enough to support many of your reporting needs.

IntraBuilder Components And Their Properties 12

Terence Goggin

Nowhere in the IntraBuilder manuals or
help files does Borland list the standard
components and their properties, so we're
including them here. This is the manual
that Borland forgot.

The ActiveX Control

Properties

alt—this property is a string to be displayed in place of the actual ActiveX
control in the event that the browser does not support ActiveX.

ClassId—the clsid string that identifies the ActiveX/OCX control.

className—a read-only property that identifies the type (class) of the
(IntraBuilder) ActiveX control. For standard IB ActiveX controls, the
className property will always be ActiveX. This property is really just
provided for your reference or to check the type (class) of an object
at runtime.

codeBase—a URL that specifies the location of the physical ActiveX/OCX file.

form—the form on which the ActiveX control is located.

left—the distance from the left edge of the ActiveX control from the left edge of the form itself.

name—the name of the ActiveX control.

pageno—the page of the form on which the ActiveX control is located. If **pageno** is 0, the control will appear on each of the form's pages.

parent—the object that owns the ActiveX control. This will typically be the form.

params—the parameters to be passed to the ActiveX/OCX control.

top—distance from the top of the ActiveX to the top of the form.

width—the width (distance from the left edge to the right edge) of the ActiveX control.

Events

onDesignLoad—triggered after the ActiveX has been loaded at design time.

onServerLoad—triggered after the ActiveX control has actually been opened.

The Button Control

Properties

className—a read-only property that identifies the type (class) of the Button. For standard Buttons, the **className** property will always be Button. This property is really just provided for your reference or to check the type (class) of an object at runtime.

form—the form on which the Button is located.

left—the distance from the left edge of the Button from the left edge of the form itself.

name—the name of the Button control.

pageno—the page of the form on which the Button is located. If **pageno** is 0, the control will appear on each of the form's pages.

parent—the object that owns the Button. This will typically be the form.

text—the text displayed on the Button itself.

top—the distance from the top of the Button to the top of the form.

visible—boolean value to indicate whether or not the Button can be seen when the form is running.

width—the width (distance from the left edge to the right edge) of the Button control.

Events

onClick—triggered when the user clicks the Button.

onDesignLoad—triggered after the Button has been loaded at design time.

onServerClick—triggered after the Button has been clicked and any code associated with the **onClick** event has already been executed.

onServerLoad—triggered after the Button has actually been opened.

The CheckBox

Properties

checked—boolean property that indicates whether or not the CheckBox control is checked.

className—a read-only property that identifies the type (class) of the CheckBox. For standard CheckBoxes, the **className** property will always be CheckBox. This property is really just provided for your reference or to check the type (class) of an object at runtime.

color—sets the color of the CheckBox's text.

dataLink—specifies a field of a Query control whose data is to be displayed via the CheckBox.

fontBold—boolean value specifying whether or not the font of the CheckBox's text should be bolded.

fontItalic—boolean value specifying whether or not the font of the CheckBox's text should be italicized.

fontName—specifies the name of the font to use for the CheckBox's text.

fontStrikeout—boolean value specifying whether or not the font of the CheckBox's text should be displayed with the Strikeout enabled.

fontUnderline—boolean value specifying whether or not the font of the CheckBox's text should be underlined.

form—the form on which the CheckBox is located.

height—the distance from the top edge of the CheckBox to the bottom edge.

left—the distance from the left edge of the CheckBox from the left edge of the form itself.

name—the name of the CheckBox control.

pageno—the page of the form on which the CheckBox is located. If **pageno** is 0, the control will appear on each of the form's pages.

parent—the object that owns the CheckBox. This will typically be the form.

text—the text displayed next to the actual box.

top—the distance from the top of the CheckBox to the top of the form.

visible—boolean value to indicate whether or not the CheckBox can be seen when the form is running.

width—the width (distance from the left edge to the right edge) of the CheckBox control.

Events

canRender—triggered before the CheckBox is rendered. If your code returns false, the CheckBox will not be drawn. Also note, this event is only triggered when the control is used in a report.

onClick—triggered when the user clicks the CheckBox.

onDesignLoad—triggered after the CheckBox has been loaded at design time.

onRender—triggered after the CheckBox is rendered. Also note, this event is only triggered when the control is in used in a report.

onServerLoad—triggered after the CheckBox has actually been opened.

The Database Control

Properties

active—boolean value specifying whether the data connection is open or closed.

cacheUpdates—boolean value specifying whether or not the BDE should cache the records or write them to disk on each update.

className—a read-only property that identifies the type (class) of the Database control. For standard Database controls, the **className** property will always be Database. This property is really just provided for your reference or to check the type (class) of an object at runtime.

databaseName—BDE alias where the table(s) are located. The **databaseName** property can also maintain certain properties of the alias.

driverName—specifies the name of the BDE driver used for the current connection. It is read-only and set automatically by the BDE when the connection is opened.

handle—the BDE handle of the Database control.

loginString—allows for transparent (i.e., no login dialog box) log into password-protected tables. The user name and password are provided in the form username/password; if either of the parameters is incorrect, the login dialog will appear.

parent—the object that owns the Database control. This will typically be the form.

session—points to a Session control already on the form. The Session control maintains additional properties relevant to the working of the Database control.

Events

The Database control has no events.

The Form "Control"

*Note: Technically, the **Form** object is not a control. However, because it appears in every project, it should be included in this list as well*

Properties

background—an image file that is to be displayed in a tiled pattern on the back of the Form (i.e., behind all controls). It's best to set this property after you've done all other visual design work in your project as this image will actually cover up the design grid.

className—a read-only property that identifies the type (class) of the Form. If you are using a standard, generic Form, the **className** property is usually the word "form" added to the Form's file name. For example, the Form in Project1.jfm would be called Project1form. This property is really just provided for your reference or to check the type (class) of an object at runtime.

color—the background color of the Form. The **color** property may not affect the Form's appearance if a background image is used.

elements—an array object that maintains a list of the controls on a Form. You might use the **elements** property to reference each of the Form's controls, one at a time.

gridLineWidth—when a browser requests a Form, IntraBuilder actually converts the .jfm Form file to an HTML document. In order to align the controls, it actually creates an HTML table and then embeds the controls in that table. The **gridLineWidth** property, then, is the width of this table's grid lines. By default, **gridLineWidth** is 0, which means that users will not see the HTML table. To show the table, simply set the **gridLineWidth** to something greater than zero. The difference between the two can easily be seen in Figure 12.1 and Figure 12.2.

height—the distance from the top edge of the Form to the bottom edge.

left—the distance of the left edge of the Form is from the left edge of the screen. Also note, this value only affects the Form at design-time or when it is being run directly from within the IntraBuilder environment. It does not in any way affect the Form when viewed through a browser.

pageno—the page that is currently visible. Although you're unlikely to ever need them all, each Form has 256 pages (numbered 0 to 255). Each page

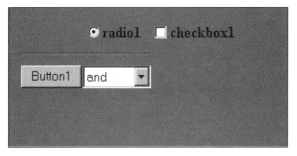

Figure 12.1   gridLineWidth = 0.

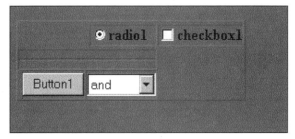

Figure 12.2   gridLineWidth = 1.

can have its own controls, but all pages share the Form's **background** and **color** properties. Setting the **pageno** property determines which of these pages is visible at any one time.

rowset—contains properties for the selected rows of a Query object.

title—the Form's caption (when run from within IntraBuilder) or the title of the Form when viewed through a browser.

top—the distance from the top of the screen to the top of the Form. Note: This value only affects the Form at design time or when it is being run directly from the IntraBuilder environment. It does not seem to affect the Form when viewed through a browser.

virtualRoot—the working directory of the project. All of your applications' file references will be relative to the **virtualRoot**.

width—the width (distance from the left edge to the right edge) of the Form.

Events

onDesignLoad—triggered after the Form has been loaded at design time.

onLoad—triggered after the document has been loaded (into the browser).

onServerLoad—triggered after the Form has actually been opened.

onServerSubmit—triggered after the Form has been submitted.

onServerUnload—triggered after the Form is closed.

preRender—triggered just before the IntraBuilder Form in converted to HTML for viewing through a browser.

The Hidden Control

Properties

className—a read-only property that identifies the type (class) of the Hidden control. For standard Hidden controls, the **className** property will always be hidden. This property is really just provided for your reference or to check the type (class) of an object at runtime.

form—the form on which the Hidden control is located.

left—the distance from the left edge of the Hidden control from the left edge of the form itself.

name—the name of the Hidden control.

pageno—the page of the form on which the Hidden control is located. If **pageno** is 0, the control will appear on each of the form's pages.

parent—the object that owns the Hidden control. This will typically be the form.

top—distance from the top of the Hidden to the top of the form.

value—the value stored in the Hidden control.

Events

onDesignLoad—triggered after the Hidden control has been loaded at design time.

onServerLoad—triggered after the Hidden control has actually been opened.

The HTML Control

Properties

alignHorizontal—sets the horizontal alignment of text contained in the HTML control. Possible values include these:

0—text is left justified

1—text is centered

2—text is right justified

3—affects the control only when the **trackJustifyThreshold** property is true

alignVertical—sets the vertical alignment of the text contained in the HTML control. Possible values include these:

0—text is flush with the top of the HTML control

1—text is centered vertically

2—text is flush with the bottom of the HTML control

3—affects the control only when the **verticalJustifyLimit** property is true

borderStyle—places of 10 possible borders around the HTML control. Also note, **borderStyle** only affects the HTML control at design time or when the form is run directly from the IntraBuilder environment. No borders whatsoever are visible when the form is viewed through a browser.

className—a read-only property that identifies the type (class) of the HTML control. For standard HTML controls, the **className** property will always be HTML. This property is really just provided for your reference or to check the type (class) of an object at runtime.

color—sets the color of the HTML's text.

fixed—boolean value specifying whether or not the text of the HTML control should be displayed with a fixed width font.

fontBold—boolean value specifying whether or not the font of the HTML control's text should be bolded.

fontItalic—boolean value specifying whether or not the font of the HTML control's text should be italicized.

fontName—specifies the name of the font to use for the HTML control's text.

fontStrikeout—boolean value specifying whether or not the font of the HTML control's text should be displayed with the Strikeout enabled.

fontUnderline—boolean value specifying whether or not the font of the HTML control's text should be underlined.

form—the form on which the HTML control is located.

height—the distance from the top edge of the HTML control to the bottom edge.

leading—the space between the lines of text contained in the HTML control.

left—the distance from the left edge of the HTML control from the left edge of the form itself.

marginHorizontal—the horizontal space between the text and the edge of the HTML control.

marginVertical—the vertical space between the text and the edge of the HTML control.

name—the name of the HTML control.

pageno—the page of the form on which the HTML control is located. If **pageno** is 0, the control will appear on each of the form's pages.

parent—the object that owns the HTML control. This will typically be the form.

rotate—rotates the text contained within the HTML control. Possible values include these:

0—no rotation

1—rotates text 90 degrees

2—rotates text 180 degrees

3—rotates text 270 degrees

> *Note: **rotate** only affects the HTML control at design time or when the form is run directly from the IntraBuilder environment. No rotation at all will be shown when the form is viewed through a browser.*

suppressIfBlank—boolean value specifying whether the HTML control should be rendered if it contains no text.

suppressIfDuplicate—boolean value specifying whether the HTML control should be rendered if it has not changed since the previous rendering.

template—via a combination of one or more control characters, the **template** property forces the characters being displayed in the HTML control to conform to a certain format. The control characters and their meanings are as follows:

X—any character, no change

!—any character, converted to uppercase

A—letters only

#—numbers, spaces, and + or -

9—numbers, and + or-only

> *Note: Additional non-control characters can be also be used where needed. The characters "-", ".", and "," would be examples of this. The template 999-99-9999, for instance, would force the text to fit a social security number format. Also note, the **template** property is equivalent to the **EditMask** property of Delphi's TDBEdit control.*

text—the raw text displayed in the HTML control, complete with formatting tags.

top—the distance from the top of the HTML control to the top of the form.

tracking—the space between characters; comparable to pitch. Also note, **tracking** affects the HTML control only at design time or when the form is run directly from the IntraBuilder environment. No special spacing will be shown when the form is viewed through a browser.

trackJustifyThreshold—the maximum space allowed between words. This inter-word space is added by IntraBuilder to try to justify the text. Also note, **trackJustifyThreshold** affects the HTML control only at design time or when the form is run directly from the IntraBuilder environment. Its effects will not be visible when the form is viewed through a browser.

variableHeight—boolean property specifying whether or not the HTML control can resize itself to show all of its text, in the event that the text is too large to be fully displayed within the HTML control's edges.

verticalJustifyLimit—the maximum space allowed between lines. This inter-line space is added by IntraBuilder to try to justify the text. Also note, **verticalJustifyLimit** affects the HTML control only at design time or when the form is run directly from the IntraBuilder environment. Its effects will not be visible when the form is viewed through a browser.

visible—boolean value to indicate whether or not the HTML can be seen when the form is running.

width—the width (distance from the left edge to the right edge) of the HTML control.

Events

canRender—triggered before the HTML control is rendered. If your code returns false, the HTML control will not be drawn. Also note, this event is only triggered when the control is used in a report.

onDesignLoad—triggered after the HTML control has been loaded at design time.

onRender—triggered after the HTML control is rendered. Note: This event is only triggered when the control is in used in a report.

onServerLoad—triggered after the HTML control has actually been opened.

The Image Control

Properties

alignment—this property determines how the picture contained in the Image control will be displayed. Possible values and their meanings are as follows:

0—the picture is resized to fit the Image control

1—if the picture is smaller than the Image control, the picture will be positioned in the upper-left-hand corner of the Image control

2—the picture will be centered in the Image control

3—the picture is resized to fit the Image control as well as it can while maintaining the height/width ratio

4—the Image control is resized to fit the picture

*Note: The **alignment** property is comparable to the **Autosize** and **Stretch** properties of Delphi's TImage.*

className—a read-only property that identifies the type (class) of the Image control. For standard Image controls, the **className** property will always be Image. This property is really just provided for your reference or to check the type (class) of an object at runtime.

dataSource—specifies picture to be displayed in the Image control. The **dataSource** can be either a file to be loaded from disk or a binary field in a table.

form—the form on which the Image control is located.

height—the distance from the top edge of the Image control to the bottom edge.

left—the distance from the left edge of the Image control from the left edge of the form itself.

name—the name of the Image control.

pageno—the page of the form on which the Image control is located. If **pageno** is 0, the control will appear on each of the form's pages.

parent—the object that owns the Image control. This will typically be the form.

text—the text displayed next to the actual box.

top—the distance from the top of the Image control to the top of the form.

visible—boolean value to indicate whether or not the Image control can be seen when the form is running.

width—the width (distance from the left edge to the right edge) of the Image control.

Events

canRender—triggered before the Image control is rendered. If your code returns false, the Image control will not be drawn. Also note, this event is only triggered when the control is used in a report.

onDesignLoad—triggered after the Image control has been loaded at design time.

onImageClick—triggered as a client-side event when the user clicks the Image control.

onImageServerClick—triggered as a server-side event when the user clicks the Image control. the **onImageServerClick** event supersedes **onImageClick**; in other words, if **onImageServerClick** is used, **onImageClick** will not be triggered. The onImageServerClick event is the one to use for image maps—do not use **onImageClick**.

onRender—triggered after the Image control is rendered. Also note that this event is only triggered when the control is in used in a report.

onServerLoad—triggered after the Image control has actually been opened.

The Java Applet Control

Properties

alt—this property is a string to be displayed in place of the Java applet in the event that the browser does not support Java.

className—a read-only property that identifies the type (class) of the JavaApplet control. For standard Java Applet controls, the **className** property will always be Java Applet. This property is really just provided for your reference or to check the type (class) of an object at runtime.

code—the name of the Java class file that contains the applet.

codeBase—the URL of the Java class file.

form—the form on which the Java Applet control is located.

left—the distance from the left edge of the Java Applet control from the left edge of the form itself.

name—the name of the Java Applet control.

pageno—the page of the form on which the Java Applet control is located. If **pageno** is 0, the control will appear on each of the form's pages.

parent—the object that owns the Java Applet control. This will typically be the form.

params—the parameters to be passed to the applet. This is comparable to the PARAM name= tag used when including applets in HTML documents.

top—distance from the top of the JavaApplet to the top of the form.

width—the width (distance from the left edge to the right edge) of the Java Applet control.

Events

onDesignLoad—triggered after the Java Applet has been loaded at design time.

onServerLoad—triggered after the Java Applet control has actually been opened.

The Password Control

Properties

className—a read-only property that identifies the type (class) of the Password control. For standard Password controls, the **className** property will always be Password. This property is really just provided for your reference or to check the type (class) of an object at runtime.

dataLink—specifies a field of a Query control whose data is to be displayed via the Password control.

form—the form on which the Password control is located.

left—the distance from the left edge of the Password control from the left edge of the form itself.

name—the name of the Password control.

pageno—the page of the form on which the Password control is located. If **pageno** is 0, the control will appear on each of the form's pages.

parent—the object that owns the Password control. This will typically be the form.

top—distance from the top of the Password to the top of the form.

value—the actual password (as opposed to the asterisks) displayed in the Password control.

visible—boolean value to indicate whether or not the Password control can be seen when the form is running.

width—the width (distance from the left edge to the right edge) of the Password control.

Events

onDesignLoad—triggered after the Password has been loaded at design time.

onServerLoad—triggered after the Password control has actually been opened.

The Query Control

Properties

active—boolean value specifying whether the connection is open or closed.

className—a read-only property that identifies the type (class) of the Query control. For standard Queries, the **className** property will always be Query. This property is really just provided for your reference or to check the type (class) of an object at runtime.

constrained—boolean value specifying whether changes to the Query's data are to be validated against portions of the SQL statement.

database—BDE alias where the table(s) are located. The **database** property can also maintain certain properties of the alias.

handle—the BDE handle of the Query control.

parent—the object that owns the Query control. This will typically be the form.

requestLive—boolean property comparable in purpose to read only. If **requestLive** is true, the data can be edited; otherwise, it is essentially read-only.

rowset—object that maintains properties about the rows (of data) retrieved by the Query's **sql** property.

session—points to a Session control already on the form. The Session control maintains additional properties relative to the working of the Query control.

sql—the SQL statement that retrieves data from the table(s) to be used in the current form.

unidirectional—boolean value that specifies whether the data will be navigated in the forward direction only. Setting **unidirectional** to true will increase the performance provided that the user only goes forward; they may or may not be able to go backwards—depending on the SQL server itself—but doing so will be very slow.

updateWhere—determines which fields are updated by the Query control.

Events

canClose—triggered before the Query is closed. Returns a value indicating whether the Query can be closed or not.

canOpen—triggered before the Query is opened. Returns a value indicating whether the Query can be opened or not.

onClose—triggered after the Query is closed.

onOpen—triggered after the Query is opened.

The Radio Control

Properties

className—a read-only property that identifies the type (class) of the Radio. For standard Radios, the **className** property will always be Radio. This property is really just provided for your reference or to check the type (class) of an object at runtime.

color—sets the color of the Radio's text.

dataLink—specifies a field (boolean type) of a Query control whose data is to be displayed via the Radio.

fontBold—boolean value specifying whether or not the font of the Radio's text should be bolded.

fontItalic—boolean value specifying whether or not the font of the Radio's text should be italicized.

fontName—specifies the name of the font to use for the Radio's text.

fontStrikeout—boolean value specifying whether or not the font of the Radio's text should be displayed with the Strikeout enabled.

fontUnderline—boolean value specifying whether or not the font of the Radio's text should be underlined.

form—the form on which the Radio is located.

GroupName—this value is used to link two or more Radios together. It is sometimes necessary to use several sets of Radios on one form. Since only one Radio can be selected at a time, this property can be used to group the Radios together.

height—the distance from the top edge of the Radio to the bottom edge.

left—the distance from the left edge of the Radio from the left edge of the form itself.

name—the name of the Radio control.

pageno—the page of the form on which the Radio is located. If **pageno** is 0, the control will appear on each of the form's pages.

parent—the object that owns the Radio. This will typically be the form.

text—the text displayed next to the actual radio button.

top—the distance from the top of the Radio to the top of the form.

value—boolean value to indicate whether the Radio button is filled in or not; i.e., has/has not been selected by the user.

visible—boolean value to indicate whether or not the Radio can be seen when the form is running.

width—the width (distance from the left edge to the right edge) of the Radio control.

Events

canRender—triggered before the Radio is rendered. If your code returns false, the Radio will not be drawn. Also note, this event is only triggered when the control is used in a report.

onClick—triggered when the user clicks the Radio.

onDesignLoad—triggered after the Radio has been loaded at design time.

onRender—triggered after the Radio is rendered. Also note, this event is only triggered when the control is in used in a report.

onServerLoad—triggered after the Radio has actually been opened.

The Reset Control

Properties

className—a read-only property that identifies the type (class) of the Reset control. For standard Reset controls, the **className** property will always be Reset. This property is really just provided for your reference or to check the type (class) of an object at runtime.

form—the form on which the Reset control is located.

left—the distance from the left edge of the Reset control from the left edge of the form itself.

name—the name of the Reset control.

pageno—the page of the form on which the Reset control is located. If **pageno** is 0, the control will appear on each of the form's pages.

parent—the object that owns the Reset control. This will typically be the form.

text—the text displayed on the Reset control itself.

top—the distance from the top of the Reset control to the top of the form.

visible—boolean value to indicate whether or not the Reset control can be seen when the form is running.

width—the width (distance from the left edge to the right edge) of the Reset control.

Events

onClick—triggered when the user clicks the Reset control.

onDesignLoad—triggered after the Reset control has been loaded at design time.

onServerLoad—triggered after the Reset control has actually been opened.

The Rule Control

Properties

className—a read-only property that identifies the type (class) of the Rule. For standard Rules, the **className** property will always be Rule. This property is really just provided for your reference or to check the type (class) of an object at runtime.

form—the form on which the Rule is located.

left—the distance from the left end of the Rule from the left edge of the form itself.

name—the name of the Rule control.

pageno—the page of the form on which the Rule is located. If **pageno** is 0, the control will appear on each of the form's pages.

parent—the object that owns the Rule. This will typically be the form.

right—distance from the right end of the Rule to the right edge of the form.

size—the thickness of the Rule.

top—distance from the top of the Rule to the top of the form.

Events

canRender—triggered before the Rule is rendered. If your code returns false, the Rule will not be drawn. Also note, this event is only triggered when the control is used in a report.

onDesignLoad—triggered after the Rule has been loaded at design time.

onRender—triggered after the Rule is rendered. Also note, this event is only triggered when the control is in used in a report.

onServerLoad—triggered after the Rule has actually been opened.

The Select Control

Properties

className—a read-only property that identifies the type (class) of the Select. For standard Selects, the **className** property will always be Select. This property is really just provided for your reference or to check the type (class) of an object at runtime.

dataLink—specifies a field of a Query control whose data is to be displayed or set via the Select control.

form—the form on which the Select control is located.

left—the distance from the left edge of the Select control from the left edge of the form itself.

name—the name of the Select control.

options—specifies the options to be displayed in the Select control. The **options** property can be used to be display an array of values or a list of files matching a criteria.

pageno—the page of the form on which the Select is located. If **pageno** is 0, the control will appear on each of the form's pages.

parent—the object that owns the Select. This will typically be the form.

top—distance from the top of the Select to the top of the form.

value—the option displayed in the Select. Usually, this is the item the user has selected from the list of options. If no item has yet been selected, the first option is used as the default value.

visible—boolean value to indicate whether or not the Select can be seen when the form is running.

width—the width (distance from the left edge to the right edge) of the Select control.

Events

onBlur—triggered when the user selects/highlights a control other than the Select control; i.e., when the Select control "loses focus."

onChange—triggered after the text displayed in the Select is changed.

onDesignLoad—triggered after the Select has been loaded at design time.

onFocus—triggered when the user selects/highlights the Select control; i.e., when the Select receives the focus.

onServerLoad—triggered after the Select has actually been opened.

The SelectList Control

Properties

className—a read-only property that identifies the type (class) of the SelectList. For standard SelectLists, the **className** property will always be ListBox. This property is really just provided for your reference or to check the type (class) of an object at runtime.

form—the form on which the SelectList control is located.

left—the distance from the left edge of the SelectList control from the left edge of the form itself.

multiple—a boolean value indicating whether the user can select only one (false) or several items at one time (true).

name—the name of the SelectList control.

options—specifies the options to be displayed in the SelectList control. The **options** property can be used to be display an array of values or a list of files matching a criteria.

pageno—the page of the form on which the SelectList is located. If **pageno** is 0, the control will appear on each of the form's pages.

parent—the object that owns the SelectList. This will typically be the form.

selected—an array property containing a list of the items the user has selected from the SelectList control.

top—distance from the top of the SelectList to the top of the form.

value—the option displayed in the SelectList. Usually, this is the item the user has SelectListed from the list of options. If no item has yet been selected, the first option is used as the default value.

visible—boolean value to indicate whether or not the SelectList can be seen when the form is running.

width—the width (distance from the left edge to the right edge) of the SelectList control.

Events

onBlur—triggered when the user selects/highlights a control other than the SelectList control; i.e., when the SelectList control loses focus.

onChange—triggered after the focus leaves the SelectList control if there has been a change with respect to which items (if any) are selected.

onDesignLoad—triggered after the SelectList has been loaded at design time.

onFocus—triggered when the user selects/highlights the SelectList control; i.e., when the SelectList receives the focus.

onServerLoad—triggered after the SelectList has actually been opened.

The Session Control

Properties

className—a read-only property that identifies the type (class) of the Session control. For standard Session controls, the **className** property will always be Session. This property is really just provided for your reference or to check the type (class) of an object at runtime.

handle—the BDE handle of the Session control.

lockRetryCount—when data in a given field is being edited, IntraBuilder attempts to lock the record so that no other users may edit it at the same time. If the attempt to lock a record fails, IntraBuilder will retry it the number of times specified in **lockRetryCount**.

lockRetryInterval—the number of seconds IntraBuilder will wait between each successive attempt to lock a record. See **lockRetryCount** above.

parent—the object that owns the Session control. This will typically be the form.

Events

The Session control has no events.

The Text Control

Properties

className—a read-only property that identifies the type (class) of the Text control. For standard Text controls, the **className** property will always be Text. This property is really just provided for your reference or to check the type (class) of an object at runtime.

dataLink—specifies a field of a Query control whose data is to be displayed via the Text control.

form—the form on which the Text control is located.

left—the distance from the left edge of the Text control from the left edge of the form itself.

name—the name of the Text control.

pageno—the page of the form on which the Text control is located. If **pageno** is 0, the control will appear on each of the form's pages.

parent—the object that owns the Text control. This will typically be the form.

template—via a combination of one or more control characters, **template** property forces the characters being displayed in the Text control to conform to a certain format. The control characters and their meanings are as follows:

X—any character, no change

!—any character, converted to uppercase

A—letters only

#—numbers, spaces, and + or -

9—numbers, and + or-only

Note: Additional non-control characters can be also be used where needed. The characters "-", ".", and "," would be examples of this. The template 999-99-9999, for instance, would force the data being entered to fit the social security format. Also note, the template property is equivalent to the EditMask property of Delphi's TDBEdit control.

top—distance from the top of the Text to the top of the form.

value—text displayed in the Text control.

visible—boolean value to indicate whether or not the Text control can be seen when the form is running.

width—the width (distance from the left edge to the right edge) of the Text control.

Events

onBlur—triggered when the user selects/highlights a control other than the Text control; i.e., when the Text control loses focus.

onChange—triggered after the text displayed in the Text control is changed.

onDesignLoad—triggered after the Text has been loaded at design time.

onFocus—triggered when the user selects/highlights the Text control; i.e., when the Text control receives the focus.

onSelect—triggered when the user marks or selects a block of text displayed within the Text control.

onServerLoad—triggered after the Text control has actually been opened.

The TextArea Control

Properties

className—a read-only property that identifies the type (class) of the TextArea. For standard TextAreas, the **className** property will always be TextArea. This property is really just provided for your reference or to check the type (class) of an object at runtime.

dataLink—specifies a field of a Query control whose data is to be displayed via the TextArea.

form—the form on which the TextArea is located.

left—the distance from the left edge of the TextArea from the left edge of the form itself.

name—the name of the TextArea control.

pageno—the page of the form on which the TextArea is located. If **pageno** is 0, the control will appear on each of the form's pages.

parent—the object that owns the TextArea. This will typically be the form.

readOnly—boolean property specifying whether or not the text contained in the TextArea control can be edited. If **readOnly** is false, the user will be allowed to edit the text.

top—distance from the top of the TextArea to the top of the form.

value—text displayed in the TextArea.

visible—boolean value to indicate whether or not the TextArea can be seen when the form is running.

width—the width (distance from the left edge to the right edge) of the TextArea control.

Events

onBlur—triggered when the user selects/highlights a control other than the TextArea control; i.e., when the TextArea control loses focus.

onChange—triggered after the text displayed in the TextArea is changed.

onDesignLoad—triggered after the TextArea has been loaded at design time.

onFocus—triggered when the user selects/highlights the TextArea control; i.e., when the TextArea receives the focus.

onSelect—triggered when the user marks or selects a block of text displayed within the TextArea.

onServerLoad—triggered after the TextArea has actually been opened.

Security and Encryption

Matt Telles

13

Controlling access to tables, access to the IntraBuilder environment, and access to data: here's how to use IntraBuilder's built-in security features.

*I*n all the hype and interest in publishing data on the Internet, the issue of data security often rears its ugly head. It is all well and good to make certain corporate information instantly available to Web browsers, but not when that information is a valuable asset like your known-buyers list and the casual browser is your direct competitor. No company wants that result from new technology.

IntraBuilder combats the problem of unintended access to your private data through the twin powers of *security* and *encryption*. Security allows you to control who has access to both IntraBuilder and the data (tables) offered within it. Encryption, on the other hand, allows you to make your data unreadable, even if a user manages to access it somehow. By using the security features built into IntraBuilder, you can tightly control who has access to specific tables, who has access to the IntraBuilder environment, and who can view the data in a meaningful way. These features, essential in any corporate environment, differentiate IntraBuilder from simple Web data-access packages.

How Does IntraBuilder Provide Security?

IntraBuilder provides the vast majority of its security features through a single object: the **_sys** object. This object, which represents the entire IntraBuilder system functionality, has a large number of functions available to it. We can browse the **_sys** object (as shown in Figure 13.1) through the Script Pad to see just what functionality is available. To do this, bring up the Script Pad by selecting View|Script Pad from the main IntraBuilder IDE menu.

> *Note: The **inspect** function is one of the most powerful commands in the IntraBuilder environment. It can be used to browse the properties, methods, and events of any object in the IntraBuilder system, or to avoid reading through the on-line help files or printed documentation. It is invaluable for browsing objects created by other programmers as well. **Inspect** is your friend; use it well.*

For purposes of security and encryption of database tables, the important functionality is found in the **protection** object embedded in the **_sys** object. Like the **_sys** object, the **protection** object can be browsed through the Script Pad by bringing up the Script Pad window (if it is not already up) and entering the following command in the edit window (followed by <ENTER>).

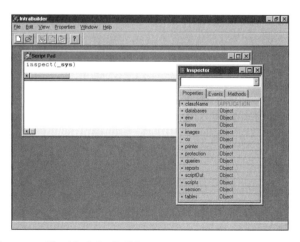

Figure 13.1   The _sys object in IntraBuilder.

```
inspect (_sys.protection)
```

Your Inspector window should now look like the one shown in Figure 13.2. As you can see, the **protection** object is quite simple. It has a single property that is its class name (as do all IntraBuilder objects) and only a single method, protect. The protect method takes no arguments.

If this object has no properties and only a single method (with no arguments—yet), where is this all-important security and encryption? How do we protect our databases and set up different users and encrypt tables? You will soon see that the single method (protect) is much more than it seems at first glance.

To invoke the protect method of the protection object and kick off the whole IntraBuilder security process, from the Script Pad window enter the following command into the command editor and press Enter.

```
_sys.protection.protect()
```

Protecting The System

When you invoke the protect method, the first visible sign that something has happened is the display of a password dialog requesting that you enter a password for entry. This dialog, shown in Figure 13.3, is titled "Administrator Password." This certainly is interesting, since you have

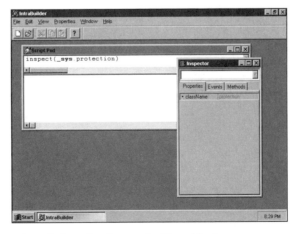

Figure 13.2   Inspector window showing protection object.

Figure 13.3 The System Administrator Password dialog.

probably never set up a password for the system administrator. Is there some sort of default password or will you need to somehow hack your way into the system to find the current password setting? The answer to both of these questions, surprisingly, is no.

The dialog displayed in Figure 13.3 will be displayed both before and after a system administrator password is defined. Actually, entering a password into the dialog and selecting OK will then display a second dialog requesting that you confirm your password choice by re-entering it. Once you have managed to enter the same password string twice, that password will become the new password for the system administrator.

Be sure to remember your password, because if you forget it you will be unable to access the IntraBuilder system. In addition, as we will see later, you will lose access to any encrypted database tables.

Once you have defined a system administrator password, you can now progress to the other properties of the security system, such as access control and user definition. When you specify the new password for the system, you will then see a brand new window appear on the IntraBuilder desktop window, the Security window.

Note: Although we went through the process programmatically, to show you how to get at the guts of the IntraBuilder system, we will show you in a moment how to get to the same point much more directly within the IntraBuilder Development Environment (IDE).

Once you have defined the system administrator password for your local IntraBuilder setup, the next logical step is to define users for the system. If you don't define users, you won't be able to get into the system to work. So you must define at least one user for the system. To add users, begin from the Security dialog (shown in Figure 13.4) and select the Users tab. Then click on the button labeled New to create a new user.

Parts To A User

As you can see from the dialog shown in Figure 13.4, each user defined within the IntraBuilder security system has several associated attributes, which, if understood, can be used to their fullest advantage.

The first choice is Group, which is a way to collect users with similar needs into a single category for use within the system. Security profiles in many systems are based around this group concept. Groups you might define within your own IntraBuilder environment, could be these:

◆ Administration—People assigned to the administration of the database environment. Administrative personnel are usually able to create new database tables, modify existing tables, or delete outdated tables. Within a database, administrators can normally add, modify, or delete records. Administrators would rarely modify forms or reports, but might need the ability to delete them.

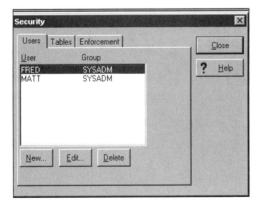

Figure 13.4   Security window in IntraBuilder.

◆ Designers—People assigned to creating new IntraBuilder applications or enhancing existing applications. Designers will quite often need the ability to add, delete, or modify existing tables, although they might not be permitted to delete tables in some environments. Mostly they will add new forms and reports or modify existing ones, and they would most likely not need the ability to delete forms, reports, or tables.

◆ Users—People who occasionally need the ability to run reports or forms within the IntraBuilder environment. Although users will normally work within Web browsers using the IntraBuilder server application, on occasion they will need to try things inside the IDE. Users will probably not be allowed to add, modify, or delete any report or form (and certainly not tables) within the IntraBuilder setup.

You are free, of course, to set up your groups in anyway that you see fit. Once you decide on a group, however, you should only use entries within your defined group list for this field (Group) entries. There is no need to do anything special to add a new group because it will automatically be added when you enter a group name within this first edit field of the New User dialog. Groups are automatically created with default permissions, which we will look at in a few moments. Group names may be up to eight characters in length.

The second attribute for a new user is the User Name (also eight characters), which represents the login name of the new user. This is a short version of Identification, which identifies the user to the IntraBuilder system. Generally, the naming convention used is the first letter of the first name, followed by up to seven characters of the last name. The user name for John Smith would be JSMITH. User names generally consist of only numbers and letters, although IntraBuilder does permit punctuation marks, spaces, and other characters (&, ^, or #, for example) in user names.

The third important component to an IntraBuilder user is the Password attribute. The password field may be up to 16 characters long and may contain numbers, letters, punctuation marks, and other keyboard characters that are printable. The password in the New User dialog is always displayed so that you can see it as you are setting up the user. When you try to log on to the system, however, the password field will not display what is entered (showing instead asterisks), so it is important that you enter it correctly here. The password field is used to identify a user and should be chosen with care. It needs to be something that a user will remember, yet something that other people will not easily guess. If you are on a networked system, consider using the same user name and password for IntraBuilder that you use for the network system in order to minimize the number of names to remember and lessen the chance that you'll resort to writing them down.

The combination of group, user name, and password are the fields required to log into the IntraBuilder system. Each user should have a separate login to the system. Further, these logins should be used to control access to the individual tables of the system. How do you control this table access? The answer lies in the next user attribute: the Access Level.

IntraBuilder provides for eight levels of access control to the tables in the system. Although it is conventional to assign access levels in decreasing order of security (level one has complete access, level eight has little access), IntraBuilder doesn't require you to assign numbers specifically. It will set up access for a minimum access level, but that level can be anything you would like. You may find that you do not need all eight levels of security, or that eight levels is too restrictive. Your mileage may vary, of course. We will look at the logistics of assigning privileges to individual access levels when we talk about the Tables tab in the Security window.

In general, you will probably want to assign access levels to users according to the groups you assign to those users. There will probably be some individual exceptions, but this is a good starting point for access level control. Once we look at how access levels are actually assigned and used, you may have a better feel for using them.

The final attribute for a user in the system is the Full Name attribute. This is simply a descriptor field that you can use, for example, to customize the screens for your users to make them feel a bit more at home. The full name field of the New User window will hold a varying number of characters based on the width (it is a non-scrolling edit box), but you can generally assume a 31-character limit on the length of the name you can enter. It is not actually required that you use this field for the name. You could, for example, enter "Matt The Magnificent" in this field. IntraBuilder considers this field to be a comment field for your exclusive use.

Where Has All The Data Gone?

When you enter a new user (or assign a system password, for that matter), IntraBuilder will create a new file called dbsystem.db in the bin directory of the IntraBuilder installation tree. As an example, if you had installed IntraBuilder in the D:\IntraBuilder directory, you will find this file as D:\IntraBuilder\bin\dbsystem.db. This file contains all of the user information. If the file is deleted or corrupted, you will lose the security access for the system and be unable to access encrypted tables.

Since the dbsystem.db file is obviously a weak point in the security system, it is recommended that you do not allow users to modify or delete this file on the system and that you back it up regularly.

Another file in the same (bin) directory that can be of interest to the system administrator is the monitor.log file. This file contains information about the running of the system. It will tell you when the system starts up, from where it is run, and when it shuts down. From a security standpoint, this file doesn't contain the total amount of information you might like, but it can be useful in tracking down issues of responsibility on your system.

Doing It The Easy Way

Up to this point we have discussed reaching the security screens in IntraBuilder the hard way—programmatically. There are two reasons why. First, it shows you how you can easily extend the power of IntraBuilder by building on the built-in components of the system. Second, it exposes the power of the built-in browsing capabilities of the system and shows you how to look at any object by using the inspect function in the Script Pad. Normally, however, you would expect the system administrator's access to the security screens to be a bit more streamlined. As we will see now, that access can be quite direct indeed.

From the main menu in IntraBuilder, select the File menu and navigate to the Database Administration menu item. Or you can press the ALT+F and

D keys. In either case, you will see the Database Administration window, as shown in Figure 13.5. In this window, you simply select the Security button to move into the familiar Password window for the system and from there to the Security window.

Normally when you enter the Database Administration window, the database type combo box will read dBase, and the only available button will be the Security button. If you select the combo box and change the selection to Paradox (at this time the only other choice), however, you will notice that the Referential Integrity button will become operational. (I'll explain more about the Referential Integrity button options just a little later in this chapter.)

Before We Were So Rudely Interrupted

A moment ago, before launching off onto a tangent about the easier ways to get to the Security window, we were talking about the tabs on the Security window. The first tab, which we just discussed, is the Users tab. The second is the Tables tab. We briefly mentioned this tab in relation to user groups and access levels. It is now time to examine this more completely.

The Tables window, shown in Figure 13.6, allows you to control access to tables in the IntraBuilder security model. Using this window, you can control who can view what tables, how they may be modified, and other esoteric functions.

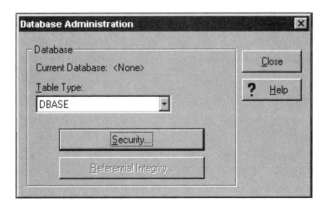

Figure 13.5 The Database Administration window.

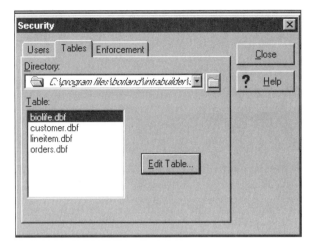

Figure 13.6   The Tables window.

The first thing that you will need to do in this window is to select a directory from which to edit tables. IntraBuilder keeps the complete path of the tables for which you define access information, which is both good and bad. It is good because it allows you to have multiple tables of the same name residing in different directories. It is bad, because if you move a table you will lose the access control you have over it. In spite of this, you can select a new directory by clicking on the browse button on the screen and navigate to the directory in which your database table files reside. Once you have moved to the directory by typing in the path or using the browse button, a list of database tables found in that directory will appear.

As a simple example, let's use the sample databases that appear in the samples directory of the IntraBuilder installation tree. If you select this directory (the default would be C:\program files\borland\intrabuilder\samples), you should see several tables shown in the list box. Select the customer.dbf table and click on the Edit button. You should now see the Edit Table Privileges window, as shown in Figure 13.7.

When you define access privileges for a table, you make use of the group and access level attributes that you defined during the new user creation phase. Basically, you define general group access and then fine-tune the access for either the entire table or for individual fields within the table.

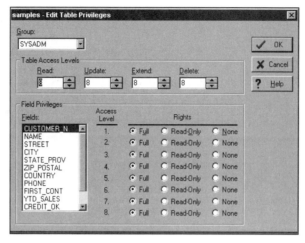

Figure 13.7   The Edit Table Privileges window.

Setting Table Level Access

The first group of access specifiers falls under the heading Table Access Levels. These specifiers refer to actions that affect the entire table. The list of possible actions that can be performed by the user are as follows: Read, Update, Extend, and Delete. Let's take a look at each category and see what you are getting yourself into.

Read access simply permits a user to open a database and view the contents of the table. Without read access, none of the other categories really matter, because the user will not be able to display the table data to do anything with it. You would normally grant read access to anyone who can log on to the system and has any reason to view the data in the table. You might deny read access if the data is confidential, such as salary information.

Update access permits the user to change existing data within the database. Where almost anyone probably was granted read access, you might be considerably more selective regarding granting update access to a table. In all likelihood, only a select group of people will be responsible for maintaining the information in tables for your system, and they would likely be placed in a single group that would be given update permission for the tables for which they are responsible. In the case of update permission, of course, we are only talking about tables related to reports, since tables for which data should be entered by the user would naturally require update permission.

Extend access permits the user to add new records to the database through the IntraBuilder system. If extend access is not granted to the user, that user will not be able to create new entries in the specified table. You could grant someone update access (which permits them to modify existing tables) without giving them extend rights. Extend privileges, which once again apply only to reporting tables, are generally reserved for the maintenance of table data.

Delete access, the highest level of change other than basic read access, permits the user to remove existing records from a table. Think carefully before allowing it to a user. When you give a group delete access, you have permitted them to remove all of the data in the table. Maintenance groups will need this capability, as will the system administration group.

Setting Field Level Access

In addition to permitting group members access to the table level, the gross—or highest—level, IntraBuilder can also control access on a much lower level, the field level. By using field-level privileges, you can protect individual fields from modification by the user. Field-level privileges are of three types: read only, delete, or full access.

Read-only access to a field permits the user to view contents and properties for a field, but does not allow them to modify or delete the field. Read-only access is most common when combined with table-level attributes. Most users will have higher than read-only access for most fields.

Delete access permits the user to delete a given field from the table but not modify the field properties, an all-or-nothing proposition. By restricting a user to delete access you are granting permission to modify the display of a table. Be careful when granting this level of permission to user groups.

Full access allows all modification privileges to a table field. Users with full access can modify the properties for a field, delete the field from the table, or view the field. Full access is the default setting for field level properties.

In general, you will probably never use field-level permissions in your own work. Large companies with serious security concerns might be interested in the field-level permission access, but few others will want to be bothered with this level of detail. In the majority of cases, if you wish to use table security at all in IntraBuilder, you will use table-level security.

Access Levels

The access level parameters we have talked about so far refer simply to a number between one and eight. Access levels allow you to screen out individual members of a group based on seniority, management level, or any other criteria you can imagine. IntraBuilder imposes no requirements on access levels, so you may assign them in any fashion you like. The one important factor in using access levels is the order in which they are used.

In IntraBuilder, access levels are in order of security level from highest to lowest, level one being the highest and level eight the lowest. This is the reason that IntraBuilder security access controls default to level eight, allowing all users access to all functions by default. While you can change this behavior by using the security screens we have been talking about, you should be careful when doing so. If you set the security access too low (requiring too many privileges), you may make it impossible for people to get their jobs done and therefore make the whole exercise rather pointless.

The Enforcement Tab

Returning for a moment to the Security window, let's close out the discussion by tackling the last tab of the window. The Enforcement tab, shown in Figure 13.8, allows you to determine when security access comes into play in the IntraBuilder system.

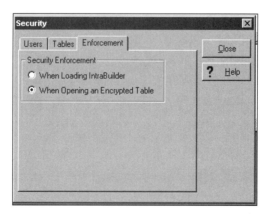

Figure 13.8 The Enforcement tab.

You have two choices when security comes into place: when IntraBuilder starts up or when an encrypted table is opened. If you elect to have security in place when IntraBuilder starts, each user will be required to log into the system before he/she can do anything else. In this traditional model for a security system, users must prove their identities before they are granted access to the system. In the second, less standard model, users will need only to log in when they try to access a table that has been protected by the IntraBuilder database administrator. In this case, the user may browse forms, reports, and unsecured database tables without being required to enter a user name or password. Obviously, this second method is not a good choice in an environment where you have users that you can't trust.

We talked about encrypted tables. How do they get that way? You will probably remember the Users window that we discussed at some length earlier in this chapter. In addition, we talked about the Tables tab and how it was used. When you went into the Tables tab, selected a table in the current database directory, and clicked the Edit button, you were brought into the Edit Table Privileges window. Selecting the settings in this dialog window—such as the table access levels—automatically encrypts the table. Once this is done, the IntraBuilder system automatically takes over and does the job of validating users and access levels. All in all, the system administrator's job is pretty easy.

Referential Integrity

The only remaining issue left in the security and encryption discussion revolves around referential integrity. What is it? Put simply, referential integrity in a database means that when one table refers to records in another table of the database, then that relationship will remain consistent regardless of changes to the database tables involved. If you delete one of the two records in the relationship, the other record must be deleted as well. This process is known as a *cascading delete*. In addition, if a record is added to one table, there must be a matching record added to the other table.

Referential integrity is not supported by all database engines. The dBase engine, for example, does not support these restrictions, while Paradox does. You enforce this integrity requirement through database rules that are stored within the database. IntraBuilder facilitates this process through the Referential Integrity Rules screen. To get to this screen, enter the database administration window by selecting File|Database Administration from the main IDE menu. In the database field, select Paradox from the drop-down combo box. This will enable the Referential Integrity button. Clicking this button will then take you to the Referential Integrity Rules window, shown in Figure 13.9.

When you initially display this window, the rule name list box is probably empty. To add a new rule, click the New button. This should bring you to the New Referential Integrity Rule window, shown in Figure 13.10, an imposing window. We will go through the pieces one at a time to make it a little less confusing. It is worth noting, however, that unless you are a database guru it is unlikely that you will ever have to deal with this window.

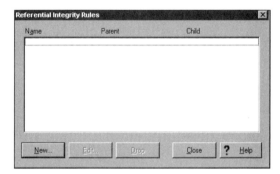

Figure 13.9   The Referential Integrity Rules window.

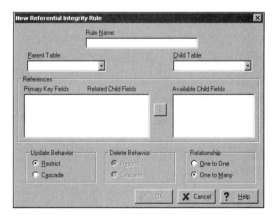

Figure 13.10   New Referential Integrity Rule window.

The first fields that you will need to set will be to select the parent and child tables for the rule. The parent table will be the master table in the equation, and will rely on entries in the child table to exist. Adding a record to the parent table that does not have an existing entry in the child table generates an error in IntraBuilder.

> *Note: If you would like to use a real live Paradox database in which you can actually view data and rules, select the Apps sub-directory in the IntraBuilder install tree and select the guestbk application directory. The guestbk.db file is a Paradox database with two tables in it that you can view.*

The next piece of the puzzle is to select the field in each table that represents the complete required relationship. This takes place with the two list boxes labeled Primary Key Fields and Related Child Fields. To create a new relationship between the two tables, select one of the fields in the Primary Key Fields list box and then the linked child field from the Related Child Fields list box. Click on the button labeled < to finish the link.

Following the fields are three radio button groups. The first radio button group, labeled Update Behavior, represents what should be done when a new record is added to the master table. The second radio button group, labeled Delete Behavior, represents what should be done when a record is deleted from the child table. In each case, the options are Cascade or Restrict.

Cascades apply to the deletion of required link records in child tables. When you enforce a cascade delete, you will cause all linked records to be deleted in order to keep the database integrity consistent. Although this is somewhat risky because you are potentially decimating a database table, you can control who has delete privileges through the Database Administration system. This ensures that you can restrict this operation to people who should at least know what they are doing.

Restricts, on the other hand, will simply generate an error message when you attempt to perform an action that violates the referential integrity of the tables in question. In this case, an error will be displayed and the operation aborted. Besides removing update and delete privileges, there are few ways to easily control this behavior when you enforce restricts.

The final radio button group in the Referential Integrity screen is entitled Relationship. In a master-child relationship there is only ever a single master record. There can, however, be multiple child records to that single master. The case in which there is only a single child record for each parent record is called a one-to-one relationship. The case in which there are multiple child records for a single parent record is called a one-to-many relationship. It is important to note, however, that a one-to-many relationship does not mean that there have to be multiple child records for each parent record, only that there can be multiples. In a one-to-one relationship, there can never be more than one child record for each parent record.

Explaining the complete rationale for referential integrity and the conditions under which it can be used are well beyond the scope of this book. If you have other questions that were not answered by this brief tutorial on the subject, please consult the reference guide for the specific database system that you are using.

The Password Object

A description of the security and encryption functionality of IntraBuilder wouldn't be complete without the mention of the password object. The password object is one of the standard component controls shown on the IntraBuilder component palette during the form design process. This object is of the class Password.

The Password class is almost entirely the same as the Text class, with one important difference. When text is typed into the password object at runtime, the text is not displayed. Instead, asterisks (*) are shown in place of the characters which are typed by the user. This makes it possible to guard the user entry from others that might be watching.

The Password object is generally used for login passwords, credit card numbers, and other information which the end-user would be unlikely to want to be seen by others in close proximity. When designing a screen that contains such information, you should strongly consider using the password object to do these kinds of jobs.

Conclusion

This chapter has been a brief, but I hope informative, introduction to the security and encryption features found in IntraBuilder. Here are some of the topics that should be somewhat familiar to you:

◆ How to create a database administrator password.

◆ How to create new users for IntraBuilder.

◆ How to encrypt tables.

◆ How to set up IntraBuilder to require user logins.

◆ How to set up access levels for different tables in IntraBuilder.

◆ A brief introduction to referential integrity and how to use IntraBuilder to enforce referential integrity rules.

Glossary

Terence Goggin

Keywords For IntraBuilder

ActiveX—Microsoft's new name for OCX controls. Also called Active Script. See OCX.

API—Acronym for Applications Programming Interface. Usually this is a set of functions or procedures that a vendor provides to developers wishing to write programs that work with the vendor's product. Microsoft, for example, provides the prospective Windows developer with several hundred functions that can be used to create Windows applications.

ASCII—Acronym for American Standard Code for Information Interchange. A binary code developed to act as a standardized means of representing plain text on computer systems. This code is used heavily in communications, especially when the communication is taking place between computers based on different platforms. Also used as a means of transferring data from one program to another, when no direct translation capability is available. Pronounced "ass-key."

Backbone—The line or set of lines that serve as the main "data pipe" for a network.

BMP—Acronym and DOS file extension for bitmapped graphics files. Pictures, in other words. This is the same type of graphics files as you might use for a Windows "wallpaper." Bmp files are not widely used over the Internet, due to the fact that only Windows machines can easily read and display them. See gif, jpeg.

CGI—Acronym for Common Gateway Interface. CGI is a standard that describes a set of rules for communication between data sent from a browser to a server.

Client—A machine typically connected to an intra-/Internet whose purpose is to retrieve some form of data from a local or remote machine (server) and process it in some way. Client can also be used to refer to software that makes this possible. See Server.

Cryptography—A way (or ways) of altering or encoding data such that it is unreadable or otherwise useless to anyone who does not have the proper mechanism to restore or decode it.

Database—A collection of information, stored in one or more electronic files.

Database Table—A file containing related information represented in the form of rows and columns, where each row describes an item and each column describes a characteristic of the item.

Data Type—In a database table, the classification of the kind of information that may be stored in a column. The type determines the operations a DBMS is permitted to perform on the column's data. Typical types are numeric, alphanumeric (character), and logical (true or false).

DBMS—Acronym for Database Management System. An application that manages the storage and retrieval of information contained in a database. DBMSs typically include the capability of working in cooperation with other applications at the code level (through the systems' API). They frequently include their own programming language, capable of producing sophisticated, standalone applications. See API.

Event—An event is a way to let your program know that *something* has happened that the program should know about. It may be anything from the user clicking a button to the system letting you know that an error has occurred. When programming for an "event-based" operating system such as Windows (3.x, 95, and NT), MacOS, etc., you typically associate a procedure or function with an event. When your program is notified of the event, this procedure or method will then be executed *in response to* the event. For example, when a user clicks a button (the event), your program responds by displaying the message "You clicked the button" (the response).

Field—In a database table, a column that contains a value that quantifies a characteristic common to each item entered in a row of the table. See Database, Database Table, Record.

Filtering—In a database context, a technique available in some DBMSs that enables the user to create a set of criteria used as a mask to select which rows in a table will be visible. See Database, DBMS.

Finger—A protocol/program that can be used over the intra-/Internet to locate people at other sites. See Protocol.

FTP—Acronym for File Transfer Protocol. File Transfer Protocol is a common method for transferring files over the intra-/Internet. See Protocol.

GIF—Acronym for Graphics Interchange Format. This is another type of graphic/picture file. Web pages commonly use gif files because they are easily viewed on a number of different operating systems. These images are limited to 256 colors and frequently have limited resolutions. However, these limitations mean that the physical gif files will usually be smaller than their jpeg counterparts. In addition, the gif format employs some internal compression to keep the files even smaller. See bmp, jpeg.

GUI—Acronym for Graphical User Interface. GUI refers to the "pretty face" that an application presents—the buttons, menus, pictures, forms, and so on.

HTML—Acronym for Hypertext Markup Language. HTML is a series of text formatting commands (Bold, Italics, Font size, color, etc.) used for the creation of Web pages.

HTTP—Acronym for Hypertext Transfer Protocol. HTTP is the protocol by which hypertext documents are transferred over the intra-/Internet. See Protocol.

IDE—Acronym for Integrated Development Environment. Strictly speaking, this means that you can write and compile code without running the compiler/interpreter from the command line (i.e., as a DOS or text mode program). However, the term IDE is nowadays often used to indicate some amount of visual design.

Indexing—In a database context, a technique of performing and maintaining a "virtual sort" on the rows of a table, using criteria based on the values stored in one or more columns of the table. Indexing is accomplished by storing the values in sorted order in a separate table, along with a pointer to the corresponding row in the data table.

ISAPI—Acronym for Internet Information Server API. A set of subroutines made available by Microsoft's Internet Information Server (IIS) program to enhance the performance of or to make it easier to write CGI applications for machines running IIS. Essentially an enhanced, Microsoft-specific version of the CGI standard. See CGI.

ISDN—Acronym for Integrated Digital Services Network. ISDN is usually the simplest and least expensive *digital* line (remember that standard phone lines are actually analog in nature) that your phone company is able to provide.

Java—Programming language created by Sun Microsystems. Originally designed to be used in remote controls and other hand-held devices, Java eventually became a way to spice up Web pages with mini-programs, called Applets.

Java Beans—An API proposed by Sun Microsystems for creating Java components, almost like OCX for Java. The advantage of the Java Beans API is that, when completed, it will, according to Sun, "be connected by bridges into existing industry component models such as Microsoft's ActiveX, OpenDoc, and Netscape's LiveConnect." The idea is then that you could write a component once, then share it across multiple platforms and programming environments, not unlike Java itself. See API, Java, OCX.

JavaScript—Scripting language created by Netscape Communications for the express purpose of allowing Web designers to enhance their pages with some additional features and small programs. Borland's IntraBuilder language is largely based on JavaScript. Note: The JavaScript language is in no way related to the Java language. Apparently Netscape simply called it JavaScript in the hopes that it might ride on the coattails of Java's popularity.

JDBC—Acronym for Java Database Connectivity. JDBC is an API (based on the ODBC API) for allowing Java programs to access multiple database formats. See ODBC.

JPEG—Yet another graphics/picture file format. Although the jpeg format uses a complex compression algorithm, files are typically much larger than gif or bmp files. This is due to the fact that jpeg files have a much greater range of colors and resolution. They are popular on web pages for images that require clarity or a high resolution. For instance, you might use a jpeg instead of a gif on a Web page that featured examples of fine art. See bmp, gif.

Locking—In a database context, a method that enables a DBMS to prevent the loss or confusion of data when multiple users are editing elements in a table. The DBMS "locks" the item so another user cannot modify it; when the first user is finished, the item is "unlocked" and the second user is free to begin an edit. Depending on the DBMS, locking/unlocking can take place at the table, row, or column level. See Database, DBMS.

Master-Detail relationship—An association between two tables in a relational database where a row in one table (called the "master" table) is inherently linked to one or more rows in a second table (the "detail" table). See Database Table.

MIME—Acronym for Multipurpose Internet Mail Extensions. MIME is a method of encoding files so that they can be attached to email messages and sent over the intra-/Internet.

Navigate—A term used in database work, meaning to move from one row to another in a table.

NSAPI—Acronym for Netscape Server API. A set of subroutines or functions made available by Netscape's Server products to enhance the performance of or to make it easier to write CGI applications for machines running Netscape Server software. Essentially an enhanced Netscape-specific version of the CGI standard. See CGI.

OCX—Object Linking and Embedding Controls. Essentially, OCX is the next generation of the VBX controls. OCX controls are visual or non-visual controls, libraries, or routines that can be added to Visual Basic, C/C++, or Delphi projects, as well as embedded in Web pages and IntraBuilder forms. Also known as ActiveX or Active Script.

ODBC—Acronym for Open Database Connectivity. ODBC is an API developed by Microsoft that gives programmers (working with any language that creates Windows programs) an interface to varied database file formats.

OS—Acronym for Operating System. Examples include MacOS, OS/2, Unix, Windows 95, and Windows NT. See Unix, Windows NT.

POP—Acronym for Post Office Protocol. POP is the protocol by which programs such as Eudora and Netscape retrieve mail from the server. See Protocol.

Protocol—A set of rules by which two computers communicate with each other, usually over a network.

QBE—Acronym for Query By Example. A method provided by some DBMSs of performing a query by specifying desired criteria in the columns of a replica of a blank row in the table to be queried. Results are returned in a table-like row and column format. See DBMS, Query.

Query—Specialized way of retrieving data from a database or table using SQL scripts. See SQL.

RAD—Acronym for Rapid Application Development. This term is used to describe visual or graphical design programming products. The idea is that you are able to get your applications developed faster by being able to design them visually. In contrast to IDE, which only indicates that the editor and compiler are somehow joined together, RAD indicates that there will be some sort of GUI designer and/or editor. See IDE.

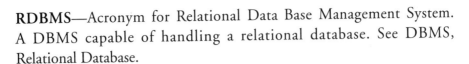

RDBMS—Acronym for Relational Data Base Management System. A DBMS capable of handling a relational database. See DBMS, Relational Database.

Record—In a database table, a row entry that represents a collection of columns quantifying various characteristics of an item. See Field.

Relational Database—A database in which an association is formed between one or more columns in one table with one or more columns in another. Using the common columns, related information may be gathered from several tables. See Database, Field, Record.

Referential Integrity—A safeguard built into DBMSs to make certain that the contents of a column in one table exactly matches the related field in another table. See DBMS.

Report Generator—A utility that facilitates the creation of reports that summarize the contents of a database. Typically included as part of a complete DBMS. See DBMS.

Server—A server is a machine whose purpose is typically to store large amounts of data, files, etc. and make them available to other machines, usually over an intra-/Internet. Server can also be used to refer to software that makes this possible. See Client, Workstation.

SMTP—Acronym for Simple Mail Transfer Protocol. SMTP is the protocol by which mail is sent from your machine to another over a network. See Protocol.

SSL—Acronym for Secure Sockets Layer. An encryption protocol developed by Netscape for the purpose of secure transactions; i.e., credit card purchases. See Protocol.

SQL—Acronym for Structured Query Language. SQL is a programming language designed specifically to modify and retrieve data from databases and tables. SQL is not really a true programming language, but rather a highly specialized language designed specifically for working with databases. SQL "programs" (scripts) are not compiled into any sort of executable. Rather, they are interpreted "on-the-fly" by the database engine.

Table—See Database Table.

Table Structure—The name given to the overall specification for the data types and sizes contained in a database table. See Database, Data Types.

TCP/IP—Acronyms for Transmission Control Protocol and Internet Protocol. TCP and IP are the protocols by which computers communicate over the intra-/Internet. Other protocols such as FTP or HTTP can be thought of as running on top of TCP/IP. See FTP, HTTP, and Protocol.

Unix—Operating system developed by Bell Labs (AT&T) in the 1960s. Commonly used on older, larger systems. A majority of the servers running on the Internet are powered by Unix. Also popular today is a PC version of Unix, called Linux.

Unlocking—See Locking.

URL—Acronym for Universal Resource Locator. URLs can be thought of as Web addresses. Typically they begin with "http://…" or "ftp://…".

WIN32—The name given to the set of API functions available on Windows 95 and Windows NT. The "32" refers to the fact that both 95 and NT are 32-bit operating systems, as opposed to DOS and Windows 3.x, which are both 16-bit. See API.

Windows NT—Microsoft's high-end 32-bit operating system. Unlike Windows 3.x and 95, NT does not run "on top of" DOS. It is an entirely new operating system built from the ground up. (Officially, NT does not stand for anything. However, it is rumored that at one time it did indeed stand for New Technology.)

Winsock—An API that provides Windows developers with a set of standard networking functions, which can then be used to implement protocols such as FTP, POP, etc. See HTTP, Finger, FTP, POP, Protocol, SMTP.

Workstation—A machine typically connected to an intra-/Internet whose purpose is to retrieve some form of data from a local or remote machine (server) and process it in some way. Similar to the hardware definition of client. See Client, Server.

Written by bestselling author John Rodley, *Developing Databases For The Web & Intranets* covers both intranet and commercial Web development.

The Example Database In Action

In Chapters 2 and 3, we looked in detail at the construction of a C/CGI Web database application, the Newfoundland Dog Database. In this chapter, we're going to take a long and critical look at how it works, what it looks like in action, and where it falls short. Far from perfect, the database suffers from many shortcomings. Here we'll look at, and sometimes implement, solutions to these problems. When we're done, we'll have closed some of the holes in the original implementation, and, at the very least, we'll have set ourselves up nicely for later chapters where we discuss newer technologies that augment or replace the Web's original HTML/CGI application model.

How It Works

Up to now, we've approached our Newfoundland Dog Database application as a disconnected set of screens and CGI queries. From the screen shots, we've seen that it most emphatically does not look like a traditional application. However, if we look back at it in a more structured fashion, we can see that it is as coherent and self-contained an application as any standalone system. Figure 1 shows a block diagram of the Newf database.

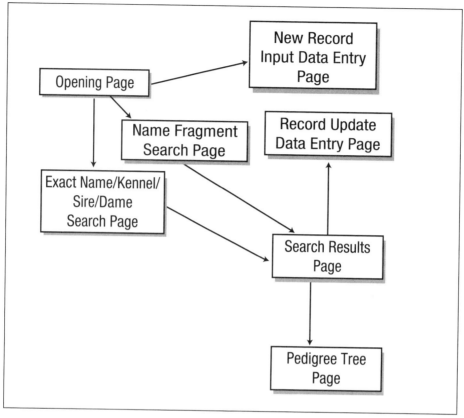

Figure 1   The Newf database application block diagram.

From the opening screen, you can go down the search branch or the insert branch. From the search branch, you can do a name-fragment search, or an exact-name search by name, kennel, sire, or dame. Searching either of the search branches takes you to a result screen. At that point, we introduce a certain amount of circularity. From the result screen, you can click on a dog's name and bring up a pedigree tree. From that pedigree tree, you can click on a dog's name and go to that dog's result screen, and so on and so on.

In fact, from any result screen, you can go to any of three different result screens—by kennel, sire, or dame—as well as to the pedigree tree and the update screen. You can think of the result screen as the endpoint of the system, the screen that contains the real information value in this application.

We've already talked about the insert screen. It's essentially a dead end, where you submit the record and receive an acknowledgment. The dead-end nature of the insert screen brings up an interesting design point. Many Web applications try to impose a hierarchical structure by providing a button bar that helps the user keep some idea of the entire application onscreen at one time. A button bar for the Newf database, for example, might provide Home, Search, and Insert buttons. However, after receiving acknowledgment for the most recent insert, a user will often want to insert another new record using many of the same values. For example, one breeder entering one litter might want to insert many records leaving the breeder, kennel, owner, date-of-birth, sire, and dame all the same. If we just slap an Insert button on the insert-acknowledgment screen without embedding the values of these variables in the hyperlinked URL, then the user clicking the Insert button will be dropped back at an empty screen. Instead, we skip the button-bar approach and simply tell the user to click the browser's Back button to go back to the form with the most recent data already filled in.

This is another example of the "stateless" nature of Web applications. This statelessness can be very confusing for users, and anything you can do to alleviate it, including button bars, is worth trying. At all points, however, you have to consider what lengths you are willing to go to in order to preserve state, and what shortcuts might be appropriate.

User Reactions To The Application

While not strictly a programming topic, user reaction to your Web application is worth considering, especially in light of the preceding section on the view from different browsers. The Newf database doesn't work properly under some browsers, as we'll see in the next section. Some browsers don't support tables, others don't support graphics, and some don't support things as silly as the background graphic.

The real difficulty, especially with low-end, mass-market Web sites, is figuring out that users are having a problem at all. There are various rules of thumb to calculate the ratio of loud complainers to silent fumers. Suffice to say that, if your site has a problem, for every user who realizes that it's your site (and not his browser) that's the problem, there are many more users who have simply given up and clicked away, frustrated, angry, and unlikely to return.

In its early days, the Newf database, for example, had a problem on the data-entry screen where perfectly good records were being rejected. At least two dozen users went away stumped before one recognized there was a problem and emailed the (properly embarrassed) administrator. The only real solution to this natural shyness of users is to provide easy, frequent, prominent, and enthusiastic opportunities to email the Webmaster if they run into a problem.

The Drawbacks Of This Approach

The heart of the Newf database's functionality is the user entering data, and our CGI program acting on that input. However, as with any real-world application, there are rules that can cause a user's input to be rejected. On the name-fragment search, the name fragment must be six characters or greater. On the data-entry screen, all dates must be formatted in one of a small set of formats.

Field Validation

What happens when the user, for whatever reason, enters bad data? If you look back at Listing 3.6, you can see a call to the function **VerifyInput**, shown in Listing 1. **VerifyInput** has one task, to make sure that the data entered by the user is useable by our CGI program.

Listing 1   VerifyInput dealing with data input errors.

```
/* VerifyDate - Take a string date (item) as entered by the user and
make sure that it fits one of our date formats:
   yyyy
   mm/yyyy
   mm/dd/yyyy
   mm/dd/yyyy hh:mm:ss AM/PM

decompose it into parts and reconstruct according to OUR one and
only format
   mm/dd/yyyy hh:mm:ss AM/PM

returns  0 if success - also reformats date into origdata and places
integer year into *pYr.
    1 if error
*/
int VerifyDate( char *item, char *origdata, int *pYr ) {
  int i;
  int component_count = 0;
  char *component[4];
```

```c
char data[1024];
char day[3];
char month[3];
char year[5];
char hhmm[80];

strcpy( data, origdata );
failed_data = origdata;
failed_item = item;

if( strlen( data ) <= 0 ) {
  failed_data = NULL;
  failed_item = NULL;
  return( 1 );
  }
component[component_count++] = data;
if( isalpha( origdata[0] )) {
  for( i = 0; origdata[i] != '\0'; i++ ) {
    if( origdata[i] == ' ' ) {
      data[i] = '\0';
      component[component_count++] = &data[i+1];
      }
    if( component_count == 4 ) {
      fprintf( errfp, "component_count rolling over\n" );
      break;
      }
    }
  if( component_count == 3 )
    component[component_count++] = "00:00:04am";
  }
else {
  for( i = 0; origdata[i] != '\0'; i++ ) {
    if( origdata[i] == '/' ) {
      data[i] = '\0';
      if( component_count == 3 )
        return( 0 );
      component[component_count++] = &data[i+1];
      }
    }
  }
switch( component_count ) {
  case 1:    // Year only, MUST be between 1700 and 2000
    strcpy( hhmm, "00:00:01am" );
    strcpy( day, "01" );
    strcpy( month, "01" );
    if( !VerifyYear( component[0] ))
```

```
          return( 0 );
        strcpy( year, component[0] );
        break;
      case 2:    // Month and year
        strcpy( hhmm, "00:00:02am" );
        strcpy( day, "01" );
        if( !VerifyMonth( component[0] ))
          return( 0 );
        strcpy( month, component[0] );
        if( !VerifyYear( component[1] ))
          return( 0 );
        strcpy( year, component[1] );
        break;
      case 3:  // Month, day and year
        if( !VerifyMonth( component[0] ))
          return( 0 );
        strcpy( month, component[0] );
        if( !VerifyDay( component[1] ))
          return( 0 );
        strcpy( day, component[1] );
        if( !VerifyYear( component[2] ))
          return( 0 );
        strcpy( year, component[2] );
        strcpy( hhmm, "00:00:03am" );
        break;
      case 4:
        for( i = 1; i <= 13; i++ ) {
          if( i == 13 )
            return( 0 );
          if( strcmp( component[0], months[i-1].shortname ) == 0 ) {
            sprintf( month, "%d", i );
            break;
            }
          if( strcmp( component[0], months[i-1].longname ) == 0 ) {
            sprintf( month, "%d", i );
            break;
            }
          }
        strcpy( day, component[1] );
        strcpy( year, component[2] );
        strcpy( hhmm, component[3] );
        break;
      }
    sprintf( origdata, "%s/%s/%s %s", month, day, year, hhmm );
    failed_data = NULL;
```

```
    failed_item = NULL;
   *pYr = atoi( year );
   return( 1 );
   }

/* VerifyYear - Verify that provided string is an integer
number between 1700 and 2000 inclusive.
return 1 if success
     0 if error
*/
int VerifyYear( char *szYear ) {
   if( atoi( szYear ) < 1700 || atoi( szYear ) > 2000 ) {
     fprintf( errfp, "bad yy %s\n", szYear );
     return( 0 );
     }
   return( 1 );
   }

/* VerifyMonth - Verify that provided string is an integer
number between 1 and 12 inclusive.
return 1 if success
     0 if error
*/
int VerifyMonth( char *szMonth ) {
   if( atoi( szMonth ) <= 0 || atoi( szMonth ) > 12 ) {
     fprintf( errfp, "bad mm %s\n", szMonth );
     return( 0 );
     }
   return( 1 );
   }

/* VerifyDay - Verify that provided string is an integer
number between 1 and 31 inclusive.
return 1 if success
     0 if error
*/
int VerifyDay( char *szDay ) {
   if( atoi( szDay ) <= 0 || atoi( szDay ) > 31 ) {
     fprintf( errfp, "bad dd %s\n", szDay );
     return( 0 );
     }
   return( 1 );
   }
```

If **VerifyInput** returns an error, the program stops processing the query and displays an HTML document detailing the field and data value that caused the error. Unfortunately, the screen that details bad data entry only comes up once the user has tried to submit the form.

Within CGI, there is literally no way around this. The data entered in a form cannot be analyzed until it reaches the CGI program on the server. In the Newf database, we deal with this as best we can, by putting up a screen that describes the problem as we've diagnosed it, and then prompting the user to click the Back button, which should bring the form back as the user filled it out. The problem diagnosis should point to the problematic field, but this approach is still less than satisfactory. It's clunky, as the user input is no longer onscreen when the problem is described, and the performance stinks, because we've fired up the entire CGI program and gone a long way down the road to doing the whole program before even detecting an invalid field value.

For users of state-of-the-art Windows programs like Quicken or Microsoft Word, this sort of batch field validation is positively barbaric. In Word, for example, my typos get corrected on the fly as I enter them. I don't have to click a button and wait for the whole document to be processed before having the typo even pointed out to me.

Field Validation Using Java

There *are* Web solutions to the field-validation problem. A Java applet, for example, could easily do field validation for us, both batch and field-by-field. In fact, this would be a trivial exercise for a Java programmer. Listing 2 shows a simple Java applet with field validation that replaces the Newf database's name-fragment search screen (Figure 3.1).

Listing 2   The Java applet for the Newf name-fragment search screen.

```
import java.awt.*;
import java.util.Hashtable;
import java.applet.*;
import java.net.*;

/* NameFragment - A class for presenting a Newf DB name-fragment
```

```
search entry screen to the user and firing off the proper
CGI query when the user hits the button.  Performs both batch
and on-the-fly field validation.
*/
public class NameFragment extends Applet {
  private final String   SEARCH_LINK = "Search";
  private TextField      tfName;
  private Choice         chCountry;
  private Button  bSearch;
  private GenericDialog  dialog;
  String sDB;  // Name of the database we're connecting to.
  String sTbl;  // Name of the db table we're using.
  String sServer;  // Name of the server the DBMS is running on.
  String sUser;  // Name of the db-user we're logging in as.
  String sBase;  // URL of the base directory of the db machine.
  Label errorLabel;  // The text appearing below the search button.
  Panel textPanel;  // The panel the name entry field is in.
  Panel errorPanel;  // The panel the error string is in.

/* constructor - Create all the visual elements and add them
to the container that is this applet.
*/
  public NameFragment() {
// Create a panel for the search button and
// error string.
    Panel bottomPanel = new Panel();
// Set it up as 2 rows, 1 column
    bottomPanel.setLayout( new GridLayout( 2, 1 ));
// Create the search button
    bSearch = new Button(SEARCH_LINK);
    bSearch.setBackground(Color.lightGray);
// Make a panel for it.
    Panel buttonPanel = new Panel();
// Add the button to the button panel
    buttonPanel.add( bSearch );
    bottomPanel.add( buttonPanel );
// Create a panel for the error string
    errorPanel = new Panel();
// Make an initial error string
    errorLabel =
      new Label( "Enter a name, and hit Search to start." );
// Add the error string to the panel
    errorPanel.add( errorLabel );
// Add the error panel to the grid panel
    bottomPanel.add( errorPanel );
```

```
// Set up the applet itself as a BorderLayout window.
   setLayout( new BorderLayout() );
// Add the Search button and error text to the applet
// via their panels at the bottom (South) part of
// the applet.
   add( "South", bottomPanel );
   textPanel = new Panel();
   tfName = new TextField( 40 );
   textPanel.add( new Label( "Name Fragment: " ));
   textPanel.add( tfName );
   add( "Center", textPanel );

// Make a panel to hold the country choice field.
   Panel pTemp = new Panel();
   chCountry = new Choice();
// Add some countries to the choice field.
   chCountry.addItem( "any" );
   chCountry.addItem( "ITALY" );
   chCountry.addItem( "UK" );
   chCountry.addItem( "USA" );
   pTemp.add( new Label( "Country: " ));
   pTemp.add( chCountry );
// Add the choice field to the applet via its panel.
   add( "North", pTemp );

// Configure the entry field.
   tfName.setEditable(true);
   tfName.setBackground(Color.lightGray);
 }


/* init - called when this screen is pulled up for the
first time.  Gets the appropriate parameters from the
HTML page setting servername, username, tablename,
databasename.  Sets the focus to the dog-name-fragment
data-entry field.
*/
public void init() {
   sServer = getParameter( "server" );
   sUser  = getParameter( "user" );
   sBase  = getParameter( "base" );
   sDB    = getParameter( "db" );
   sTbl   = getParameter( "tbl" );
   tfName.requestFocus();
 }
```

```
/* handleEvent - called whenever the user hits a key in
our applet.  Deals with forward and back tab by moving the
focus and calling field-validation routines.  Deals with
the Return key by formulating our CGI query from the
data in the entry fields and using AppletContext.showDocument
to hyperlink to the results of the query.
*/
public boolean handleEvent(Event evt)
  {
    switch (evt.id)
    {
// Here's the Tab key
      case Event.KEY_PRESS:
        if (evt.key == 9)
        {
// If Shift is set, we're back-tabbing
          if (evt.shiftDown())
            tabBack(evt.target);
          else
// Otherwise, we're forward tabbing
            tabAhead(evt.target);

          return true;
        }


// If the Return key is hit, batch validate the fields
        if (evt.key == 10) {
          if( !nameValid(tfName.getText())) {
            showError(
              "Name MUST be at least 6 characters! Try again." );
            tfName.requestFocus();
          }
        else {
// Get the AppletContext (the browser)
          AppletContext ac = getAppletContext();
// Construct the CGI query
          String sURL = new String( "http://katie/cgi-bin/
newfq.exe?country="+chCountry.getSelectedItem()+"&dog.text=
  "+tfName.getText()+
            "&base="+sBase+"&QueryType=partial&db=
              "+sDB+"&server="+sServer+
              "&user="+sUser+"&tbl="+sTbl);
// Try executing the CGI query
          try {
            URL uURL = new URL(sURL);
```

```
// Link to the document.  Our applet disappears from screen
// right now.
                ac.showDocument( uURL );
                }
// We should do something more friendly, but for now just
// print a message to stdout if the CGI query fails on
// connection.
           catch( Exception e )
             { System.out.println( "bad URL "+sURL ); }
           }
          return true;
        }

        break;
    }

    return false;
  }


/* nameValid - Check if the supplied string meets our criteria
for dog names in a name-fragment search.  In this case, we only
check for the fragment being greater than 6 chars in length.
*/
public boolean nameValid( String dogName ) {
   if( dogName.length() < 6 )
      return( false );
   else
      return( true );
   }


// tabAhead - Move the focus to the next field in the list.
// If we're on the name field, and it has bad data in it,
// then don't move the focus, just show an error and return
// the focus to the name field.
void tabAhead(Object from)
  {
   if( from == chCountry ) {
      tfName.requestFocus();
      showError( "" );
      }
   if( from == tfName ) {
      if( nameValid(tfName.getText())) {
        bSearch.requestFocus();
        showError( "" );
        }
```

```
      else {
        showError( "Name field MUST be 6 characters or greater" );
        tfName.requestFocus();
        }
      }
   if( from == bSearch ) {
      chCountry.requestFocus();
      showError( "" );
      }
  }


// tabBack - Move the focus to the previous field in the list.
// If we're on the name field, and it has bad data in it,
// then don't move the focus, just show an error and return
// the focus to the name field.
void tabBack(Object from)
  {
   if( from == chCountry ) {
      bSearch.requestFocus();
      showError( "" );
      }
   if( from == tfName ) {
      if( nameValid(tfName.getText())) {
        chCountry.requestFocus();
        showError( "" );
        }
      else {
        showError( "Name field MUST be 6 characters or greater" );
        tfName.requestFocus();
        }
      }
   if( from == bSearch ) {
      tfName.requestFocus();
      showError( "" );
      }
  }


// showError - change the string in the errorLabel under
// the Search button to be the string supplied.
public void showError( String s ) {
  errorLabel.setText( s );
  errorPanel.layout();
  }


// action - handle any button presses in the applet, specifically
// the Search button.
```

```
public boolean action(Event evt, Object obj) {
    if( evt.target instanceof Button ) {
      String label = (String) obj;
      if( label.equals(SEARCH_LINK) ) {
        if( !nameValid(tfName.getText())) {
      showError( "Name MUST be at least 6 characters! Try again." );
          tfName.requestFocus();
          }
        else {
          AppletContext ac = getAppletContext();
// Create a URL for the CGI query and jump to it
          String sURL =
           new String("http://katie/cgi-bin/newfq.exe?country="+
             chCountry.getSelectedItem()+
              "&dog.text="+tfName.getText()+
               "&base="+sBase+"&QueryType=partial&db="+
                sDB+"&server="+sServer+"&user="+sUser+
                 "&tbl="+sTbl);
          try {
            URL uURL = new URL(sURL);
            ac.showDocument( uURL );
            }
          catch( Exception e )
            { System.out.println( "bad URL "+sURL ); }
          }
        return true;
      }
      else {
// return false if we didn't handle the event.
        return false;
      }
    }
    else {
      return super.action(evt, obj);
    }

  }
}
```

If you look back at our original name-fragment search screen in Figure 3.1, this solution, in Figure 2, looks quite familiar. Looking at the HTML source for the screen, Listing 3, you can see that the main difference is that it entirely eliminates the HTML **<FORM>** element that used to gather our data.

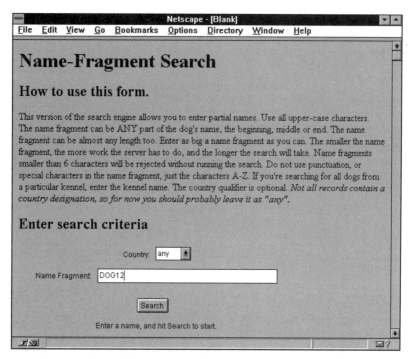

Figure 2   The Java field-validating applet in action, before data entry.

Listing 3   The new name-fragment HTML source, using a Java applet for validation.

```
<!DOCTYPE
HTML PUBLIC "-//SQ//DTD HTML 2.0 + all extensions//EN" "hmpro3.dtd">
<HTML>
<HEAD>
<TITLE>Blank</TITLE></HEAD>
<BODY BACKGROUND="images/background.jpg">
<H1>Name-Fragment Search</H1>
<H2>How to use this form.</H2>
<P>This version of the engine allows you to enter partial names.
Use all uppercase characters. The name fragment can be ANY part of
the dog's name, the beginning, middle, or end.The name fragment can
be almost any length, too. Enter as big a name fragment as you can.
The smaller the name fragment, the more work the server has to do,
and the longer the search will take. Name fragments smaller than 6
characters will be rejected without running the search. Do not use
punctuation or special characters in the name fragment, just the
characters A-Z. If you're searching for all dogs from a particular
```

```
kennel, enter the kennel name. The country qualifier is optional.
<I>Not all records contain a country designation, so for now you
should probably leave it as &quot;any&quot;.</I></P>

<H2>Enter search criteria</H2>
<P>
<APPLET
    CODE="NameFragment.class" ALT="This browser is not Java enabled!"
    WIDTH="450" HEIGHT="150" ALIGN="MIDDLE" ID="NameFragment">
<PARAM NAME="base" VALUE="http://www.realink.com">
<PARAM NAME="server" VALUE="marconi">
<PARAM NAME="tbl" VALUE="shortdog">
<PARAM NAME="user" VALUE="sa">
<PARAM NAME="db" VALUE="newf"></APPLET></P>
<HR>
<P><A HREF="NewfDB.html">Return to Newf DB top level</A></P>
</BODY></HTML>
```

The **<FORM>** element has disappeared, replaced by an **<APPLET>** element. And what of the information that was inside the **<FORM>** element? The two **<INPUT>** elements, **country** and **dog.text**, as well as the Search button have all disappeared inside our Java applet. The **<ACTION>** attribute that described our CGI query has also been written into the applet. Some of the old **<FORM>** items have remained in the HTML source, though, most notably the five hidden inputs, **base**, **server**, **tbl**, **user**, and **db**. We embedded these in the original form in order to avoid hardwiring them into the C CGI program, and we set them as Java applet parameters here for the same reason, to avoid having to hardwire them into the applet.

Everything else is inside our Java source. The form **<INPUT>** elements have been replaced by Java objects: the Java Button instance **bSearch**, the Java Choice named **chCountry**, and the Java TextField named **tfName**. These are instantiated and positioned within the applet's window by the rather wordy code in the **NameFragment** constructor.

The constructor is more complicated than it probably seems like it needs to be. This is because we need to create multiple Java Panels in order to position our input elements sensibly. We divide the applet window into three Panels:

- The top (or North) Panel contains two elements, the Label **"Country"** and the Choice that contains a list of countries to choose from.

- The bottom (or South) Panel contains two elements, the Search button (**bSearch**) and the error string.

- The middle (or Center) Panel contains two elements, the Label **"Name"** and the text-entry field **tfName**.

Figure 3 shows the division of applet window space into panels and elements.

We've already explained the **chCountry**, **tfName**, and **bSearch** objects, but the error string "Enter a name, and click Search to start." is something new. Basically, we've reserved a little window at the bottom of our applet to display messages to the user. When we first come up, the message displayed is "Enter a dog name ...". If, however, the user enters bad data, we can explain that mistake in this window.

There are two points where we perform field validation in this applet— when the user tries to leave the **tfName** text field, and when the user clicks

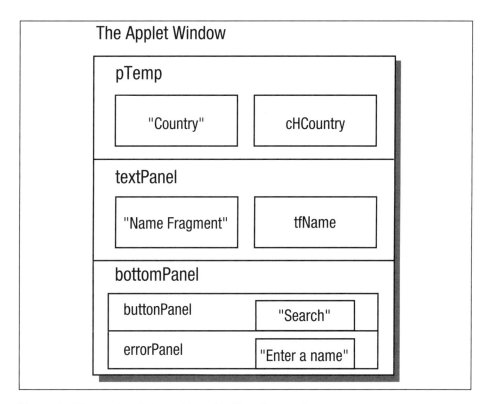

Figure 3   The panel and element layout in NameFragment.java.

the Search button. If a user clicks the Search button, the screen of data input does not go away. Instead, Java automatically invokes the action method. Within the action method, we perform a batch validation on the input fields. If the dog-name fragment entered does not meet our validation rule (at least six characters long), we simply display the error string and continue. In that case, the user gets the screen in Figure 4, which details the error very quickly, while the bad data remains visible.

In addition to displaying the error message, our field validation also resets the current field to be the field that violated validation, in this case **tfName**. Users are stuck in the invalid field until they correct it or hyperlink away.

If the fields do meet our validation rule, then the applet constructs a CGI URL, then calls **AppletContext.showDocument**, passing that URL. That CGI URL is the same URL that our **<FORM>** tag from Listing 2.4 would access in its ACTION attribute.

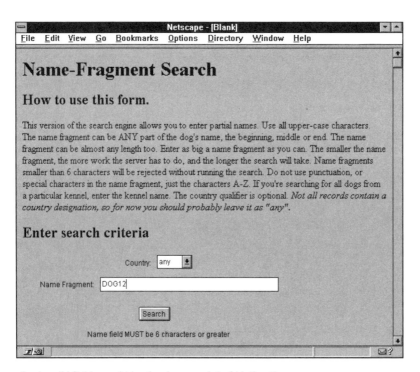

Figure 4 Invalid field caught by the Java applet of Listing 3.

We go through the same validation/rejection process when the user tries to tab from field to field in our form. When the user presses the Tab (or Shift-Tab) key, Java automatically invokes the **handleEvent** method, where we check to see which key was pressed. For tabs and back-tabs, if the user is in the **tfName** text field and attempts to tab away from there, we check the data in the field. If it is less than six characters, we do not allow the user to leave the field, displaying the error message and remaining in place.

Obviously, with only a single field, this is a simplistic example. However, you can extend it as far as you want, to forms like our data-entry screen, which has 35 fields with dozens of different rules to satisfy. The more field validation you have, and the more immediate it is, the more efficient users will become in filling it out. Efficient users are happy users, and happy users are return customers.

Response Limiting

Another huge problem with the Newfoundland Dog Database, as written, is that it doesn't automatically limit the length of the HTML documents that it tries to send back to users. For instance, a user who does a kennel search on POUCH COVE might get thousands of hits, producing an HTML document well over 1 MB in size. This doesn't work. Browsers typically only perform acceptably for documents 100 K and under, and at more than 250 K, even the heftiest hardware is not enough to bring the entire document onto the screen within the user's lifetime.

A good example of how most Web applications deal with this problem is Digital Equipment Corporation's outstanding Internet search engine, Alta Vista, shown in Figure 5.

Alta Vista is a database of Web pages and Usenet messages, indexed so as to be full-text searchable. Users fill in a search form, then kick off a CGI process by clicking the Search button. In the example of Figure 5, we've searched on two terms, Java and JDBC, and Alta Vista has found over 200 matches. In order to make the results manageable, Alta Vista arbitrarily limits the results of a search to 200 matches. It also divides those 200 matches into 20 screens of 10. At any one time, the user can only be viewing a single screen of 10 matches. What this means is that, especially if you view listings in "compact" format, all you see is approximately one screen's worth of information.

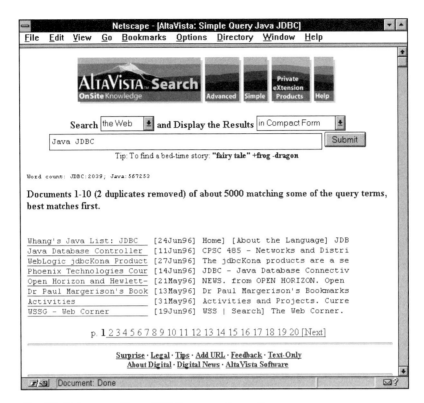

Figure 5   Alta Vista presenting a 200-item search result.

The user has a number of action options from any page: going to the next page, going to the previous page, or picking a page at random from the list of available pages. Maintaining this system of search-result page creation is relatively simple. Take, as an example, the CGI query that results if we choose page 3 from the results page of Figure 5. The resulting CGI query is:

```
http://altavista.digital.com/cgi-bin/query?pg=q&what=web&stq=
    20&fmt=c&q=Java+JDBC
```

This query has two name value pairs—**q=Java+ODBC&stq=30**—that tell Alta Vista exactly what page of results we want to see. The number of listings per page is set to 10, and the starting item, **startq**, is set to 20. So we get 10 results starting with number 20—page 3. Listing 4 shows the HTML source for this screen.

Listing 4   The HTML source for the Alta Vista screen of Figure 5.

```
<html>
<head>

<title>
AltaVista: Simple Query Java JDBC</title>
</head>
<body  bgcolor="#ffffff"  text="#000000"  link="#0000ee"
vlink="551a8b" alink="ff0000">
<CENTER>
<a href="/cgi-bin/query?pg=about&what=web">
 <IMG src="/av/pix/av-logo.gif" alt="[AltaVista] "
BORDER=0 ALIGN=middle  HEIGHT=73 WIDTH=204>
</a>
<a href="/cgi-bin/query?pg=aq&what=web">
 <IMG src="/av/pix/av-adv.gif" alt="[Advanced Search]  "
BORDER=0 ALIGN=middle  HEIGHT=73 WIDTH=59>
</a>
<a href="/cgi-bin/query?pg=q&what=web">
 <IMG src="/av/pix/av-sim.gif" alt="[SIMPLE QUERY] "
BORDER=0 ALIGN=middle  HEIGHT=73 WIDTH=42>
</a>
<a href=
   "http://altavista.software.digital.com/products/search/choice.htm">
 <IMG src="/av/pix/av-pex.gif" alt="[Private eXtension Products] "
  BORDER=0 ALIGN=middle  HEIGHT=73 WIDTH=65>
</a>
<a href="/cgi-bin/query?pg=h&what=web">
 <IMG src="/av/pix/av-help.gif" alt="[Help with Query]  "
BORDER=0 ALIGN=middle  HEIGHT=73 WIDTH=35>
</a>
</CENTER>
<CENTER>
<FORM method=GET action="/cgi-bin/query">
<INPUT TYPE=hidden NAME=pg VALUE=q>
<B>
Search <SELECT NAME=what>
<OPTION VALUE=web  SELECTED>
the Web<OPTION VALUE=news >
Usenet</SELECT>
 and Display the Results <SELECT NAME=fmt>
<OPTION VALUE="." >
in Standard Form<OPTION VALUE=c SELECTED>
```

```
in Compact Form<OPTION VALUE=d >
in Detailed Form</SELECT>
</B>
<BR>
<INPUT NAME=q size=55 maxlength=200 VALUE="Java JDBC">
<INPUT TYPE=submit VALUE=Submit>
<br>
<FONT size=-1>
Tip: To find a bed-time story: <B>
"fairy tale" +frog -dragon</B>
</FONT>
</FORM>
</CENTER>
<FONT size=-1>
<PRE>
Word count: JDBC:2039; Java:567253<BR>
</PRE>
</FONT>
<P>
<b>
Documents 1-10 (2 duplicates removed) of about 5000 matching
some of the query terms, best matches first.</b>
<br>
<pre>
<a href="http://www.sicc.co.kr/~sjwhang/javalist/lang/jdbc.htm">
Whang's Java List: JDBC  </a>
 [24Jun96] Home] [About the Language] JDB
<a href="http://www.cs.tamu.edu/people/jhamann/jdbc/">
Java Database Controller </a>
 [11Jun96] CPSC 485 - Networks and Distri
<a href="http://www.weblogic.com/products/jdbckona_noframe.html">
WebLogic jdbcKona Product</a>
 [27Jun96] The jdbcKona products are a se
<a href="http://www.phoenixtech.com/JDBC.html">
Phoenix Technologies Cour</a>
 [14Jun96] JDBC - Java Database Connectiv
<a href="http://www.openhorizon.com/pressrel/praesidm.htm">
Open Horizon and Hewlett-</a>
 [21May96] NEWS. from OPEN HORIZON. Open
<a href="http://www-tec.open.ac.uk/design/book.html">
Dr Paul Margerison's Book</a>
 [13May96] Dr Paul Margerison's Bookmarks
<a href="http://www.iei.pi.cnr.it/GRANT/ligonzo/activ.html">
Activities           </a>
```

```
  [31May96] Activities and Projects. Curre
<a href="http://tuna2.berkeley.edu/Webcorner/webcorner.html">
WSSG - Web Corner       </a>
 [19Jun96] WSS | Search] The Web Corner.
</pre>
<CENTER>
      p. <b>
1</b>
<a href="/cgi-bin/query?pg=q&what=web&stq=10&fmt=c&q=Java+JDBC">
 2</a>
<a href="/cgi-bin/query?pg=q&what=web&stq=20&fmt=c&q=Java+JDBC">
 3</a>
<a href="/cgi-bin/query?pg=q&what=web&stq=30&fmt=c&q=Java+JDBC">
 4</a>
<a href="/cgi-bin/query?pg=q&what=web&stq=40&fmt=c&q=Java+JDBC">
 5</a>
<a href="/cgi-bin/query?pg=q&what=web&stq=50&fmt=c&q=Java+JDBC">
 6</a>
<a href="/cgi-bin/query?pg=q&what=web&stq=60&fmt=c&q=Java+JDBC">
 7</a>
<a href="/cgi-bin/query?pg=q&what=web&stq=70&fmt=c&q=Java+JDBC">
 8</a>
<a href="/cgi-bin/query?pg=q&what=web&stq=80&fmt=c&q=Java+JDBC">
 9</a>
<a href="/cgi-bin/query?pg=q&what=web&stq=90&fmt=c&q=Java+JDBC">
 10</a>
<a href="/cgi-bin/query?pg=q&what=web&stq=100&fmt=c&q=Java+JDBC">
 11</a>
<a href="/cgi-bin/query?pg=q&what=web&stq=110&fmt=c&q=Java+JDBC">
 12</a>
<a href="/cgi-bin/query?pg=q&what=web&stq=120&fmt=c&q=Java+JDBC">
 13</a>
<a href="/cgi-bin/query?pg=q&what=web&stq=130&fmt=c&q=Java+JDBC">
 14</a>
<a href="/cgi-bin/query?pg=q&what=web&stq=140&fmt=c&q=Java+JDBC">
 15</a>
<a href="/cgi-bin/query?pg=q&what=web&stq=150&fmt=c&q=Java+JDBC">
 16</a>
<a href="/cgi-bin/query?pg=q&what=web&stq=160&fmt=c&q=Java+JDBC">
 17</a>
<a href="/cgi-bin/query?pg=q&what=web&stq=170&fmt=c&q=Java+JDBC">
 18</a>
<a href="/cgi-bin/query?pg=q&what=web&stq=180&fmt=c&q=Java+JDBC">
 19</a>
<a href="/cgi-bin/query?pg=q&what=web&stq=190&fmt=c&q=Java+JDBC">
```

```
 20</a>
<a href="/cgi-bin/query?pg=q&what=web&stq=10&fmt=c&q=Java+JDBC">
  [Next]</a>
</CENTER>
<CENTER>
<HR>
<FONT size=-1>
<B>
<a href="/cgi-bin/query?pg=s">
Surprise</a>
 &#183;
<a href="/cgi-bin/query?pg=legal">
Legal</a>
 &#183;
<a href="/cgi-bin/query?pg=tips">
Tips</a>
 &#183;
<a href="/cgi-bin/query?pg=addurl">
Add URL</a>
 &#183;
<a href="/cgi-bin/query?pg=fb">
Feedback</a>
 &#183;
<a href="/cgi-bin/query?pg=q&what=web&fmt=c&q=Java+JDBC&text=yes">
 Text-Only</a>
<BR>
<a href="/cgi-bin/query?pg=digital">
About Digital</a>
 &#183;
<a href="/cgi-bin/query?pg=whatsnew">
Digital News</a>
 &#183;
<a href="http://altavista.software.digital.com">
  AltaVista Software</a>
</B>
<hr>
<a href="http://www.digital.com/">
<IMG src=/av/pix/logo22pt.gif alt=" "
BORDER=0 ALIGN=middle  HEIGHT=17 WIDTH=50>
</a>
 <a href="/cgi-bin/query?pg=legal">
Copyright</a>
 &#169; 1996 <a href="http://www.digital.com/">
    Digital Equipment Corporation.</a>
    All rights reserved.
```

```
</FONT>
</CENTER>
</body>
</html>
```

As you can see, all of the hyperlinks from Previous all the way through page 20 to Next are hardwired CGI queries. Now, creating these links by hand would be a daunting task, but doing it programmatically within the CGI query is just a small matter of programming. *Note that the lines in the* ***<PRE>*** *elements have been broken arbitrarily to comply with the publisher's restrictions on line length.*

While the 10-item restriction can be somewhat annoying from a user's perspective, overall, this is excellent Web design, and well worth imitating. Implementing this in the Newf database would require a couple of fairly simple changes. In Listing 2.8, in the function **ProcessArgs**, we'd need to add a variable like Alta Vista's **startq**, to tell us which item to start at. Then, within **Query**, we'd need to output result rows only when we're fetching the right 10 items. And, within the HTML output, of course, we'd need to add hyperlinks to all the other pages, as well as Next and Previous. All in all, not rocket science, but a considerable chunk of code.

Display Limitations

HTML was developed as an easy way to present and link simple types of static data. When you deal with visual items more complicated than static text or black-box image files, HTML quickly becomes unwieldy. A great example of this is the Newfoundland Dog Database's pedigree-tree screen.

The point of the pedigree-tree screen is to present the user with a graphical view of the ancestry of a particular dog going back five generations. This is an important function for breeders to see where various genetic lines intersect and on which side, dame or sire. You reach the pedigree-tree screen by clicking on a dog's name in a search-results screen. Via a new CGI query, with **QueryType** set to Pedigree, the system will bring up a pedigree tree such as that in Figure 6. Listing 5 shows the code we use to generate this tree, a single recursive function named **PedigreeSearch**.

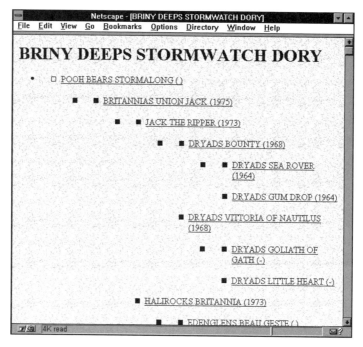

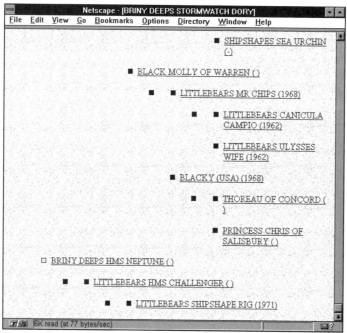

Figure 6   A pedigree tree—two screens worth.

Listing 5   The pedigree search function.

```
/* PedigreeSearch - Output HTML list items <LI> corresponding
to the sire and dame of the specified dog (tname), then call
this function recursively, specifying the sire and dame.  This
will result in a list of lists where each level of
indentation shows a different generation in the pedigree tree.
If we reach MAX_DEPTH, simply return, cutting off the
recursion at a certain depth.
*/
void PedigreeSearch( char *tname ) {
  int i;
  char sought_dam[256];
  char sought_sire[256];
  char buffer[1024];
  EXEC SQL BEGIN DECLARE SECTION;
  char yob[256];
  EXEC SQL  END DECLARE SECTION;

// If we've reached the maximum recursion, simply return.
  if( current_depth == MAX_DEPTH ) {
    return;
    }
  current_depth++;

// Null our parents out.
  sought_dam[0] = '\0';
  sought_sire[0] = '\0';

// sought_name is a global, set it here, use later.
  strcpy( sought_name, tname );

// Get the sire and dame from the DB.
    EXEC SQL
      SELECT NAME, SNAME, DNAME, DOB2
      INTO :temp_name, :temp_sire, :temp_dam, :yob
      FROM shortdog
      WHERE name = :sought_name;

// Output the sire and dame list items and
// recurse down their branches.
    if (SQLCODE == 0 || SQLCODE == 1 ) {
    if( strcmp( yob, "0" ) == 0 )
      yob[0] = '-';
```

```
// Start the list item for sire.
    printf("<LI><UL>\n" );
  if( strlen( temp_sire ) > 0 )
    strcpy( sought_sire, temp_sire );
  if( strlen( temp_dam ) > 0 )
    strcpy( sought_dam, temp_dam );
  if( strlen( sought_sire ) == 0 ||
      strcmp( sought_sire, "NOT YET RECORDED" ) == 0 )
    printf( "<LI>unknown</LI>\n" );
  else
    {
      sprintf( buffer, sought_sire );
      for( i = 0; i < strlen( buffer ); i++ )
        if( buffer[i] == ' ' )
          buffer[i] = '+';
    sprintf( slink, "<A HREF=\"%s%s/newfq.exe?dog.text=%s&\
      QueryType=Name&%s\">%s (%s)</A></P>",
        documentbase, cgi_directory, buffer,query_args,
        sought_sire, yob );
      printf( "<LI>%s\n<UL>", slink );
// Recurse down the sire's branch of the tree
      PedigreeSearch( sought_sire );
      printf( "</UL></LI>\n" );
      }
  if( strlen( sought_dam ) == 0 ||
      strcmp( sought_dam, "NOT YET RECORDED" ) == 0 )
    printf( "<LI>unknown</LI>\n" );
  else
    {
      sprintf( buffer, sought_dam );
      for( i = 0; i < strlen( buffer ); i++ )
        if( buffer[i] == ' ' )
          buffer[i] = '+';
    sprintf( dlink, "<A HREF=\"%s%s/newfq.exe?dog.text=%s&\
      QueryType=Name&%s\">%s (%s)</A></P>",
        documentbase, cgi_directory, buffer,
          query_args,sought_dam, yob );
      printf( "<LI>%s\n<UL>\n", dlink );
// Recurse down the dame's branch of the tree.
      PedigreeSearch( sought_dam );
      printf( "</UL></LI>\n" );
      }
  printf( "</UL></LI>\n" );
  }
// If we errored out, output an error message.
  else {
```

```
    if (SQLCODE == 100 )
        printf("Dog (%s) not found!\n", tname);
    else
        ErrorMsg();
    }

// Pop back up a level.
  current_depth--;
}
```

This function is deceptively simple. We get the dog's sire and dame from the database via a simple SELECT. Then, for the sire, we output a list-item giving his name and the year he was bred. Then we call **PedigreeSearch** recursively to do the same thing for the parents of the sire. These recursions continue until **current_depth** reaches **MAX_DEPTH**. This is our generational limit. When **current_depth** reaches **MAX_DEPTH** for the first time, we've followed the male line back **MAX_DEPTH** generations. Thus, the first five lines of the pedigree screen will always be the male line—father, grandfather, great-grandfather....

The pedigree screen shows the two parents of the named dog, then the parents of each of those dogs as indented lists under each of those dogs. HTML coders will instantly recognize this as a brutally simple application of unordered lists. While dyed-in-the-wool C programmers can easily follow the meaning of an indented list like this, it is much less obvious to our target audience—dog people. They're used to a much more explicit graphic, where each dog name is boxed and solid lines lead from one generation to the next.

HTML doesn't provide any built-in element to deal with problems like this; it is beyond the scope. Within a strict HTML framework, items like this should be dealt with by creating an image file. We could deal with it that way. In fact, if we could create a stream of bytes in GIF or JPEG format, then we could simply change our **startStream** function such that it outputs a line that says something like

```
printf( "Content-type: image/gif\n\n");
```

instead of:

```
printf( "Content-type: text/html\n\n");
```

This changes the stream type from **HTML/text** to **GIF/image**, and causes the browser to expect and display a GIF stream. However, within our current, unordered list implementation, the user can click on individual dogs and get the record for that dog. If we output a GIF representation of the tree, then we'd have to create a corresponding image map to make that image clickable. You can see how this exercise quickly becomes unmanageable.

At the point where you're considering outputting a GIF image with a corresponding image map, you're very close in complexity to a Java applet that could take the data and draw the tree by itself, including handling clickable hyperlinks. Factors such as your users' ability to run Java applets should drive this choice, but the trend is clearly away from server-based image processing like the GIF/image-map model and toward client-based graphics via technologies like Java and ActiveX.

Performance

As we've said before, by current industry standards for standalone applications, the performance of the Newfoundland Dog Database is awful, barely tolerable even for those who really, really, want the data and can't get it anywhere else. There are four approaches to improving the real and perceived performance of the Newf database:

- Process creation
- Database connection
- Nonparsed headers
- Table row dimensioning

Process creation is an easy problem to understand. A process is what the operating system calls a running program. Whenever you run a program such as Netscape, you're creating a process. If you run another copy of Netscape, you create another process. Processes are expensive. They take time to create, since the operating system needs to read the file off disk, interpret its header, and set it up to run. Before our CGI program even executes the first line of source, a considerable amount of real time has been spent just loading it into memory.

This is something to think about if you're considering writing CGI programs in an interpreted language like Java. In order to run a Java program, you have to load both the Java interpreter and the Java program itself. Thus, though it may take a lot longer to write, an executable written in C or C++ will almost always load faster than the equivalent Java program.

There are a couple of solutions currently in the works to the process problem: NSAPI and ISAPI. Basically, these solutions require that you write your CGI program as a Dynamic Link Library (DLL) that can then be called by the Web server as NSAPI or ISAPI requests come in. Operating systems treat DLLs differently than executable programs (like our CGI program). A DLL is typically loaded into memory just once, and it stays there forever. Executable programs, like the Web server, can call into the DLL just by using a function name. Thus, we've almost entirely eliminated the process-creation overhead. It remains to be seen which of these technologies will win greatest acceptance.

The database-connection problem is very similar to the process-creation problem. Creating a connection to the database is an expensive operation in terms of real time, often taking up to four or five seconds. Again, under most operating systems, the preferred solution is to use a DLL or a daemon to consolidate the process. The theory is that your DLL opens a connection to the database, then holds that connection open forever. Every time a CGI program or NSAPI function wants to use the database, it uses that open connection, thus eliminating the database-connection time.

This is a solution that most Web database tools like NetDynamics employ. With multiple users calling the database at the same time, this is a trickier problem than it might appear. You must somehow serialize access to the connection such that conflicting operations do not occur at the same time. Under JDBC, for example, if you try to do a new select against a connection while there are still results pending from a previous selection, you'll throw an exception. There are ways to deal with this, especially in Java, but it takes some planning and some work. It is not a simple matter of opening a single connection and handing it out to whatever process asks for it.

Having seen two areas where performance improvement entails a significant amount of work, we now come to a couple of cherries ripe for the picking. Server pass-through is an easy one that would never occur to you if you didn't know how Web servers work. In the **StartStream** function of Listing 3.10, we output a string "Content-type: text/html\n\n". This is a partial HTTP header.

The Web server and the browser speak HTTP protocol to each other, and the HTTP protocol specifies that a header block can have a certain amount of information in it. When we output the string "Content-type: text/html\n\n", what actually goes out over the socket to the browser is something more like this:

```
HTTP/1.0 200 OK
Date: DayOfWeek, DD-Mon-YY nn:nn:nn GMT
Server: Netscape-Communications/1.1
MIME-version: 1.0
Content-type: text/HTML
```

What happens is that the Web server sees (and expects) a partial header, and prepends the other headers to it before sending the whole block off to the browser. This means that the Web server must handle every byte of information flowing back to the browser from the CGI program.

Almost all Web servers allow you to get around this using nonparsed headers. Essentially, with nonparsed headers, your CGI program agrees to send a complete header, and the Web server gives you direct access to the socket connection to the browser. Usually, in order to use nonparsed headers, you have to name your CGI program with a specified sequence. For Netscape, NCSA, and CERN servers, this means starting your program name with the letters nph.

For our CGI program to use nonparsed headers, we'd need to make two changes. First, we'd rename the program from newfq.exe to nph-newfq.exe. We'd then change the ACTION attributes in the forms that call the program to call the new, nonparsed version. Finally, we'd have to have a new version of **StartStream** to output the complete header, as in Listing 6. This version outputs various interesting header fields, creating a proper date using **strftime**. We also need to call this version instead of the parsed version from **startQuery** in Listing 3.4.

Listing 6 The nonparsed version of StartStream.

```
/* StartStreamNonParsed - Tell the browser we're sending back HTML. */
void StartStreamNonParsed() {
  char szdate[256];
  struct tm *today;
  time_t long_time;

  printf( "HTTP/1.0 200 OK\n" );

  time(&long_time);
  today = localtime( &long_time );
  strftime( szdate, sizeof( szdate ), "%A, %d-%b-%y %H:%M:%S GMT", today
);
  printf( "Date: %s\n", szdate );
  printf( "Server: Netscape-Communications/1.1\n" );
  printf( "MIME-version: 1.0\n" );
  printf( "Content-type: text/html\n\n");
  }
```

Nonparsed headers seem like an unvarnished gain, but they have a down-side, mostly related to error handling. In the event of abnormal termination of the CGI program, the server usually deals with it by sending its own error message off to the browser, and logging the error in its log. It can't do this, however, if it doesn't "see" the stream you're sending to the browser. Thus, implementing a nonparsed-header performance enhancement is best reserved for a time when the program has been running successfully for some time and all, or most, bugs have been wrung out.

The other easy picking in the performance arena is not so much an enhancement in performance as an enhancement in perceived performance. Where our last enhancement required a knowledge of Web servers, this one requires an understanding of how browsers work, especially how they process table rows, **<TR>** elements.

Most visual elements in HTML allow you to specify a height and width as an attribute of the element. Thus, for an image **<IMG>** element, you can say **<IMG HEIGHT=200 WIDTH=100>** to tell the browser that the image is 200 pixels high and 100 pixels wide. Why does HTML do this?

Actually, this is one of the best, and least, well understood features of HTML. For our 200 by 100 image, for example, that image may be 100 K bytes, and take a full minute to download. Depending on the image type, the browser might have to download a large part of the file before it can know the dimensions of this image. The browser can't render any of the visual elements that follow that image until it knows how big the image is. If it knows how big the image is, it can just reserve a space 200 by 100 pixels, download the image in the background, then continue rendering all the text surrounding and following the image. You've undoubtedly seen this on hundreds of Web pages, where the text appears surrounding a blank box that eventually fills with an image.

In our Newf application, you may notice that even for a query returning hundreds of rows, the browser doesn't display *any* of the data until all the data has been downloaded. This is because table rows operate much the same way as images. If you don't specify the dimensions of the table cells, then the browser scales them on the fly depending on the size of the data within all the cells. Thus, it has to wait for all the cells to be downloaded before it can render *any* of the cells. Netscape, for example, will try to size a column of text cells to be just as wide as needed to hold the single biggest word in any of the cells of that column.

If, however, we size the table cells ourselves, then the browser has no decision to make and can render the row as soon as the data for that row arrives. Table data cells, **<TD>** elements, only allow setting of the width. Thus, if we add a simple attribute, say **WIDTH=100**, to each of our table data cells, our table rows will appear to flow onto the screen one by one, as opposed to appearing all at once in a lump.

Conclusion

In this chapter, we've stepped back a bit and looked critically at the Newfoundland Dog Database as a real-world application. In the process, we've discovered a number of interrelated problems, including performance, input validation, browser incompatibility, display-capacity limitations, and, for the pedigree tree, inadequate display capabilities. Each of these symptoms has a root cause based in the architecture of the Web and its components, the browser, Web server, and CGI program. And for each of these symptoms, there are measures that can be taken to alleviate the problem, as shown in Table 1.

Table 1 Problems with the Newf application, and possible solutions.

Problem	Possible Solutions
Performance	Nonparsed HTTP headers
	Semi-permanent open database connections
	Statically sized HTML visual elements
	NSAPI
Input validation	Client-side input validation via Java
Browser incompatibility	Least-common-denominator HTML design
	Separate branches of execution based on browser capability
Display capacity limitations	Response limiting via multipart result screens
Inadequate display capability	Client-side graphic processing via Java

Hopefully, through the work of this chapter, we've seen how to take a basic, fairly primitive Web database application and tune it to look and perform more like a halfway-decent standalone application. As tools like Java and ActiveX develop, Web applications should be able to take much better advantage of the client-side capabilities, and thus perform more up to the standard set so far by standalone, graphical applications.

Webliography

- http://www.ncsa.uiuc.edu/SDG/Software/WinMosaic/HomePage.html   NCSA Mosaic browser.

- http://www.cc.ukans.edu/about_doslynx/doslynx.html   About the Lynx browser.

- http://www.microsoft.com/ie/   Microsoft's Internet Explorer browser.

- http://altavista.digital.com   Digital Equipment's Alta Vista search engine.

- http://www9.netscape.com/
  newsref/std/server_api.html

  An in-depth explanation of
  Netscape Server API, NSAPI.

- http://www.microsoft.com/
  infoserv/docs/PROGRAM.
  HTM#27081

  Microsoft's Win32 extension for
  its Web server, called Internet
  Server API (ISAPI).

- http://www.javasoft.com

  The Java home page.

- http://www.microsoft.com/
  activex/actx-gen/awhatis.htm

  Microsoft's ActiveX client-side
  controls technology.

Index